Praise for Te

The Dogs Were Rescued (and So was I)

"A literary masterpiece! Teresa Rhyne writes from the heart and soul in a way that draws you in so deeply, you can't help but physically feel her pain, her love, her sorrow, her fear, her excitement, and her inspiration. Her true 'tails' of loss and newfound life are not to be missed. I laughed, I cried. I felt relief and enthusiasm. This is a must-read not only for dog lovers, but also for anyone with a passion for animals."

—Shannon Keith, Beagle Freedom Project president

"*The Dogs Were Rescued* is a love letter to our animals, to who they are and who they make us want to be. Teresa has written a wonderfully funny story about change, transformation, and unexpected second acts. She also reminds us of what her beagles always knew: love deeply, move forward, and never turn down a snack."

—Quinn Cummings, author of *The Year of Learning Dangerously* and *Pet Sounds*

"*The Dogs Were Rescued* is far more than a dog book. It's a book about how all of us who love animals can understand, and do, more to make their lives better. After reading this book, I want to do more than love my own dog. I want to live in a way that shows my love for all dogs."

—Kim Kavin, author of *Little Boy Blue: A Puppy's Rescue from Death Row and His Owner's Journey for Truth*

"You may never look at a glass of milk or a slice of meat in the same way again! In her new memoir, Ms. Rhyne opens the window into her life, post–cancer victories, but Seamus's recurrent battles with the disease make Teresa reevaluate the foods they both eat and the lifestyle choices she has been making. With Teresa's characteristic intelligence, humor, and intensity, she explores food production; the horrors of animal testing in cosmetics, cleaning supplies, and more; and determines that the vegan life is the only choice that makes sense for her. Beautifully woven throughout are the challenges that her beagle loves—Seamus, Percival, and Daphne—present to both her and the wonderfully patient Chris. This book will change you…and you'll have Teresa to thank."

—Linda Sherman-Nurick, Cellar Door Books, Riverside, CA

The Dog Lived (and So Will I)

"This book does a great thing: it shows us how to make room in our lives for disease and then to get on with the important business at hand—falling madly in love and spoiling a beloved dog rotten. It's a book that dares to be honest and sad and hilarious all at once. It will help inspire many people to respond to the unexpected in their own lives with humor and grace."

—Susan Conley, author of *The Foremost Good Fortune*

"A story about the courage to confront the adversities we all encounter and about love, both human and canine, and the strength love gives us to go on."

—Larry Levin, *New York Times* bestselling author of *Oogy: The Dog Only a Family Could Love*

"Funny, smart, uplifting, and fun, *The Dog Lived (and So Will I)* reminds us that animals are among our best teachers, our most powerful healers, and our most steadfast friends. This unforgettable story of an irrepressible beagle, a tough lawyer, and her unlikely boyfriend will make you cry a little and laugh a lot. Whether you're facing a scary illness or just a blah Monday, this book is good medicine. I loved it!"

—Sy Montgomery, author of *The Good Good Pig*

"This poignant and fast-moving memoir of Teresa and Seamus—both definitely Type A personalities—is proof that even a hard-charging lawyer is no match for a big-hearted beagle. Their mutual triumph over terrible trials is a testament to the healing power of dogs. Four paws up!"

—Martin Kihn, author of *Bad Dog (A Love Story)*

THE DOGS WERE RESCUED

(and So Was I)

TERESA J. RHYNE

Published by Sourcebooks, Inc.
P.O. Box 4410, Naperville, Illinois 60567-4410
(630) 961-3900
Fax: (630) 961-2168
www.sourcebooks.com

Library of Congress Cataloging-in-Publication data is on file with the publisher.

Printed and bound in the United States of America.
VP 10 9 8 7 6 5 4 3 2 1

For the animals.

And always, for Chris, my favorite animal.

"I hold that the more helpless a creature, the more entitled it is to protection by man from the cruelty of man."

—*Mahatma Gandhi*

CONTENTS

AUTHOR'S NOTE

THIS IS MY MEMOIR. AS SUCH, IT IS MY STORY FROM MY EXPERIENCES and memories, and mine alone. Most names have been changed, some characters are composites of people, and occasionally, for the sake of story, timelines or dates of events have been altered or events combined—because life doesn't always make sense, but a book should.

This is my memoir. As such, it is not a how-to guide, nor a cookbook, nor a psychological thriller. (You were expecting that, right?) This is the story of how I came to live a more compassionate lifestyle, inspired by some adorable beagles, and the struggles we all had along the way. It's also a love story. But in neither instance do I intend to be giving you advice. (Maybe warnings, but not advice.)

This is my memoir. As such, I hope it brings you pleasure while you read it. And if it causes you to think about the animals a little more than you used to, well, that will bring me pleasure in return.

Chapter 1

SEEING RED

My dog Seamus and I were sitting in the backyard of a friend's home—the same home where I'd celebrated the end of my cancer treatments in a *Survivor*-themed party—when I saw red. It was a bright, clear fall day in 2011. As Seamus wiggled in my lap, the sun illuminated a pool of blood deep in his eye.

I immediately denied what I was seeing, unable to believe there could be another health issue. *Not now.* This was a shadow, a reflection of my fuchsia sweater, an illusion. This was anything but what I knew it was. If I hadn't been so shocked, I would have seen the irony in finding that spot in his eye just then.

We were posing for the author photo for my memoir about how he—my beagle, my love, my hilarious, spirited guide to life—had survived his own cancer and given me the strength and courage to survive mine. As soon as the photo shoot was over, in what was a familiar routine for me, I scheduled a vet appointment. The vet just as quickly sent us to a specialist.

I was back in a sterile, white room with my dog—trusting and fearless—standing on a metal table. The initial evaluation was done by an intern. He was polite, quiet, and appeared to be thorough in his exam, but he said very little to me. Seamus stayed calm on the table, as he always did, glancing my way only occasionally. When the exam was over, Seamus howled.

"He wants a cookie," I said. "He's well-trained to know he gets a treat when the exam is over. Preferably a green dog bone, if you have one."

The intern smiled. "Poor guy. I'll get him a treat, but I don't know about green. I'll bring it back when the doctor comes in."

Several minutes later, the intern, the doctor, and a tech came in the room—an entire, foreboding team. The intern handed Seamus a cookie.

It wasn't green, but Seamus merrily took it and howled for more. The intern laughed and petted Seamus's head. The doctor promised he'd give him more later. Other than that, though, the doctor was all business. And maybe that should have been a clue too.

Seamus had first been diagnosed with cancer a year after I adopted him. He was only two, maybe three years old at the time. He spent a year in treatment—two surgeries, many months of chemotherapy, and then another year and a half of follow-ups and blood tests before he was deemed cancer-free and released from treatment. Six months after that, I was diagnosed with triple-negative breast cancer and spent nearly a year in treatment myself. I was still going for semiannual oncology checkups. So, it's not like I was new to doctors and devastating diagnoses. You'd think I'd get used to this.

"I don't like this," he said, peering with the ophthalmoscope, its pinpoint light shining in Seamus's left eye. "Did you see this…?" And here he switched into the medical jargon that some medical personnel use so easily without any thought that the patient—or, in this case, the patient's guardian—cannot understand it and therefore would only be frightened by it.

"I did see that," the intern said, glancing quickly in my direction and away again.

Of course there's something to see. It's why I brought him in. I tried to stay calm, but the doctor's approach was not helping.

"Yeah, that's not good at all. I don't like what I'm seeing," he said to no one in particular as he was still looking into Seamus's eye.

I wanted to smack him. *I'm sitting right here. Hold your editorial until you are ready to talk to me.* But I have a history of wanting to lash out at doctors. I'd felt that way about Seamus's first oncologist (I not so fondly referred to her as Dr. Sorority Bitch) and the oncologist I did chemo with (Dr. B…no explanation needed, I trust, though clearly I could use some creativity in my anger).

The intern switched the exam room lights back on.

Finally, the doctor turned to me. "This isn't good. What I see is most likely—I'm almost certain—a melanoma."

I had long ago noticed, in my vast experience with cancer, that very few people, medical personnel included, actually say the "C" word.

"Cancer?" I said.

"I'm afraid so."

Shit! I am so sick of cancer. How bad is it? This cannot be happening. How bad is it? Can. Not. Be happening. Not again. How bad is it?

I stayed quiet, stroking Seamus's head while I steadied myself. "Can you give him that other cookie now?" *And maybe one for me?*

The doctor pulled a dog biscuit from the pocket of his lab coat and fed it to Seamus, who gladly ate it in only a few quick bites and then howled, wagging his tail.

"He's a really cute dog," the doctor said.

"He is. And he has already survived cancer once—a mast cell tumor. He's been through two surgeries and months of chemotherapy." While one hand held Seamus, my other was clenched in a fist at my side. "Is this related to that cancer? A recurrence now—seven years later?"

The doctor's eyebrows shot up, but he was quick to recover. "No, not related. This is a different cancer altogether. He's just not very lucky."

Luck? It was only luck or, more to the point, bad luck that determined who got cancer? "I guess I'm not very lucky either. I'm also a cancer survivor."

Now the doctor's surprise stayed on his face. "Wow. Um, wow. That's a lot of cancer in one house. Do you live near a nuclear reactor or something?"

I was no amateur at hearing a cancer diagnosis—I'd experienced it done both better and worse than this. I couldn't tell if he thought he was making a joke, but whether he was or not, it was an entirely inappropriate comment. Now we'd swung from "luck" to where we live maybe being the cause of cancer. Time to bring the doc's focus back to where it should be—to *what next?*

"So where do we go from here? What's the treatment? Do you know for certain it is cancer?"

He gave a long explanation, with the usual amount of confusing and frightening medical terms. It came down to surgery. The doctor was 99 percent certain there was a melanoma on Seamus's eye. Whatever it was, it had to be removed. Chemo and radiation were not options for this cancer. They could remove the eye and likely be done with it. Or they could try shaving the tumor off and saving the eye, but if it grew back, they'd have to remove the eye then. Chances were it would grow back; the only issue would be how long it took. The longer it took, of course, the longer he'd keep the eye—could be weeks, could be months, could be years.

Seamus was nine, maybe ten, years old then. Since I'd adopted him from a shelter, I was uncertain of his actual age. But still, at nine or ten, he could live four, five years longer, maybe more. Trying to save the eye seemed the right thing to do. If he were older, maybe I'd worry more about the possibility of two surgeries and the toll that would take. But he'd been such a trooper during all he'd been through that I had great faith in his recovery abilities. Plus, I'd become accustomed to beating the cancer odds, maybe even, inexplicably, cocky about it.

"I want to try to save his eye," I said.

"That's what I'd do too." The doctor moved toward the door. "We'll get you an estimate of the cost and schedule the surgery."

We scheduled the surgery for December. I considered waiting until January, because December is when all bad things seem to happen in my life. My entire family has a bad history with the time between Thanksgiving and Christmas—accidents, deaths, cancer diagnoses (note the plural on all of those events). I dread the entire holiday season, but particularly the month of December. And now, another reason to despise it. But I didn't want to just leave cancer hanging around in the poor dog's eye any more than I had wanted to leave it hanging out in my right breast when I was diagnosed in December 2008.

Seamus, in his usual style, and as I had counted on, recovered from this surgery quickly. But he still needed care—bandages changed, pain medication, and eye drops—so I resumed our old routine. I was his caretaker, working from home, and he was his rascally self, using his diabolical cuteness and now his new swashbuckling eye patch to work me over for more treats. And for those days, at home with Seamus, the doctor's words ate at my brain.

"Do you live near a nuclear reactor or something?"

We didn't, of course. Does anybody anymore? I lived in a townhome, up on a ridge in Riverside, a suburb in Southern California (usually described as halfway between Los Angeles and Palm Springs). I lived there with Seamus and Chris, the beagle and human loves of my life. There was no nuclear reactor. But three cancers in one household over seven years was a lot of cancer. Too much cancer. *Was* I doing something wrong? And, of course, I'd tied my own cancer recovery so closely to Seamus's it was difficult not to think I might have a recurrence too. "The dog lived and so will I" had been my mantra as I went through a breast lumpectomy, three months of chemotherapy, and thirty-six rounds of radiation. "The Dog Lived" was the name of my blog, and eventually *The Dog Lived (and So Will I)* was the name of the memoir I'd written. And now the dog had cancer again. It was impossible not to feel "…and so will I." Maybe I had done everything wrong.

With Seamus's original cancer and again with my own, I never spent a lot of time wondering why the cancer had occurred. I didn't spend time attaching blame or wondering why me. But now it was getting hard to avoid the thought that maybe there *was* a reason this was happening to us.

What was I doing wrong? Why was this happening?

When I had finished my cancer treatments, I quickly resumed my old lifestyle. I had not had the great epiphany one hears many cancer patients have: I kept waiting for the urge to run marathons, rescue orphans, or quit my job and travel the world, but I was waiting while reading magazines, sipping a martini, and feasting on fried calamari. And my cancer had been triple-negative—which means not responsive to hormones—so the doctors had not given me any dietary restrictions. Naturally, I used that as an excuse for many celebratory meals of dubious nutritional value. Now, though, with Seamus on the couch next to me, curled up and sleeping soundly, his eye patch clearly visible, the bottles of pain medication and antibiotics lined up on the kitchen counter, and with me only a few months away from my own oncology visit, I knew I had to do something. I had to change. I vowed—for Seamus, for me, for our household—that I'd find a way to do better.

I'd find a way to fight for us all.

Chapter 2

THIS IS PERSONAL

Since I had a few days at home with Seamus while he recovered, and because I rely on reading like I rely on coffee (I could not live without either of them), I began to read all that I could find on fighting cancer. I read like my life—and my dog's—depended on it.

Though I wanted to avoid this answer, very quickly it became obvious that diet and exercise were essential foot soldiers in the assault on cancer I was about to launch. I'd never been good at either of these things. If I didn't have Seamus, I'd never exercise at all. I'd celebrated oncology checkups at the Cheese Store of Beverly Hills. I considered potato chips and chardonnay a meal, and a darn fine one. Comfort food was macaroni and cheese, fettuccine Alfredo, or, of course, fast food— cheeseburgers and fries, burritos, nachos, all of it. I'd never been one of those girls who ate small, dainty foods in tiny, cute portions. The more carbs, cream, and fat, the better, as far as I was concerned. And as I'm nearly six feet tall, I'd always told myself it was okay that I ate like a guy. That guy may have been a linebacker, but whatever. I loved heavy, processed, fatty food.

I wasn't that way as a child, though. As a kid, my favorite food was apples. That's even what I gave up for Lent at the height of my Catholic years, and nobody accused me of trying to make it easy on myself. I wasn't much of a meat eater, didn't like candy, desserts, kids' breakfast cereals, or Thanksgiving dinner (except the mashed potatoes and the cranberry jelly). I loved fruits, salads, and nuts. Somewhere along the line, that changed. And I couldn't even recall when, let alone why.

By high school, I was living off fast food. Bacon cheeseburgers, meat-and-cheese burritos slathered in sour cream, chili cheese dogs, and French fries were constants in my life. That didn't change in college, though pizza and potato chips joined the lineup. Law school did not improve my diet, unless one considered a tuna melt at the greasy diner down the street an improvement. (It wasn't, and still, there were the fries.) Until I hit my forties, my metabolism kept up with all of this just fine, so I'd never been on a diet of any kind either. I simply never paid attention to what I ate.

And then along came Chris.

Chris had gone through Seamus's and my cancers every step of the way. And he is a wonderful cook who loves food—all kinds of food. So when he moved in with me and began doing the cooking, my tastes shifted again to more of what he liked and prepared. He is a man who loves steak, hamburgers, a pastrami sandwich, hearty omelets, and anything with bacon. And so I began to eat red meat—steak slathered with blue cheese was a signature dish of Chris's that I favored. He also made a phenomenal *paella* that became our traditional "Mas-Chris" meal (the weekend before the dreaded "Christ-mas"). I had my limits, though—I did not eat veal, venison, duck, lamb, or, as Chris claimed was my standard, "any cute animals."

Fine. Diet is an obvious and important factor in this battle we didn't ask for. My diet could certainly improve, despite my years of denial. So it was time I paid attention to that. Fine. And I'd pay attention to Seamus's diet too. Though the surgery had been successful and Seamus recovered quickly, we'd been told the chances were high that the tumor would come back. It was just a matter of time. In the meantime, we administered eye drops twice a day.

Naturally, I started our nutritional boot camp with changes to Seamus's diet. This seemed both easier and more immediate. I was right about the immediacy, less so about the simplicity.

There was, it seemed, a prescribed cancer-fighting diet for dogs. Many articles, books, and websites sang the virtues of certain foods as cancer-fighting and best for dogs all around. My problem was that they were gross. There were a lot of animal organs, bones, and raw meats involved. It was hard to imagine doing this. I ate meat, sure, but I preferred not to think of it as ever having been alive. "Organs" were just not something I wanted to touch. If it would help Seamus, I'd do it, but I hoped to find a better answer.

I found several dog food brands that sounded promising. But now the problem was that they were raw foods packaged and shipped frozen, so they were very expensive, as one might imagine shipping organs would be. And I didn't have a very large freezer. Not like one of those in which you'd store, say, a year's worth of venison you'd hunted and killed yourself. Eventually, I found a food that seemed perfect: human-grade, grain-free, whole foods. The ingredients were much the same as the abhorrent diet I'd prefer not to make myself, and because the food was dehydrated, I could afford to have it shipped. Now, where to find it? I checked the list of suppliers, but neither had it on their own websites. I emailed both companies and that evening had a response from a man named River. (No, not an old man.)

River was poetically effusive about holistic methods for fighting cancer and proudly stated homeopathy had been curing cancer since the 1600s. He proclaimed that every item his shop sold was toxin-free, safe for the environment and my animal companion. He also mentioned he spent his time caring for his farm, saving animals, and finding grace, so he hadn't updated his site, but he was sure he could get me what I needed.

I was new to this concept of clean living and caring about the environment, so the cynic in me could only think, *Oh, forget the dog food. Please do tell me where one searches for grace.* Or, given that his name was River, perhaps Grace was his daughter or his wife, in which case, I hoped he found her, and Harmony, who no doubt lived on the sanctuary too. It was tempting to run off on one of the many tangents such an email offered a mind like mine, but I opted to stay with the dog food aspect. I emailed back to order the particular formula I wanted. I got this response:

> Are you putting Seamus on a BARF diet?
>
> Peace,
> River

A *what* diet? And no, definitely not. Whatever that was, Seamus would not be eating it. That was not a river I was going down, River.

A winding, drifty, unfocused but enthusiastic ten emails later, I knew that a "BARF" diet meant a "Biologically Appropriate Raw Food" diet. I had ordered two four-pound boxes of The Honest Kitchen dehydrated food, and River had effused about things like alternating proteins and adding colostrums and probiotics, because, as he said, he was "a healer and messenger and my path is to end all the needless suffering that occurs. To have the knowledge I have and not share it seems selfish, esp. when it makes such a huge difference and can cure cancer, etc."

I particularly loved the "cure cancer, *etc.*" You know all those things like curing cancer? He did that too. But I did love his passion. I could use some of that. Best to just start with the dehydrated food, though, especially since bottled passion was not listed on his website. On second thought, perhaps that was a different website entirely.

When the boxes arrived, shipped from his green corner sanctuary on the East Coast all the way across the country to me in California, I could not help but laugh. My research had not been thorough, and his "nontoxic to earth" statement was not quite accurate. The product was manufactured in San Diego, California—about sixty miles southwest of me. The Honest Kitchen had shipped eight pounds of dehydrated food to the East Coast, so he could turn around and ship it back to the West Coast. I didn't know a lot about carbon footprints, but I was pretty sure I had some carbon karma points to make up. I was also sure that, sadly, it did not make economic or carbon sense to do further business with my new River friend when I could simply order directly from the company sixty miles away. It wouldn't have been my style to just figure that out in the first place.

Seamus loved the food. Well, Seamus loved all food, so that was not a surprise, but he did seem pretty excited about this new feast. The hardest part for him—as it must be for any self-respecting beagle—was waiting the five minutes it took for the food to reconstitute after warm water was added. He howled and cursed at me for every second of the five minutes. (Chris and I had long ago given Seamus a human voice that was part Irish brogue, part Bill Murray's Carl Spackler character in *Caddyshack*; consequently, he howled "*fooooooooooooook*" a lot.)

Spurred on once again by a beagle's battle with cancer, I launched my own healthier lifestyle as well. I cut out fast food and was determined to limit glasses of wine throughout the week. (Notice my specificity! I should note here that Chris owns an online wine store that also has a tasting room retail location in Riverside, which kept him working long hours, eating [fast food] without me, and frequently bringing home his wine wares for us both to sample—*hey, it was a job requirement!*) And I walked Seamus more. The walking would be good for Seamus and me, I told myself. But then, I also told myself *Five more minutes* every time the alarm went off following my repeated hits on the snooze button. I did get up and walk him, though. A few times. On one of those walks, impressed by my three consecutive days of progress, I decided there was something more I could do. I would try a different kind of exercise. Fresh air does strange things to me.

I hate participating in sports, and gyms make me crazy—all that sweat and locker rooms harkening back to junior high are just not my thing. Well, who am I kidding? Exercise is not my thing. But yoga, I imagined, would not be sweaty and would not be a competition. It would, I hoped, be relaxing. I needed exercise, and stress relief couldn't be a bad thing. Yoga seemed like a wise choice, shocked as everyone was to whom I mentioned it.

As it turned out, I shocked myself. I *liked* yoga. And the classes were *not* filled with dreadlocked hippies (we don't actually have those in Riverside); Zenlike, lithe, blond women lifting their eighty-pound bodies into the air, balanced only on slender wrists with their legs wrapped around their ears (those were only the instructors); or men with hair longer than mine (and silkier…*bastards!*). No, these were average folks who, like me, were tired of being puffy, bloated, and, well, ravaged by disease. But I did sweat. Man, did I sweat. And while I liked yoga, the feeling did not appear to be mutual.

One Saturday morning, as the instructor demonstrated a particularly impossible and unnatural-looking pose, I burst out laughing. Hey, at least I was getting the stress relief down. The instructor looked my way, as did the rest of the class.

Hmmm. A yoga faux pas. "I'm sorry. I'm just pretty sure my body can't do that. I don't think I've ever been that flexible in my life."

"No," he agreed. "You'll have to work on your flexibility. You may want to look at one of our stretching classes."

Or a different yoga studio.

I struggled through, chastened, and rigid in oh so many ways. Afterward I overheard a woman who had to be at least twenty years older than me explaining to the instructor that she really wanted to work on her flexibility. She wanted to know about the stretching classes too. "I mean," she said, "I'm worse than her!" She pointed to me, the new standard for inflexibility.

My yoga hobby was starting to look short-lived.

On top of the embarrassment of my performance, I was terrible at sticking to a schedule and frequently missed classes. Yoga once a week was great, but it was hardly going to stave off cancer. To increase my chances of more regular sessions, I hired one of the yoga instructors— tall, thin, impossibly elastic, but very amiable Lauren—to teach private classes at my office, and I roped a few friends into joining me. If yoga came directly to me, I could not hide. And my friends were not likely to be much more flexible than I was. When it came to yoga, I mean.

Wednesday nights and Saturday mornings found my law office reception area covered in yoga mats with middle-aged women trying to Warrior Pose our way through to Corpse Pose—the only one we were any good at. One friend's inability to achieve Happy Baby Pose (lying on your back, grabbing the soles of your feet with your hands, knees toward your face) caused us to dub the pose "angry baby" instead. And Lauren's insistence that we hold Warrior Pose far longer than any of us felt necessary or attainable caused us to dub her "Yoga Bitch." She was Zen enough to accept and wear the title proudly.

On Saturday mornings, I walked Seamus and then brought him with me to the office. He moved from person to person, checking our poses and wondering if we happened to have brought any food with us. By the end of the session, he could be found seated in Yoga Bitch's lap, enjoying a belly rub and oblivious to my pain. I think Lauren snuck him treats so at least he wouldn't think of her as Yoga Bitch. He thought of her as Snack Bitch.

On my little dog and I marched in our war against cancer. Chris

looked on, mostly encouraging and definitely amused, but not participating in the fight himself. He's twelve years younger than me and thus,
perhaps, not as ready to look at his own immortality.

But springtime saw us launch new counterattacks. And I surprised
myself as much as I did Chris.

Chapter 3

HONEY AND ANCHOVIES

My CONTINUING RESEARCH LED ME TO A HOLISTIC SUPPLEMENT study for canine cancer that was sponsored by the National Canine Cancer Foundation. I immediately enrolled Seamus, and he was accepted into the group of "currently fighting cancer" dogs. He took the supplements twice a day, and we restricted his treats to one or two a day. Instead of the snacks he loved, we gave him apple slices or celery or broccoli, which were becoming my snacks too. As a consequence, there were chewed remains of spit-up greens dotting our kitchen floor regularly (some of them left by Seamus). I had even lost a few pounds and was only inches away from touching my toes in yoga class.

I continued my search for more ways to wage war on cancer myself as well.

Although in my precancer life I would have avoided both a "women's conference" and a "health conference," I now willingly attended a women's health conference at a local hospital not far from where I had undergone my chemotherapy treatments. My search for weapons was going to be thorough, if a tad imprecise.

In the late morning I found I had two choices for the break-out session. One featured none other than the icicle of a woman who'd been in charge (albeit only on paper) of my chemotherapy—Dr. B herself, talking about who knows what, but I was certain I didn't want to hear it and didn't want to see her. By default, I headed to the other session.

I walked into the conference room and saw that the presentation would be by Julieanna Hever, the author of *The Complete Idiot's Guide to Plant-Based Nutrition*. I seemed to fit the target market as I'd never even heard the term "plant-based diet." I forced myself to keep an open mind. I'd told myself that I was going to explore all options for Seamus and me to fight our cancers, and a plant-based diet was certainly an option, just not one I thought I was capable of.

I was early, so I approached the table in the back of the room where books were stacked. I picked up the *Idiot's Guide* and began to flip pages.

"Hi. Thanks for being here."

I looked up and saw what can only be described as a glowing woman. Her skin shone, her hair shone—massively thick and dark, falling just below her shoulders—her eyes twinkled and her teeth gleamed from her…right…from her shining smile. I don't think I'd ever seen anyone exude *health* like this woman did. Of course, I'd been spending a lot of time in oncology wards, so what did I know.

"Hi." I put the book down and extended my hand. "You must be the speaker?"

She shook my hand. "I am. I'm Julieanna Hever. I'm so glad you're here."

"I'll admit I know nothing about this. I am the complete idiot. But I'm also a cancer survivor, so I feel like I need to do something…more."

We spoke for ten minutes; she was all sunshine and rainbows, and I was all clouds of doubt and rainstorms (give up *cheese*?). But *man*, I wanted to be like this woman. That doesn't happen to me a lot. So I pushed on. I told her about Seamus, our book coming out, and my search to stave off cancer taking over our lives. She extolled the virtues of plants and mentioned the various studies that had been done, referring me to the documentary *Forks Over Knives*. She swore the plant-based lifestyle was easy.

I was feeling—what was that feeling? An unfamiliar…tingling… sort of…ins…inspi…*inspired*. I was feeling inspired! That was it! But wait…

"What about wine and coffee? Or, as I think of them, 'water and air,'" I said.

She laughed. "Both are plant-based. You're good. Everything in moderation, but that goes for any diet."

Define moderation. No, never mind. Don't.

I bought her book and took a seat in the second row. I was two days away from my oncology checkup; what did I have to lose?

When Chris got home that night, I pounced. "I'm going to try a plant-based diet!"

"A what?"

"Plant-based diet. Just food that comes from plants. Not animals."

"So vegan?"

I paused. *Huh?* "I don't think so, no. Nobody said anything about vegan."

"But isn't that vegan? No animal products?"

Maybe. I grabbed the book and handed it to him. "No. It doesn't say that. Vegan sounds way too intimidating."

"Beans. Vegetables. Lentils. Tofu. What part of this does not sound vegan to you?" he said, flipping pages.

"Um, the cover of the book? The presentation I listened to today?"

He handed the book back to me. "You know this means no cheese, right?"

I'd already had to scrape the cheese off my vegetarian pasta at lunch, so yes, I knew that. "I said I was going to try healthier lifestyle choices to figure out what works. I figure if I do this—go cold tofu—and totally hate it, I can gradually add things back in and figure out the best balance. Maybe I go back to eating cheese, or fish, or eggs. Who knows? But it makes more sense to me to cut it all out and see how I like it. See how my body responds."

"Because that's harder, so of course that makes more sense to you."

"It's more logical."

We both laughed. My greatest strength was logic, but overdone, I've been told it becomes a point of weakness. I am generally more logical than emotional, and this is sometimes a problem (um, *for others*). I thought my logic here was sound. If I tried vegetarian or, as I'd been doing, just "eating healthier," I'd still find a way to melt cheese on everything and pile on the cream, as I'd been doing for months. I'd be eating broccoli, but it would be dipped in ranch dressing, just as my salad would be swimming in blue cheese. This way I at least had a guide, a nutritionist I could talk to (Julieanna, it turned out, was infinitely accessible through social media), and some solid evidence that this was an appropriate diet for fighting cancer.

"I'm shocked. And worried. Yoga and now this. You're still going to shave your legs, right?" Chris said.

"Yes. I'm just going to use an artichoke."

"What?"

"Totally kidding. But here's the good news: I haven't completely lost my mind—wine is plant-based!"

"Oh thank god." He moved toward the wine refrigerator. "I'm pouring the plants now."

A day and a half later, having eaten nothing but surprisingly delicious plants—Julieanna's "Easy Beans and Quinoa" with onion, garlic, corn, and cilantro; kale and broccoli salad; and a breakfast of almond butter on whole wheat toast with my old friend a red apple—and drinking a lot of water, I felt the effects. Not only did I have more energy, but I'd also lost two pounds. And I wasn't hungry! This was a great start. Other than having to go to the restroom four times during the night (cleansing, anyone?), I slept soundly. That normally did not happen in the nights preceding my oncology checkups.

I was three years out from my cancer diagnosis by this point. I'd almost stopped even thinking of myself as a cancer patient except in the twenty-four hours or so preceding a doctor's visit: it is hard not to think of oneself as a cancer patient when "oncology appointment" is on the calendar. Every six months, I'd been going for these checkups, and I'd always kept my date with NED ("no evidence of disease"). My anxiety decreased each time.

Then I was hit with Seamus's new diagnosis.

It had only been four months since his surgery and our gradual diet and exercise changes. That probably wasn't enough to discourage any cancer cells in my body thinking about making a comeback. Or maybe I was fooling myself and they'd long ago started the reunion, probably back when Seamus's diagnosis came. This would be a great time for my logic to kick in, but it wasn't happening. In my mind, our destinies were locked. The feeling that what happened to Seamus would happen to me was not logical, but when it came to dogs, and Seamus in particular, well, that's where logic failed me.

And there really is no logic to cancer anyway.

Making matters more difficult, Chris would not be accompanying me to my appointment. When I was in treatment, he'd gone with me to every appointment, even my blood tests, and he'd humored and cared for me through it all. Since he'd opened Chris Kern's Forgotten Grapes online wine shop and I was years out from my diagnosis, I began going myself. I much preferred his company, of course, but he had a business to run and I wanted him to succeed. He deserved it. Besides, there'd be no cheese shop visit for us this time.

I flipped magazine pages in the waiting room and tried not to look at the other patients. When I weighed in with the nurse, the scale showed a loss of four pounds. I wanted to boast about my seventy-two-hour-long plant-based diet, but in addition to that sounding nuts, I thought I might be answered with "weight loss is a sign of cancer," which is actually even more nuts. But one is entitled to such thoughts during an oncology checkup. I'd had crazier thoughts.

A blood pressure check, an exam, and a blood test later, and the physician's assistant said, "That's it. You're all clear."

I sat up straighter in my paper-towel dress. "That's it?"

"That's it. You can get dressed now," she said, closing my file. "Except one other thing."

I knew it. I only had six months to live. Maybe less. Or just a general "there's cancer everywhere" statement. *Because that happens from a blood test.* "One other thing?"

"We'll move you to annual checkups now. You'll still have your mammogram in October and then your checkup with us in April, so technically someone's checking on you every six months still, but you don't have to see us every six months."

Huh. Okay, well, that would be good, right? Fewer oncology appointments can't be a bad thing. And I'd found the lump myself the first time, so I certainly know what I'm looking for. Plus, now I had plant-based superpowers on my side!

Back at home I celebrated by cuddling with Seamus; making a mango, avocado, and black bean salad with lime juice, olive oil, and cilantro dressing; and going online to join Farm Fresh to You, a community-supported agriculture group that would deliver local, farm-fresh produce to my door every other week. I was feeling good and becoming a believer. Perhaps even an evangelist. My cancer wasn't back! We were winning the war! *All hail kale!*

Emboldened, I continued to arm us for battle. Though there was a misfire. Inevitable, I suppose. For Seamus, an important part of my troops, I bought a thirty-dollar, one-hundred-page, holistic canine-cancer-fighting book online that seemed to be everything I was looking for, and it was written by a doctor. When the book arrived, though, I soon noted that nowhere did it say what kind of doctor the author was. Technically, as I have a Juris Doctor degree, I am a "doctor" too. Please don't ever take medical advice from me. Blood makes me pass out, as does the word "stitches." (Hang on while I come to again…) And I've had no medical training whatsoever, except as a patient.

As I read the book, I began to question, as the author intended, not just the proper feeding of a domesticated dog, but also much of the traditional gospel of pet care. Could neutering dogs really increase the risk of cancer? Seamus was already neutered when I got him, so it hadn't been my choice. Was adding apple cider vinegar to his drinking water really going to fight off fleas *and* cancer (*win-win!*)? But then the author started to lose me. He was adamantly against chemotherapy treatments for dogs or for anyone. This seemed too far outside the norm for me, especially since chemotherapy had been the only treatment available to both Seamus and me following our respective cancer surgeries.

When I read his "muscle testing" procedure for determining areas of health concern, he completely lost me. It seemed to be a version of the Ouija board where, instead of passing hands over an alphabet on a board to receive messages from a spirit, one passed their hands over a dog and asked certain true-or-false questions. "My name is Tippy St. Clair" would be a warm-up question to make sure I had the technique down. (And if I did, the circle I'd make with my index finger and thumb would easily break when I passed my other index finger through the point where the fingers touched since this was a false statement…or my middle finger would rise, something like that.)

I had wasted thirty dollars. Thirty dollars I'd never get back, and frankly I didn't deserve to. I hadn't done my homework once again.

Summer arrived. Our battle with cancer looked less like a war and more like a truce. Despite my misfiring, Seamus was thriving. He looked lean and muscular, and he was clearly enjoying his new food, supplements, and exercise. Chris was still the one primarily responsible for taking Seamus on the "serious" walks, but I like to think Seamus enjoyed the more casual walks with me, sniffing anything and everything as he pleased. And I was clearly thriving on my plant-based diet. In just over three months, I'd lost thirty pounds. It had not even been difficult. Sure, occasionally I looked longingly at what Chris was eating, and occasionally I accused him of eating my old favorites (steak and blue cheese!) just to tease me, but mostly, the effects of my diet were so instantaneous and rewarding, I stuck to it with relative ease.

I enjoyed the foods I was eating. I enjoyed preparing my meals. In the past I'd been a decent cook, as long as I was following a recipe. But it wasn't something I was passionate about, and I was never one of those people who could look in the cupboard or refrigerator and say, "Oh yes, I have red pepper, dill pickles, and beef; therefore, I'll make my delicious pepper-dill-steak casserole gourmet meal!" (See, I couldn't even cook properly with words! Seriously, who would eat that?) I didn't have any understanding of what flavors went with what or how, when, or why meats should be prepared, and I never liked looking at raw meat, let alone handling it. I just figured the kitchen wasn't my forte. I left that to Chris.

Now, though, I was enjoying the kitchen. I bought a separate cutting board (no meat!) for my veggies, and I learned about quinoa, lentils, hemp, and the miracle of kale. I began to follow vegans on Twitter and Facebook, all of whom regularly shared delicious-sounding recipes. I was constantly printing off new recipes (ahem, with apologies to the environment—and Pinterest, which clearly I needed to join).

I prepared lemony quinoa with pine nuts and spinach; gingered quinoa with dates and watercress; fig and blue "cheese" pita sandwiches; a rainbow salad of kale, cabbage, oranges, red onion, bell pepper, and sunflower seeds in a Dijon mustard and orange juice dressing; a curried quinoa wrap with avocado-citrus slaw; and, every morning, a delicious, energizing kale (or other leafy green) smoothie. Mix up pineapple, mango, coconut water, kale, and chia seeds, and it was as if I were on a tropical vacation. Frozen bananas, almond butter, almond milk, and cinnamon whipped together was far more like a milkshake than the healthy drink it was. And frozen cherries, cabbage, and cinnamon blended with coconut water? 7-Eleven could sell it as a Slurpee.

I convinced a group of plant-curious friends to get together on Sundays and prepare various dishes that we could divide up and take with us for lunches at work over the next few days, in addition to enjoying one fabulous, healthy, energizing dinner together.

And, most importantly, Chris joined me for many of the meals. Occasionally he'd still insist on a chicken breast next to my quinoa creation, or he'd throw a steak on top of my kale concoction, but he was eating far better than I think he realized. *I* realized, though, exactly what was happening to my body.

My energy was way up, I was sleeping through the night, and as I told anyone who listened (willingly or not), everything chemo had done to my body, the plant-based diet reversed (except for the part about killing off the cancer cells…that part was sticking). I could have starred in any one of the food and health documentaries I'd been watching—the same documentaries that now had me thinking about the animals in our food system in a way I never had before

I still made mistakes—like forgetting that honey was an animal product. I had to research that one. Was there actually a health problem with eating honey? Turned out, opinions vary. Not everyone thinks an insect is an animal, for one. But there is the theory that honey is an animal protein that contains something distastefully (on purpose, I assume) known as "animal ferments" and therefore is not good for human health. I also learned that bees make honey by continually eating and regurgitating it. Lovely! And then there was the vegan approach—the production and harvesting of honey involves enslaving and exploiting the bees, which are removed from their natural environment and can be harmed in the harvest process; therefore, if one is vegan, one does not eat honey. Eating honey is apparently the gateway to the slippery slope away from a true vegan ethic (a bee's pain is okay; therefore, maybe a fish's is too, and then perhaps a quail, a rabbit, a pig…).

The difference between the plant-based diet I'd been following and a vegan lifestyle began to crystallize. A plant-based diet was about me. A vegan lifestyle was about the animals. I tucked that thought away in the back of my mind. And I tucked the honey away in the back of the pantry.

Then I went to a wine dinner at Chris's wine shop. The winemaker from one of our favorite Paso Robles wineries, Dubost Winery, was there to share and discuss her wine while her husband grilled and served wild game he'd shot and prepared himself. We loved Kate and Curt and their wines, so there was no way I was missing this event, even with the thought of grilled boar to discourage me. Chris resolved my dilemma when he asked Curt to grill some additional vegetables for me.

The salad course was delicious, and while the others enjoyed the grilled oysters and Kate's Sauvignon Blanc, I nibbled on bread in a delicious, garlicky olive oil dip. And then I had more bread. And then more. And perhaps some wine.

Chris stopped by my table to see how I was faring.

"I can't believe you aren't eating oysters. You love oysters," he said.

"They're an animal. I'm sticking to this."

"I don't think they even feel pain. Aren't they lacking a central nervous system?"

"Well, that's not really the point. Or true. I don't think. Anyway, I'm fine. Besides, this bread and olive oil is delicious."

"So you'll eat anchovies but not oysters?"

I dropped my yummy-soaked bread. "Anchovies? What?" I vaguely recalled Kate mentioning anchovy-something when she discussed the menu. I had not thought anchovy equaled animal. Nor had I thought that salty, savory taste in my dipping sauce was anchovy.

Chris pointed to the nearly empty saucer in front of me. "May as well eat the oysters at this point."

I was crestfallen. I'd done so well! First honey, now anchovies. *Who knew?* Well, of course, anyone who thinks about what they're eating before they stick it in their mouths would know. I pushed the bread plate away, though part of me wondered how much empathy I could really muster for an anchovy.

It was a learning process, and I had a lifetime of eating habits to get over. But I was determined to do it. I was vain enough to be inspired by the weight loss, but smart enough to know my physical well-being had greatly improved, so I was sticking to the plant-based diet, stumble though I may. I was just going to have to think things through a bit more.

Already it took me twice as long to grocery shop than it ever had before. I started shopping at Trader Joe's and Sprouts, which were farther away from me, and fervently hoped for a Whole Foods or Gelson's to magically appear in my city. I visited a local farm stand as frequently as I could and drove downtown on Saturday mornings for the farmers' market. In the stores, I had to read ingredient lists diligently (they sneak milk, eggs, and cheese into just about everything, and why is there honey in wheat bread?), which meant a constant on-and-off with my reading glasses, which I viewed as a mocking symbol of my middle-aged-ness. I was also learning about ingredients I'd never heard of before. Where does one find nutritional yeast? Is it with bread yeast? (No, it's with the vitamins and protein powder.) There is such a thing as dairy-free yogurt? Yes, yes there is; it's made from nut milks. Tempeh? Seitan? Yep, over near the tofu, which is, ironically, over near the refrigerated dairy section. Chia seeds? Flaxseed? Hemp? Bags of it, and again over near the vitamins and supplements. And now, my favorite aisles were the bulk-food aisles: raw cashews, walnuts, grains, quinoa galore, all to my heart's content. And fresh ground almond butter! And wait…macadamia nut butter! Heaven! I'd also discovered the joys and many uses of coconut oil, which I now cooked with and also used as a moisturizer and makeup remover. On the other hand, there were entire rows and sections at the grocery store that no longer applied to me. I could sail past all the processed foods and the dairy and meat departments (in other words, three-fourths of the grocery store).

The shopping part I was getting down pat; I'd have to work on eating out. But I'd get the hang of this sooner or later. I'd watched *Forks Over Knives*, the documentary Julieanna had recommended, and I was more determined than ever, both for my health and for the animals.

Buoyed by my new lifestyle, inspired by my ability to change, and with Seamus doing well, I had another life-changing idea around midsummer. I shared it with Chris in the hot tub one evening, perhaps surprising myself as much as him.

"I'm thinking of going to India."

"Huh?"

Fair enough response. Chris and I both love to travel, and we'd both traveled a fair amount. There was a long and ever-expanding list of places we wanted to visit, but India was not yet on it. Given that some of my least favorite past travel experiences were in Asia, it's understandable that "India" might catch him off guard.

"I can explain."

"Please do."

"One of the breast cancer blogs I follow is written by a young woman who, post–breast cancer, did a sort of trip around the world by volunteering. She went to something like four countries on three continents, volunteering in orphanages and whatnot, as a way to refocus her post-treatment life."

"This is not explaining India at all. In fact the mention of 'orphanages' just makes me think you have a high fever and none of this can or should be explained. Though I do love your clarity on the stranger you met on the Internet who maybe sorta did, you know, stuff," Chris said.

Dang, I hate it when he makes sense! That was perhaps not my best, most impassioned statement. I was new at this. I was not the kind of person who travels the globe doing volunteer work and living in youth hostels, and certainly not anywhere near an orphanage. I *want* to be that person; I just also want my blow-dryer, plenty of quiet, relaxing down time, room service, and cute outfits. And no children around. But I pressed on.

"So this young woman, Terri, she's formed a nonprofit called A Fresh Chapter. And she's putting together a group of twelve cancer survivors from around the world for a volunteer program for two weeks in India. Mornings are spent volunteering and afternoons are spent learning the culture and touring about, including a cancer center in Delhi. I think it sounds kind of amazing."

"Who *are* you?"

"I know. I know. But—and this is key—the trip happens over my fiftieth birthday. So I kinda think it's perfect. This is my first 'big' birthday since the whole cancer thing, and remember I said I wanted to do something spectacular, but something that wasn't all about me. Not a party or a weekend away. Celebrating with other cancer survivors, doing hands-on volunteer work, and seeing one of the Wonders of the World in a country I consider both frightening and fascinating…that seems to fit the bill."

"It does." He was quiet for a short moment. "I'm kind of amazed. But it might be a great idea. Certainly an experience. How much does it cost?"

"Well, that's being worked out. It's a nonprofit and gets some grants that underwrite part of the trip, but we're also supposed to raise funds. It's like a crowdsourcing thing. I was thinking that if I get selected, I'd just tell friends and family if they want to know what to get me for my birthday, they can pitch in there."

"Not a bad idea. Definitely a once-in-a-lifetime trip. I think you should do it."

One of the many things I love about Chris is that he can respond like that. Just a supportive "you should do it," without days of angst and agonizing or picking the idea apart, finding a million reasons why it was crazy. No, that would be my job, and he knew that. His job was the supportive, upbeat "go for it" part.

"I have to apply. I might not even get selected. I imagine she'll have a lot of breast cancer survivors applying, just because of her blog. And she's trying to get a good mix of people—men, women, folks from different countries, survivors of different cancers. So who knows?"

"Right. You won't know unless you apply."

"I'm going to seriously consider it."

"You, India, forced togetherness with a group of strangers, touchy-feely cancer discussions, volunteer work with kids… What could possibly go wrong?"

One of the other things I love about Chris is his sarcasm. It's a good thing I love that.

We literally and figuratively enjoyed the salad days of summer. My memoir would be published in October, and we were excitedly making plans for that. I even managed to not talk myself out of applying for the India trip. I was proud of myself for recognizing a great summer when it happened without simultaneously expecting a disastrous fall or winter.

I should never let my guard down like that.

Chapter 4

WORDS, WINE, AND WAGS

IN EARLY SEPTEMBER A PHOTOGRAPHER FOR A NATIONAL MAGAZINE came to our home to photograph Seamus and me for an article on our story. He took several shots inside the house and then wanted to move to the back patio, which has an expansive view of the city.

"Can you pick him up?" he asked.

"Well, I can try, but he hates to be picked up. You'll have to shoot fast before he starts struggling."

I picked Seamus up, and he fought me just as expected. I wrestled him into position, and we faced the camera.

"Turn slightly to your right."

I turned. Seamus squirmed. But I held him tight. Glancing at him, though, I noticed he was blinking. "I need to turn him out of the direct sun."

"Just a few more."

In a few more clicks of the shutter, it was over. I looked at Seamus, still holding him in my arms, and I saw it.

What is it with photographers and sunlight and pools of red blood in this dog's eyes? It seemed too ridiculous to be true. But by the end of the day, the eye was swollen and visibly bothering him. He was no longer blinking so much as holding the eye shut.

We took him to his specialist the next day, and they increased the eye drop medication. We were up to four drops a day. Then one morning shortly thereafter, I woke up and headed downstairs with Seamus following behind me as usual. When I turned on the kitchen light and looked down at him, I was horrified. His eye had swollen to nearly the size of a golf ball.

I had been hoping for more time. I had even begun to think the tumor might not come back, that we might beat this back with all we'd been doing. But now I knew: Seamus was going to lose his eye.

The vet made arrangements for the surgery two days later. And just like that, I was back in a vet's office, waiting for the results of a cancer surgery and wondering where we'd gone wrong. Maybe the diet and supplements and exercise were why he had nine months instead of nine days. Or maybe they didn't change a thing. Or maybe we'd irritated the eye and shortened the timeline. Who knew? Who ever knew with cancer?

I tried to distract myself from the worry and the anger by flipping through magazines in the waiting room. I'd come early so I could take Seamus home the moment he recovered enough to leave. I didn't want to be stuck in traffic while he waited for me to come get him.

"Ms. Rhyne?"

I stood and walked toward the receptionist. "Yes. That's me."

"Great. Just follow me."

She led me back to the exam room, the same room where Seamus had been diagnosed. "They will be with you shortly."

I sat again. By now, I was familiar with the reading material in this room, and since I wasn't in the market for a speed boat and couldn't bear to see the photo album of the stages of eye surgery and recovery, I didn't even bother to pick one up. Instead I texted Chris with an update, though I had little in the way of information. Just: I'm here. Should have Seamus soon.

I tried to ready myself for what Seamus might look like. Bandaged, of course. And woozy. But he'd always been such a trooper. Rarely did anything get him down or slow him down. But losing an eye was grave. He never knew he had cancer, but he'd certainly know he was missing an eye. What would the adjustment be like? Would he have balance issues? Would he be confused now that he couldn't see on his left side? I hated that I couldn't explain to him what had happened and why.

The vet tech came into the room.

"Seamus is doing great. Still a little groggy. We'll bring him to you in a few minutes. First, I wanted to go over the medicines and aftercare with you."

"Okay. Great. He's doing okay?"

"Yes, he did well. Surgery was a success." She explained the medications—pain pills, antibiotics, the usual—and handed me a small white bag filled with his prescriptions. "Now, because of the anesthesia, he may not want to eat tonight or even tomorrow morning. As long as he drinks a little water, that's fine—totally normal."

Seamus not eating? I'd probably have to keep checking that it was really my dog. Seamus ate all the time. He was never not hungry. Not even after surgeries in the past, not after chemo, never. This dog always wants food. Always. I listened to her, but I was thinking, *If he doesn't eat by tonight, I'm going to be freaked out.*

"I can't imagine that," I said.

"Perfectly normal. He's had anesthesia and he'll be on pain medication. Sometimes that upsets their tummies too. So just remember it's nothing to be concerned about."

Oh, I'll be concerned. "Okay."

"If you want to pay at the front desk, I'll go get Seamus and bring him to you there."

At the front desk I handed over my credit card, adding to the frequent-flier miles Seamus and I had so regularly accrued in years past. As I signed the bill, I heard the jingle of his collar and the four-pawed pitter-patter come down the hallway. A little slower than usual, and no howling, but there was my boy. He picked up his pace when he saw me and came right to me. The bandage was not as frightening as I thought it would be, and I'd gotten used to the brightly colored wrap applied to the front leg where they insert the IV. I bent down to pet him, and in return he lifted his face to mine, sniffed me, wagged his tail, and then turned, went straight for the reception desk, put his two front paws up on the desk, and *AAARRROOOOOO*'d away at the treat jar.

I laughed. "So much for no appetite."

"I guess so!" the vet tech said.

The receptionist opened the jar and handed him a treat. He ate it quickly and looked at her for another, wagging his tail in approval. Then he howled again. She gave him another cookie.

"Okay, that's enough for now." The tech turned back to me. "So, in Seamus's case, since he *does* seem to have an appetite, just make sure he eats small portions. You don't want to upset his stomach."

"Nearly impossible. He has a stomach of steel, but I won't take any chances."

Seamus's recovery was speedy. He needed only a day or two of rest before he was up to his usual antics. When we finally had the bandage removed—though of course he was missing an eye—I was impressed with the surgeon's skill. Seamus looked like he was winking. There was no sunken hole, no jagged scar, nothing brutal or terrible-looking. He was still a diabolically cute dog. Now he just had a permanent wink. The vet told me Seamus had probably gradually lost sight in the eye in previous months, so the adjustment was likely already complete. As we watched Seamus's swift return to normal, it was easy to believe that was true. He was breaking into cupboards, stealing our food, and howling his demands, just as he'd always done. And we, of course, were no better in our corrections of him. We'd lost that battle long ago, and now with his one-eyed swashbuckling look, we were entirely disarmed.

Two weeks after the surgery, he'd recovered well enough to be at the launch party when our memoir came out and even howled on cue when I read out loud from the scene wherein I first met and adopted Seamus.

"'And again there was the howling. He sounded as though he'd suckled whiskey from his mother's teats and had been chain-smoking since birth,'" I read.

"*AAAARRRRROOOOOO*," Seamus said.

He was going to be just fine. He'd adjusted again—my little trooper. I was so proud.

And I could begin to look forward to my trip to India. With everything going on, and despite the fact that I'd driven all the way into Los Angeles to interview as part of my application, I'd nearly forgotten I'd applied. But then came the news: I'd been selected as one of the Delhi Dozen. I'd be leaving on Valentine's Day.

My memoir was published, and from October through December, Seamus joined me at book events and, without fail, charmed the audience with his antics and energy. He hadn't slowed down one bit. In January, we had one last book event to do before I left for India.

And even in that room full of beagles and other dogs, Seamus was the loudest. He stretched up on his hind legs, front paws on the table, and howled his indignation that the platters of appetizers had all been pushed back out of a beagle tongue's reach. A well-dressed, petite woman reached for one of the multicolored dog treats, baked and decorated to look like doughnuts and cupcakes, and handed it to him, just as he knew would happen. He gulped it down and lunged for more. The woman laughed.

I tugged Seamus away from the table, but with half effort. After all, this was his party too. Seamus, Chris, and I had been on a tour we called "Words, Wine, and Wags." We'd done over a dozen events, helping to raise funds for various animal rescues by combining my book signings with "celebrity" appearances and paw-tographing from Seamus (due to the popular demand, we'd had a stamp of Seamus's paw print made), and a wine tasting from Chris Kern's Forgotten Grapes. I was the words, Chris was the wine, and Seamus was the wag. It was the way our little family worked. And we were having a blast—much to my continued amazement.

Years ago, when I was going through a divorce, I'd said I wanted an alphabet life composed solely of A for "Alcohol," B for "Books," C for "Coffee," and D for "Dogs." Chris had thrown that off a bit by adding "L" for "Love," and I'd taken a very circuitous route, but it seemed now I'd landed right where I wanted to be. This tour had brought it all together, and the event on this day was particularly special, because it was held at Ruff House, the doggie day care and resort where Seamus had the honor of being the first customer and, due to his severe separation anxiety, a regular visitor. In addition, the event was for an organization called Beagle Freedom Project.

I'd heard about Beagle Freedom Project from other beagle-loving friends. So when Chris and I put our tour together, I reached out to them. I knew they worked to rescue beagles used in animal experimentation in research laboratories. And I knew I wanted to help. I didn't think too much more about "animal experimentation" or what that meant when I reached out to the organization. But at our event, there were two of these victims right in front of me. There was Bogart—rescued in May 2012 from a lab in San Diego, California, and now in the loving home of Kelle and her husband, Manos—who calmly greeted everyone. Bogart was the perfect yin of calm to Seamus's yang of chaos. And then there was Comet, a little slip of a beagle with dark, almond-shaped eyes, long soft ears, and the cutest little way of sticking his paw out at you. Comet was there with his foster mom, Vanessa, who had been caring for him since he and ten other beagles were rescued from a Northern California laboratory on December 11, 2012. Barely a month free and here he was, standing, running, and playing in a crowd of people with several other dogs and a lot of food, noise, and commotion. He didn't seem frightened at all, just reserved.

I saw Chris hold Comet more than a few times that afternoon, which made me smile. Beagles always make me smile, but Chris picking up and holding a beagle, well…that makes me glow with happiness.

When I first met Chris, he wasn't much of a dog person. But after all the three of us had been through—years of fighting first Seamus's and then my cancer—well, Chris came to love Seamus every bit as much as I did. He became a dog person. And more specifically, Chris became a beagle man.

Shannon Keith, founder and president of Beagle Freedom Project, stepped forward. In a soft but firm voice, she thanked the guests for attending and then began to explain the work of her organization.

"We work behind the scenes, legally, to rescue the animals that survive vivisection—that's the term for testing on live animals."

Shannon is a lawyer. I could recognize her training. Using the word "vivisection" gets the listeners' attention. It got mine. "Animal testing" is vague and allows one to think the beagles are asked to identify flash cards or count to three with their paw. "Vivisection" is, well, vivid.

"Testing done on beagles in university and other research facilities includes medical, pharmaceutical, household products, and cosmetics. When the beagles are no longer wanted for research purposes, some labs kill the dogs."

I noticed Kelle pulling Bogart closer.

"Other labs attempt to find homes for adoptable, healthy beagles. Working directly with these labs, Beagle Freedom Project is able to remove and transport beagles to place them in loving homes. All rescues are done legally with the cooperation of the facility," she said.

Shannon was an attractive blond woman in her late thirties who radiated competence, compassion, and tenacity. I liked her instantly. I loved what she was doing, though hated that she had to. And, no surprise, I loved those beagles. Appalled by what I was hearing, I listened intently to the plight of these poor dogs. Shannon lifted Comet from Vanessa's lap and picked up one of his floppy ears. She showed us inside, where a long number had been tattooed.

"This is the federal ID number that was given to Comet. This is as close to a name as he had until we rescued him in December. Bogart has a similar tattoo. And do you notice how quiet Comet is?"

I had noticed. Neither Comet nor Bogart made a noise—in stark contrast to the steady *AAARRRRROOOOOOOOO* coming from a certain beagle at the hors d'oeuvres table.

"They don't howl because the labs have the beagles debarked—a cruel practice of cutting the vocal cords," Shannon said.

I cringed. A beagle's howl is intrinsic to a beagle. I couldn't imagine Seamus without his signature howl. It had been one of the first things I'd noticed about him. Well before I had even seen him in his kennel at the shelter, I had heard him. My neighbors could have done without his howl, but that was beside the point. Beagles howl. It's their thing.

I watched Bogart, cuddled in Kelle's lap, content and calm, and Comet, now returned to Vanessa's lap, leaning far into her and resting his head on her chest.

"The reason beagles are used in the research is not just because of their size, short hair, and good nature, but precisely because they are so trusting and forgiving. The labs use those very characteristics against them to subject them to a shortened lifetime of cruel testing. There are seventy thousand beagles in labs across America being tested on every year."

Seventy thousand. Beagles.

I was stunned.

I knew then I wanted to help—needed to help. I instantly thought about adopting one of these dogs and glanced over at that sweet-faced Comet who still needed a home. But this wasn't the time. Seamus was an only-dog kind of dog. He'd shown no interest in sharing his time and total dominion of our household with any other dog. Maybe one day, after Seamus was gone, I'd look at adopting a Beagle Freedom Project dog. But that wasn't a day I wanted to think about just then. I filed the thought away. It was my turn to address the audience.

I handed Seamus's leash to our friend Todd, aka "the beagle whisperer." He and his wife, Tiffany, have six beagles, and Todd can magically make them all behave. (And Seamus was in many ways the equivalent of six beagles.) I walked to the front of the room.

"Well, you may have all noticed that Seamus looks a little different than he does on the cover of the book," I said. And I saw several people nodding, though no one had mentioned it during the wine tasting.

"Seamus had another bout of cancer last year. And this time it was an eye melanoma. He had one surgery last December—a month I hate, as many of you know—but unfortunately the tumor grew back, and in September we had to have the eye removed." I could hear the crowd wince and say "ooh," and I could see the sympathetic faces. I'd gotten used to that in our cancer years. I knew Seamus, though, and he was not a dog who needed or expected sympathy. He'd adapted to his circumstances immediately and seemed to inherently understand that this was something he could use to his advantage. *More treats!*

"But as you can see, it hasn't slowed him down. And it definitely hasn't affected his appetite." At this the audience laughed. Seamus had a legendary appetite—an inescapable fact that everyone present had learned early in the event when he'd knocked over more than one plate and quickly gobbled up the spoils.

"And he is cancer-free at this point. Luckily, eye melanomas very rarely spread to other parts of the body. So, Seamus, in his Seamus-esque way, has just added this permanent wink to his repertoire of cuteness."

Seamus howled on cue, as he was wont to do in these events. And, likewise on cue, another guest handed him a green-sprinkled doggie doughnut.

"He is my little survivor, and that's really what we are here celebrating today. Seamus, Comet, Bogart… They are all survivors. And so am I."

In that moment, I really believed that.

Chapter 5

BREATHING IN

A T LEAST THIS TIME WHEN I WAS CHARTING OUT PILLS AND DOCTOR appointments, it wasn't because of cancer. This time it was for travel. Two hepatitis shots, a tetanus shot, malaria pills, and two shelves of over-the-counter-oh-my-god-you'll-catch-everything drugs later, and I was ready for India. I began packing three nights before I was to leave, partially because I was nervous and partially because I knew I'd have difficulty shoveling it all into only one suitcase. This did not seem to be the sort of trip where one should arrive with her entire closet in tow, nor did I think much of a wardrobe would be necessary. We'd be taken shopping shortly after arriving so we could purchase traditional, appropriate clothing for our volunteer time. Still, I had to bring something to wear, and it was hard to figure out what made sense. This was unlike any travel I'd done before.

I was diligently eliminating any leather. (That would be rude, wouldn't it? In a country that revered cows?) I bought my first pair of canvas TOMS Shoes and even managed to resist buying the sparkly silver ones in favor of a simple cornflower blue pair. I dug out a fabric purse I had in the closet and packed jeans, khakis, T-shirts. Then I unpacked a sundress, sandals, a silk blouse, and two tank tops.

After a few hours of decision making, folding, unfolding, packing, unpacking, I decided to give it a rest. I had two more nights to get it right. I got dressed for bed and joined Chris.

"Have you noticed Seamus's breathing tonight?"

I looked over at Seamus, lying curled up in his bed. "Not really. Why?"

"I don't know. It sounds funny to me. Shallow or something."

I walked over to Seamus's bed and listened. Chris was right. Seamus was taking shorter breaths. "Did you just notice that tonight?"

"No. I noticed it last night too, and when he was at the shop with me today."

"That's not good. I guess I was too busy with all this India stuff." I wanted to pet Seamus now, but I resisted. I didn't want to wake him. Normally I noticed every change in Seamus's behavior or body. I was shocked I hadn't noticed this one.

"I think maybe we should take him to Dr. Davis. Do dogs get colds?" Chris said.

"I don't think so." I'd long ago learned not to panic with every lump, bump, or change in Seamus. I tried not to rush him to the vet constantly, though with his history that was often hard to do. Four months had passed since his eye surgery, and other than checkups for that, he'd been vet-free and doing fine. Up until that moment, he seemed healthy and happy. "I'll call Dr. Davis's office in the morning."

When Dr. Davis examined Seamus and did chest X-rays, his response was swift and decisive. We needed to get Seamus to a specialist right away—and not the eye specialist. He was sending us back to the cancer center.

My world stopped for a moment, but then I swung into action. I called the Veterinary Cancer Group where we'd first taken Seamus, and when I learned they had no available appointments for the next ten days, I called their other location. They had an appointment available the next day—the day I was supposed to fly to India.

I walked into our bedroom and sat down on the bed, my packed luggage only a few feet away. I told Chris I'd made the appointment.

"So that's it. I'm not going to India," I said.

"You have to go. It's all set. I can take Seamus," Chris said.

"No, this is serious. I can't go if there is something seriously wrong with him. We're not being sent to the cancer center because he has allergies." I dropped my head into my hands.

"I know. But I can handle it, and your trip is only for two weeks."

I looked up. "But what if—"

"He won't."

"But—"

"He won't." Chris reached over and held my hand.

I had less than twenty-four hours to decide if I was getting on the plane, and I still didn't feel like I'd made a final decision when Chris took me to the airport, with Seamus in his crate in the backseat. I'd spent much longer kissing and saying good-bye to Seamus than I spent with Chris, though I knew Chris understood. After dropping me off, Chris took Seamus to his appointment, not far from Los Angeles International Airport.

For two hours I sat in the terminal, waiting for my flight to Amsterdam and then on to Delhi, wondering if I was really going to board the plane. I'd gone back and forth on whether I even wanted the call to come. *Would it mean bad or good news if the call came this soon?*

It didn't matter what I decided. As my plane was boarding, my phone rang. I stepped out of line to answer the phone.

"Hi."

"Hi," Chris said. I could tell nothing from his voice, though I was trying to read everything into it. "The good news is Seamus will be here when you get back. But there is bad news."

I'm not getting on the plane. I moved to an empty seat in the terminal and sat, heavy in heart and body.

This cancer was supposed to have been gone. It wasn't supposed to have metastasized. That only happens in five percent of the cases. *Five lousy percent.* We'd beaten odds far worse than that.

"Seamus will be here when you get back. But it is cancer. It's spread to his lungs." I could hear Chris inhale. "They said stage four. Unfortunately, it is terminal."

"I can't believe this. I just can't believe it."

"I know. I feel the same way. They said he has two to four months. We can try chemotherapy, and that may give him six months, if it works. It doesn't work on all dogs."

When devastating news is heard, there is a moment where the brain pushes back, protects the heart by refusing to believe it, by grasping at hope, by denying, by closing. But that moment ends and the heart is defenseless.

I slumped down in my chair. "Only *two* months?"

"Two to four. But maybe six months. And this is Seamus—he's beaten the odds before."

"He was younger then. And the odds weren't this bad."

"I know, baby. I'm sorry."

"I'm supposed to be getting on the plane right now. They're boarding. I can't go. I can't do this."

"You can go. You should go. I'll be here with him. They can start the chemo today and that may shrink the tumor and make him more comfortable. He'll be here when you get back. It's only two weeks."

"How can I leave? I can't leave him."

"You're there. The group is expecting you. I promise I'll take good care of da Moose." Chris had many nicknames for Seamus, but "Moose" was a favorite. Normally it would have made me smile. But this time I was in too much shock. And the flight attendant was calling for my section to board the plane.

This wasn't just a vacation or it would have been easy to turn around and never board the plane. Friends and family had contributed to the cost of the trip—the birthday gift I'd asked for. There were people counting on me, people who supported me, and there were folks who had applied to go who weren't selected. Not fulfilling my obligation didn't seem right either.

"I don't know how I can enjoy the trip. I don't know what to do." I closed my eyes and dropped my head.

"It's your birthday. It's your special trip. It's paid for. And it's only two weeks. Seamus will be here when you get back, I promise. He's got months. And I'll be here too. I'll keep you updated every day. You should go. Get on the plane. I've got this."

"Oh god. I hate this." I looked toward the plane. There were only a few people left to board.

"Go ahead and go, baby. You just need to tell me if you want them to start his chemo today. At least we know he can handle chemo, right?"

"He shouldn't have to go through this again."

"I know."

We were both quiet until finally, with no one else in line to board

the plane, I said, "Start the chemo. I'm getting on the plane, but I will
fly home in an instant if anything goes wrong. So please let me know."

"I think that's the right thing to do."

"I hope so. I love you. I love Seamus. Please take care of him."

"I love you too. And I will."

I boarded the plane in a state of shock. My seat was in the middle of
a row of five, sandwiched between a young boy to my left and an older
Indian man on my right. This would not be the time or place to break
down in tears, so instead I remained immobilized. I stared ahead, blinking back tears, my hand covering my mouth.

Once the plane was in the air and there was no turning back, I tried
to journal and then tried to sleep. I succeeded at neither. Closing my
eyes just made me think of Seamus and what a mistake it had been to
get on the plane. Writing in my journal had the same effect; I wanted
to write my thoughts on starting this adventure to India, but all I could
think or write about was what was happening with Seamus and how
angry and despondent I felt. I am normally not bothered flying coach
on long journeys, despite my height and the tight quarters. I'm happy
enough to be traveling and have a long, uninterrupted period of time
to write or read. But this time the flight was long and uncomfortable,
and my energy was entirely absorbed by my struggle not to break out
in violent sobs.

The connecting flight from Amsterdam to Delhi was delayed. As I
dutifully called Sahil, our contact with Cultural Volunteer Vacations, to
let him know my plane would be late, I began to realize I'd be arriving
in Delhi alone, tired, and distraught at three o'clock in the morning.
Despite weeks of preparing, I suddenly felt very ill-equipped to handle
the events to come.

My flight from Amsterdam to Delhi was just as crowded and my seat
was just as poorly located, but exhaustion weighed in and I slept for an
hour or two. The bright spot to the flight had been the Hindu meal I
was served—piping hot, savory, delicious, and brought to me first as it
was considered a special dietary order on KLM Airlines.

As the captain announced our imminent landing, I remembered to
apply mosquito repellent with the travel wipes in my purse. I then sat in

quiet horror as the plane was fumigated on the tarmac. What were they spraying down on us through these vents? What were they worried was carried from Amsterdam to Delhi?

What had I gotten myself into?

Chapter 6

ALONE IN A CROWD

I APPROACHED THE DELHI CUSTOMS DESK, HOPING THAT MY VISA wasn't correct and I'd be sent back home. I'd be where I wanted to be, and it would be out of my hands. Whatever happened wouldn't be because of a decision I made. The customs official did not see things the same way and instead warmly welcomed my weary self to his country and sent me on my way.

While I waited for my luggage, I reviewed the instructions for meeting the group guide. I was supposed to be wearing the T-shirt they had sent so I could be recognized. I figured as a nearly six-foot-tall blond, I'd be easy enough to recognize in the Delhi airport, and I did not feel like being a billboard for anyone, so I was not in the T-shirt. It would thus be up to me to find the guide carrying the "Cultural Volunteer Vacation" sign. My welcome packet said they would be waiting for me after I picked up my luggage and cleared the long hallway. I was to walk to the end and they would be there.

Hundreds of people were there swarming about, and many were carrying signs, but none with the "CVV" I needed. I was quickly annoyed. Then a thought occurred to me: Couldn't anyone easily just stand at the airport with a CVV sign and pick up unsuspecting Western women gamely here alone for volunteer work and willing to leave an airport with a strange man, provided he was flashing the right sign? The horrific gang rape and murder of a young girl on a bus in New Delhi had occurred only a month prior. Stories of attacks on women in India had been bombarding the news, and phrases like "rape culture" were being used. I hated to generalize or stereotype, but it was the middle of the night and I was alone, tired, and distraught.

I walked until I found a place to sit to phone Sahil.

Two men, both small, came rushing toward me. One wore a Sikh turban; the other held a "Cultural Volunteer Vacation" sign in front of his chest. Without thinking, I stood and said, "I'm Teresa." Too late I realized it would have been smarter to let them identify me. If they knew who I was, knew who they were there to pick up, it was likely because they had indeed been sent by CVV. These two could have just made that sign in the bathroom and sat waiting for some idiot to volunteer to be kidnapped. *Like I just did.*

The Sikh gentleman introduced himself, but I did not understand his name. Nor did I catch the name of the other man. They grabbed my bags and began quickly walking out of the airport. I followed, my vague sense of possible danger increasing. Now not only was I following strange men (but with the right sign!), I was heading to a parking lot and had willingly handed over my luggage.

Naturally, they were driving a white van (*the better to kidnap you with, my dear!*). One lifted my luggage into the back while the other held the side door open for me. I climbed in. (*It's what my paperwork said to do!*) We drove for about half an hour, but I had no idea where we were. It was drizzling rain and very dark, even on some of the larger highways. My initial impression of India was simply gray. I had expected bursts of color and vibrancy, but everywhere I looked was gray, beige, and wet, as if my mood had colored it all.

The two men made the usual small talk about my flight, whether this was my first time to India and some tidbits about the others they'd picked up before me. *Aha! So there are others.* I hoped he meant other members of our group and not other human-trafficking victims. Whoever they were, a few of them had been there for a day, one had arrived a few hours before me, and another two would be coming later that morning. The rest would arrive, like civilized folks, the following afternoon. If these men were kidnappers or rapists, they were very organized and chatty.

We drove into a large apartment complex through a security guard station (I noted the guard waved like he knew them…*but he could have been in on the whole crime ring!*) and turned down several narrow streets of identical muted yellow buildings before stopping in front of one of them.

"This is your apartment. You are just down there." The Sikh man pointed down a dark walkway. "I'll show you."

In for a penny and all… I got out of the van and followed him.

My apartment, my home for the next two weeks (or a lifetime, depending on how this went), had a large metal door with several locks. It was four in the morning—anything would have looked ominous to me, but if there was a bed inside, I would be relieved. He opened the door and moved my luggage just inside. I stepped through the doorway and, noticing the pile of shoes next to the door, stepped out of mine. Since I'd been in the same clothes and footwear for well over twenty-four hours, that too came as a relief. *Unless I needed to run.*

But then Terri stepped out of a doorway and into the living room. This trip was her vision, her dream. She was the one who had put the trip together, interviewed the applicants, selected the group, and was now here, standing before me, smiling and welcoming, though it was four in the morning for her too, of course. I felt comfortable that this was not a coincidence.

Terri and I said our hellos and my driver departed. "Three of our participants are in that room," Terri said, pointing to the far right door. "And you're in that room." She pointed to the middle door in the short hallway. The apartment was one large living room, a dining area, a small kitchen, three bedrooms, a sink in the hallway, and a bathroom. If I had been more awake, I might have focused on the decided lack of bathrooms for the number of women in the apartment. In my then-state, I just wanted a bed. Terri continued, "Your roommates are not part of A Fresh Chapter, and they're gone for the weekend. So you get the room to yourself for now."

"I will not complain about that," I said, though my brain was struggling with the plural. More than one roommate? Even in college, I'd only shared a room with one person. But there they were—three twin beds (and I think "twin" is being generous) maybe eighteen inches apart, with little stands next to each one. There were reading lights attached to the wall above each bed, a linoleum floor, a coat tree, and…well, there's no *and*. That was it. There was no decor save the bright blue bed coverings, and no dressers or shelves, though there appeared to be closets against the far wall—two narrow closets.

I set my bags down and surveyed the room. My roommates had

each wisely chosen a bed near a wall, leaving me with the middle bed. I walked over to the closets and opened them. The doors banged into the bed next to them, and I had to maneuver my body to the other side of the door to see whether there was any space available for me. Each closet was really more of a cupboard, with a bar on top to hang at least a few items, and then two shelves below. The cupboards below were locked. One closet was full and the other was half full—the clothing pushed to one side. I took that as a sign that the empty side was my designated space. But I was too tired to unpack any further than getting out pajamas, a toothbrush, and face wash and leaving my suitcase on the floor. I climbed into bed. I did not know what the plans for the next day were, and I did not care. My exhausted thoughts were solely about Seamus. Finally, I could let out the pain. As the tears came, I was thankful again that I did not have roommates that first night.

I awoke late that first morning, jet-lagged, swollen-eyed, disoriented, and deeply sad. We'd been waging our war against cancer, Seamus and I, for the past year. We'd made significant changes; I'd thought I'd armed us well. But I knew now that Seamus was going to lose his battle. *We* were going to lose our battle. And I was halfway around the world, unable to fight alongside him. I didn't have it in me to be a gracious loser.

I headed to the kitchen to see what I might be able to assemble for breakfast and coffee. Some comforting foods and liquids would be good. I figured a plant-based diet in India would be easy, given the variety of vegetable-based meals I'd seen when perusing my guidebooks. I knew I wouldn't likely be able to have the kale smoothies I normally had for breakfast, but I assumed there would be vegetables of some sort, or fruit, maybe some grains. This was my new comfort food, and I needed it.

The apartment was quiet. In the kitchen I found cookies, bread, and a few bananas. Not perfect, but I could make do. At least a toaster and a jar of peanut butter were available. I searched for a coffee maker.

Terri poked her head into the kitchen. "They serve breakfast over in the office area. You've probably got another fifteen minutes to get there. Everybody else already went. I can show you."

I quickly threw on some clothes and followed Terri. The spread on the breakfast room table consisted of eggs, naan (a flatbread) with *ghee* (clarified butter), some cereals with milk, chai tea (made with cream and sugar), and fruit. Not exactly a plant-based paradise. Had they adjusted the menu for the Americans and Canadians now descended upon them? I grabbed a banana and poured myself some mango juice. I just wanted to return to my apartment and make my backup instant Starbucks coffee while checking for emails from Chris. I wanted to crawl back into my little cubbyhole of a bed. But there was no time for that. Terri was explaining the schedule to the group and, I learned, I'd have about twenty minutes, half an hour if I was lucky, to get showered and ready to go out for the day's tour. There was barely time to eat the banana. I raced back to my apartment.

During the daytime tour of temples, I met the other members of the Delhi Dozen. Most of the group was much younger than me—in their twenties and thirties—which is tragic when you consider this was a group of cancer survivors. And, though naturally the first connection the twelve of us had was as cancer survivors, I quickly found I could not hear the word "cancer." I couldn't tolerate a discussion of "stages" or treatment, or, worst of all, fears of recurrence. I was barely holding it together and still feeling very strongly that I should be home with Seamus, yet I was also aware, of course, that I was grieving for a dog, and not everyone—perhaps least of all human cancer patients—would get or respect that.

I've never been much of a "group person." I hate crowds, noise, and anything that confines me to a "majority rules" situation. I much prefer one-on-one engagement and conversations. I thought this trip would be different simply because of a shared, traumatic experience. I could already sense how wrong I was. I wouldn't be able to talk about cancer now. *I shouldn't have come.*

At dinner, my concerns increased when I learned that I had to be up, dressed, and waiting at the office by seven the following morning to be driven to Mother Teresa's Home for the Destitute and Dying.

Immediately, I began to worry that I wouldn't be ready in time and that even if I were, I wouldn't be able to handle my assignment. I am not a morning person, and as far as I know, I'm not much of a caretaker either. I'd done plenty of volunteer work, but it was more in the fund-raising, board of directors, big-picture sort of way. Also, I was really wimpy when it came to medical issues. Well, human medical issues.

I hoped sleep and an adjustment to the time-zone change and jet lag would adjust my mental state. Until then, I'd just keep to myself; I'd keep taking deep breaths and holding on as long as I could. But it did not feel like that would be long. I did not need my cell phone alarm to wake me in the morning.

Chapter 7

NAMASTE

I AWOKE AT FOUR A.M. AND WAS UNABLE TO RETURN TO SLEEP. INSTEAD, I got up and tiptoed out of the room, taking my iPad with me. I sipped my coffee alone in the living room. Chris's email telling me Seamus was doing well and seemed to be improving helped my mood. It wouldn't be like Chris to make that up or try to fool me, so I relaxed a bit. Then I went to the bathroom and clipped my fingernails down to nothing.

We'd been told lice were a problem at Mother Teresa's, and in order to avoid getting the lice caught in our fingernails, we should cut them as short as possible. My nails after chemo had more ridges, were weaker, and frequently broke or tore. After changing my diet, that was finally improving, but I still willingly clipped my nails. Never had there been better motivation to give up vanity.

I showered quickly, as we'd been told to do, and I remembered to preserve the water in the large bucket kept in the shower stall in case the water ran out. I was also careful to keep my mouth closed and not swallow any of the water for the same reason we were told to eat only cooked food and fruit we peeled ourselves. Delhi belly is the more aggressive Indian cousin of Montezuma's revenge.

I couldn't dry my hair—the noise would have awakened the house (they all didn't report to their volunteer positions until nine or ten a.m.), and I couldn't find an outlet near a mirror anyway. I hadn't counted on the wet weather—my hair wouldn't dry in the damp air. Finally, I opted to use the blow-dryer quickly, in the far corner of the living room. I plugged it in, flipped the switch, and aimed at the back of my neck. The hot air swept over my shoulder in a comforting rush and then *Pop!* Sparks flew, the scent of burned hair wafted, and the dryer stopped. The puff of smoke and the dim light fixture confirmed that I had blown the fuse. *That figures.* I pulled my hair into a damp ponytail.

I dressed in the traditional Indian attire I'd purchased the day before: blue *salwar* pants, a long purple *kameez* tunic, and a blue, purple, and orange scarf covering my head. When there was enough daylight in the room, I looked at myself in the mirror. I was hardly recognizable even to myself. I looked like I was the one dying. (I could have been mistaken for a resident at Mother Teresa's.) The bright color of the clothing washed out my pale face, and while the bags under my small, bloodshot eyes should not have been a surprise, they were. Tendrils of my limp, damp hair escaped the ponytail and stuck to my cheek. I applied tinted moisturizer, blush, a little eyeliner and mascara, and finally some lip gloss. Nothing helped. I made it to the office apartment in time to let Sahil know about the blown fuse and to gulp down a cup of chai tea specially made without the milk. The other three volunteers for Mother Teresa's—Mary, Lisa, and Helene—were also there, and each looked more fresh and excited than I looked or felt. They also had dry hair.

The drive took a little over half an hour. Plenty of time to view the streets of Delhi as they came to life early in the morning. As I expected, cows were everywhere. But so were dogs, monkeys, pigs, chickens, and goats. And massive swarms of humans and cars. Everybody and everything moving quickly and crowded together. There was chaos, and yet a vaguely discernible rhythm. Our driver, Ashwani, played a Shiva chants CD, providing the perfect background music for our journey. Mary chatted, on and on, excited and nervous. I was glad to see I wasn't the only one with a bit of trepidation, though mine was expressed differently.

I stayed quiet, tired, and observant, wondering what we might be doing once we arrived, what the patients would be like, while simultaneously questioning myself. *What was I doing here? Could I possibly do this?* And, of course, again the answer to my rhetoric didn't matter. I saw the large sign outside the heavy iron gates of a private compound. We'd arrived. I'd be spending the morning with the Sisters of Mercy and the destitute and dying.

The gates opened, and we drove down the long driveway.

Even though the sky was overcast and drizzling, the place was surprisingly beautiful. Wildflowers were abundant, and the wall down the right side of the drive was covered in flowering vines. And I could see there were animals—chickens, a goat, and most surprising of all, peacocks. My immediate impression was one of peace, not distress. We came in off the crazy, hurly-burly streets to a serene calm, and the change was immediate.

Ashwani parked the car and we tumbled out, adding our bright clothing to the wildflower scenery in the midst of the lifting fog. "You will meet Mother Superior first. Here." He pointed to the smaller of the two buildings.

There was a perfunctory welcome, where we learned each of the sisters included "Teresa" in their name, which would not be confusing at all. *Ahem.* We were quickly taken to the second building—a much larger structure built around a center courtyard with locked gates. This was the residents' building. The Home for the Destitute and Dying.

Excited exclamations of *"Didi!"*—the Hindi word for "older sister" and a term of respect—followed us as we walked. We smiled and waved as we hurried to keep up with the sister. Some of the residents were sitting in the courtyard, wrapped in jewel-toned shawls against the chill that still hung in the morning air. Others were washing the floors, which caused me to note, almost immediately, how very clean the place was. Some approached us, wanting to hold our hands, walk with us, or simply look at us. Most were smiling. Some were laughing.

This was not what I had expected. This was not a hospital. There was no medicinal smell, other than the floor cleaner; people were up and walking, talking; there was no screaming, no crying, and there was great beauty in the simplicity of the place. The beauty was only emphasized by the peacock strutting through the breezeway. I'd seen far worse when, as an estate planning attorney, I'd visited clients in nursing homes or assisted-living facilities.

But as we approached the living area, that changed. Four women, two who seemed very young, were in wheelchairs, lined up against the wall. Two of them were severely disabled—cerebral palsy, I guessed. Two women were still in bed, one crying out and the other rocking back and forth. I froze, immediately assuming things would get worse; we'd walk deeper and deeper into a sad, depressing hospital atmosphere.

Yet the rest of the room had the same simple tranquillity as the courtyard. The room housed beds for fifty-eight of the seventy residents. The cots were lined up in rows, each with a brightly colored, matching bed covering and pillow. Most of the beds were made, but not all of them. Diffused sunlight streamed in from the windows on the far wall, casting a warm golden hue across the beds. It looked comfortable, homey. And that is not a small feat for a room with fifty-eight metal cots.

Before we could take it all in, the sister was gone.

As the four of us stood, slack-jawed and immobile, trying to conceive of what we should possibly be doing, a young, smiling girl approached and grabbed my hand. She pulled me down the row of cots. "Come, come," she was saying. Or, at least, I thought that's what she was saying.

Still smiling, she dropped my hand and stretched her right arm out toward a partially made bed. I could see that she had limited use of her left arm, which was bent and tucked up near her chest, her hand hanging limp. *Ah, okay. Make the bed.* This I could do. Well… maybe. My own bed only gets made maybe twice a week (and I'm exaggerating that number.). But this was a small cot and it was something to do, so I made the bed. Or, I thought I made the bed. There seemed to be an extra pillowcase.

The young woman laughed and said something, presumably in Hindi, that I could not understand. But she was clearly amused at my efforts, so I smiled as well. I held up the extra pillowcase. She nodded. *Hmmm…* I looked around to see if there was a pillow nearby missing a pillowcase. The bed next to hers was also unmade, so I moved to make that bed. She quickly grabbed my arm and, laughing now, shook her head no. She took the pillowcase from my hand and put it back on her bed, and then, through a series of hand movements on her part, bad guesses on mine, and with much laughter, I was able to figure out that the extra case was to be folded and placed under her pillow. I did as I was so comically instructed. She then guided me to the next bed, and the process started over again—though now she helped by pulling up covers, handing me the extra pillowcase, and always laughing.

I was able to determine my new friend's name, Ranjana. My name was, of course, easy for all of them. Ranjana seemed to have a pretty

good grasp of English as well—she (or her family) may have been destitute, but she was not dying. Watching her, I realized that in the United
States, she likely would have been mainstreamed into public school. I
wondered what her story was but, of course, did not ask. Instead, I followed her again as she led me to the front of the room.

Sitting on a bamboo mat, I drew in coloring books with the ladies,
helped Ranjana and one other young woman learn to pronounce the
English names of the animals in the coloring books, and smiled until it
hurt. Later I walked about with some of the women, arm in arm as they
seemed to prefer, and periodically I huddled with my fellow volunteers
to wonder if we were doing this right. We gathered in the smaller room,
east of the large dormitory room we'd been in. This smaller room had
twelve cots and a small office space. We later surmised that the higher
functioning women were housed in this room.

It didn't seem like much, what we'd been doing. And it seemed too
easy—other than the uncomfortable feeling of naïveté and the language
barrier, which was less than I imagined. There were several women who
knew enough English to converse. I was thankful to learn this as, despite
my good intentions when I applied for the trip, I had not managed to
learn a single Hindi word beyond *namaste*, which I, like most middle-
aged, suburban American women, had learned in yoga class.

When the sun came out, we all went out to the courtyard where
Ranjana showed us the balls and paddles and a plastic cricket set. The
courtyard wasn't large enough for any organized game, especially with
the number of women who joined us. But playing catch and "batting" a
ball back and forth worked well. The fresh air, the movement, the simple
joy of playing momentarily relieved my grief and fatigue.

The spicy, fragrant scent of lunch began to drift from the kitchen to
the courtyard. The sisters reappeared at eleven thirty, and the women
began to line up for lunch. We were handed plates of food and spoons.
Then each of us was guided by one of the residents to one of the women
in wheelchairs. With a few hand motions indicating we were to spoon-
feed them, we were again left to figure it out.

I don't have kids. I don't recall feeding kids. My parents are only
seventy years old and quite able-bodied, so I've never had to assist with

their care and feeding. I have, however, fed myself on more than one occasion, and this I fervently hoped would be sufficient experience. I leaned over the plate, scooped up a spoonful (*Enough? Too much? Should I mix the items?*), and moved the spoon toward the young woman's waiting mouth. She chewed, drooled, chewed, and opened her mouth again. I spooned. We repeated the motions unchanged until another of the residents came by and moved the plate in my hand so that it was farther under my charge's chin. Then she motioned for me to squat or kneel down, and when I did, I realized how tense my back was from standing over the wheelchair. I had a lot to learn about some very simple things. It was too soon to be patting myself on my sore back for my one day of volunteering.

I was quiet on the drive home, lost in my thoughts as the others chatted. All I'd done was spend four hours playing catch, making a few beds, coloring in a book, naming animals, and feeding a disabled young woman. I was ridiculously proud of myself for having completed the first day with no horrible mistakes or wildly uncomfortable moments, but I was also aware that I'd been quite tense and nervous. The point of the trip was to get me out of my comfort zone, but I hadn't expected that to happen on the first day of volunteering, nor over such simple actions. I rested my head on the window and watched as the Delhi street scenes unfolded.

It was easy to do. We were moving slowly, much more slowly than we had during our drive in that morning. I watched for the animals—the cows, the pigs, and particularly the dogs. Piles of trash were deposited along the roadsides, and the cows and pigs rummaged through them at will. Cows meandered across the streets, and dogs dashed in and out of the slow-moving traffic, nimble and quick. I'm an animal lover through and through—all animals, but of course dogs in particular. And each dog on the streets—and there were many—brought my thoughts back to Seamus. These dogs did not look healthy, nor did they look particularly sick; they weren't fat and they weren't thin. None were any discernible breed, and they were generally all medium-sized. The males were not neutered. Some were injured, some were still puppies, and some were nursing mothers with a few (never a lot) of puppies nearby. I wondered about their care and how long they survived on the streets. And did they get cancer? If they did, would anyone know? Again, I choked back tears—tears for them, tears for Seamus, and tears of exhaustion. I closed my eyes and pretended to sleep.

Our driver leaned on his horn, as did every other driver in India, but to no visible avail. We did not arrive back at CVV home base until one thirty p.m. There was no time to head to our apartments and freshen up. No time for me to check emails or text messages to see how Seamus was doing. We had to eat lunch and be ready for the two o'clock lecture. Luckily, for us, if not for her, Lisa had a room in the apartment that was also used as the main kitchen and dining room by the entire group. The four of us dashed into her room and bathroom to wash our hands, remove our head scarves, and run the electric delousing comb through our hair. Prior to that moment, I did not know there was such a thing as a delousing comb. This was not exactly what I meant by "out of my comfort zone," but it was certainly one version.

I inhaled a lunch of *dal* (split lentils in an aromatic blend of spices), sliced vegetable crudités, naan, and a masala rice dish. The cook had been made aware there were three vegans in our group and adjusted the meals accordingly, serving vegan versions alongside the dishes that contained butter or milk or cream or egg. My options were now varied, and each was delicious. Or at least I was ravenous enough to think so.

I sat for the afternoon lecture, which began immediately after we cleared our dishes from the table. Fifteen minutes later, I nodded off, my head bobbing forward and jerking back as I tried to wake myself. I moved in my chair so that the post in front of me would block me from the view of the lecturer. "*The people of India are a diverse…*" My head snapped forward. "*…witness to the migration of the bucolic…*" My eyes closed again and my mind drifted. "*…under the famous Gupta dynasty…*" I pried my eyes open and tried to focus. Looking around the room, I saw I was not the only one struggling to stay awake. An early morning, a long car ride, and a quick meal followed by a lecture was not a prescription for a perky me (there is, in fact, no such prescription), and I was not alone. I observed many heads slowly falling forward and then jerking upright. "...*the virtues of the Indian people...*" My eyes closed. I'd have to discover their virtues for myself some other time.

Following the lecture, we had time only to run to our room, freshen up slightly, grab our cameras or other personal items, and head back to the meeting room before we were off on our next excursion. This time, it was a cultural exercise that had us shopping for ordinary household items and food in the local village.

It was a worthwhile exercise if only because it allowed me to find a coffee shop, which allowed me a much-needed shot of life (also known as espresso). I could then finish the challenge of finding a bag of potato chips, a single can of cola, bread, and six eggs, with only the three hundred rupees we'd been given. (Hint: there is no "grocery store," and who knew there were "bake-it-yourself" potato chips?) The discussion that followed back at the home base was lively and humorous, though we were all limp in our chairs from exhaustion. Yet still, there was another Hindi lesson—words and phrases that would be useful to those in the group volunteering at the schools and teaching young children. The four of us at Mother Teresa's were not likely to need to say *"Cupa rahō!"* (keep quiet) or *"Mata mārō"* (don't hit), or at least I hoped not. But we did at least learn how to ask someone's name. *"Nāma?"* Okay, it wasn't the most polite way of asking, but it would do. I also figured *"Mujhē nahīṁ patā"* (I don't know) would come in handy, so I tried to remember those two expressions. Those were all the brain cells I had left.

Finally in bed at eleven that evening, I checked my iPad and saw that Chris had sent a photo of Seamus and a note. Seamus was doing better, howling more (always a good sign), and eating well. At last, I could sleep—if only for a few hours.

Chapter 8

EENY, MEENY, MINA

THE GRINDING SCHEDULE CONTINUED FOR TWO MORE DAYS. OUR work at Mother Teresa's became more serious.

Mother Superior learned that among our group there was a doctor, a physical therapist, and a physical education teacher. I'm sure she prayed for the strength to overlook the one disappointment…me, the lawyer. She requested that we obtain the weight and blood sugar levels of each of the seventy women and tasked Sister Margaret Theresa to organize us and the project.

My fellow volunteers were up for the task and then some. They were thrilled. I tried to devise ways to be helpful without being too near the pinpricks of blood for testing glucose levels as I was certain my fainting would not be deemed helpful.

There was one strength I could put to use—my logic. I became the organizer, enlisting one of the residents, Fatima, to help me figure out the women's names so I could chart the statistics. Fatima's English was sufficient, certainly far better than my Hindi. And she had shown herself to be congenial and helpful despite having lost three of her limbs to complications from diabetes (which made the task at hand that much more serious). There was no computer printout to work from, only a large old-fashioned ledger book with light green pages and thin red-lined columns. Sister Margaret Theresa instructed me to put a date at the top of each page and list each woman's name, weight, and blood sugar level.

While I worked on the system, Mary and Lisa struggled to find enough various working parts and latex gloves to comprise a functioning glucose test system, and Helene found the scale and talked with and soothed the women lining up. Even I was soothed by Helene's aura. It was calming just to stand next to her in her state of grace and compassion. Maybe it would rub off on me—me, the one next to her with a clipboard, a plan, and a fear of blood.

Not that much went according to my plan. We only got halfway through before it was time for lunch the first day and then our departure. Lunch could not wait, no matter what my process was. Apparently the sisters love a certain efficiency too, even if it meant we left without completing our task.

On the second day when we finished the blood sugar and weight statistics, Mother Superior then informed us we needed to do their blood pressure as well. My system would have worked far better, of course, if all three of those things had been done at the same time. Perhaps Mother S didn't think we'd get it all done, so she had started with the most important tests. Crafty Mother. But now I'd have to be certain that this "Mina" or "Meena" or "Meha" was the same "Mina" or "Meena" or "Meha" as the one who'd weighed 54 kg and had a blood sugar level of 80 mg. Or was this the other one? And it seemed I was not hearing the names the same way. Mina now sounded like Dina, but I didn't have a Dina on my list. I did have a Nina and a Meena, though. Adding to my confusion, but certainly making the whole process more fun, the ladies were now mentioning their nicknames.

Now one woman was referred to as "vegetable Jaya" (her job was to peel vegetables), and there were several "Chotis," which I heard as "shorty" but in reality meant "small" or "younger sister" (I thought I was close enough). We were taken aback, and duly warned, when we learned one woman's nickname meant "biter" because of her habit of biting… well, the hands that fed her.

On it went. I learned bits of both the culture and the language simply by compiling my list. And I found a kind of comfort in the process. I was emboldened enough to try to pronounce the names as I was told them. Luckily, I am able to laugh at myself.

Fatima stated the name of the next woman in line: "Poppy."

"Poppy?" I said.

Fatima giggled. So did her friend Santi.

"No." Fatima was smiling broadly. "Pa-pee."

"Pa-pee," I repeated.

Now several of the women were giggling.

"No. Po-pee," she said with an emphasis on the last syllable.

Bravely I tried again, though I could not decipher any difference between what she was saying and what I'd already said. But perhaps with volume and enthusiasm my pronunciation would sound the same. "PA-PEE!" I said, the way nervous people speak to blind people.

The room of women burst out laughing. I tried it yet again and hoped I was not swearing inadvertently. "PAW-PEE!"

The ladies' eyes widened and they laughed and covered their mouths with their hands. Fatima explained that *pappii* is a cute word for a kiss and is most assuredly not a woman's name. The roomful of women laughed louder now. I could see that I would easily elicit laughter all morning by playing the fool, exuberantly shouting *pappii* at random moments. And so, when I got frustrated with my failed system or lack of progress, I shouted, *"Pappii!"* and joined in the laughter. No one kissed me, though.

It took the rest of my morning to sort out my notes and the charts and figure out which women still needed to have their blood pressure taken. Some were willing to volunteer over and over again, and others hid. Both approaches wreaked havoc with my system. Only one woman kicked and screamed; she was dragged in by two other patients, each holding an arm and a leg, swinging the screaming, squirming woman between them like children on a playground. Still, the woman would not be quiet or still enough to have her blood pressure taken (which was high, we were sure). This was not playing catch in the courtyard.

And yet Mother Teresa's Home was quiet, relatively calm, and certainly beautiful in its own way. My mornings there were the best part of the trip.

Because the afternoons were hard and the nights were unbearable.

The schedule, combined with the difficulty of carving out any alone time to process India and what I'd left behind in Riverside, was wearing me down, weighing so heavily mentally that I could feel it physically—though I had not yet caught the cold or the Delhi belly that was knocking down our group one by one.

I was isolated, in part because I roomed with two wonderful, interesting women who happened to be part of another group and thus on an entirely different schedule. So in addition to having to keep my next day's clothes and toiletries in the living room to avoid waking them hours before they needed to leave in the morning, I had no roommate to talk things over with, to discuss the next day's schedule with, or to invite me to run out for coffee or to dinner, to shop, explore, or eat in town. The women in my Fresh Chapter group and in my apartment were on different schedules, leaving two hours after I did and generally arriving back from their volunteer placements before I did. Thus, they spent their days together, bonding as women do, and I was never comfortable enough to just walk into their bedroom and join in on those rare occasions we were in the apartment together.

But my isolation was also a result of being grief-stricken over my dog. And I was angry. Tired and angry, and not hiding it well. The combination left me without friends, and the circumstances left me without solace or the energy to do anything about it.

I assure you, I am not normally this way. While Chris teases me that I can be a bit of a hermit (the whole "Alcohol, Books, Coffee, and Dogs is all I need" thing), I generally have a good social game face and enjoy meeting and talking with new people. But even in the best of circumstances, I do not do well without time alone. That's where I get my fuel. That's how I can function. The welcoming gift of blank journals seemed like a mockery now. Worst of all, I didn't have enough contact with Chris for him to humor me out of the dark cloud I felt descending on me. He could not lead me to the light, as he has always done in our years together.

I was on my own.

I'd learned a lot in my odyssey through cancer, and here—across the globe, traveling with a group of fellow cancer survivors—I'd need to draw on that. One of the things I thought I'd learned was to adjust to circumstances I can't control, to look for the good, and to cling to what I valued most. That night I skipped dinner so I could carve out a few moments alone in my room. Finally, I was able to email Chris, alternating between descriptions of my exhaustion and begging for news (*lie to me, please, if need be*) that Seamus was well. It was only five in the morning his time, so I knew Chris wouldn't answer. He was no more a morning person than I was. I picked up my journal and began to scribble my random thoughts, trying to make sense of anything. I had only half an hour before Terri was back in our flat.

And then Terri poked her head in my room. "Do you know how to get to apartment 330?"

Only then did I remember that we were to have yet another group meeting following dinner. I didn't want to go.

"No," I said in a tone that also said, *"And I don't care."* Maybe my time alone had only increased my need to be left alone.

"Okay, then I'll wait for you," she said. Of course, she didn't know where I'd gone in my head. She didn't know how much of my brain had now been consumed by that dark, descending cloud.

I wanted to scream *"It's going to be a long damn wait!"* but I didn't. This, it turned out, was a mistake. It would have been better to have lost it then and there with minimal witnesses. Or to have told her frankly what was going on with me. But I'm at best reluctant to talk about my feelings. Really, really reluctant. Instead, I dutifully, and against every screaming nerve in my body, followed Terri to apartment 330. Bad idea. *Very, very bad idea.*

We settled in on couches and chairs, gathered in a circle. The meeting began with what I swore I was promised would not be happening: talking about feelings with near strangers. I barely discuss feelings with people I know well (I write about them and share them with total strangers, but that's just different…somehow). Perhaps some people are willing to discuss their feelings about having had cancer. I am not one of those people. I sat, boiling and churning inside. I could not talk about cancer at that moment. I could not hear about cancer. And I was captive in a room of cancer survivors who wanted to talk about…cancer. Yes, I should have excused myself, but I didn't.

The discussion turned to how the trip was going and how we were feeling. I had heard many of the participants complain to one another about their exhaustion, their difficulty with the volunteer assignments, and the living conditions. Now many of them voiced their concerns, and finally, for one brief moment, I was not alone. I was not the only

one suffering. But when I heard the CVV leader's response to the suffering—a smile and simplistic "India is hard"—I lost it. And not one
bit graciously.

I *thought* I was saying that when one of the participants, a single
mother of two teenagers, expressed anger that she was diagnosed with
stage IV lung cancer and given two years to live, she is allowed to be
mad as holy hell and no one should try to temper that. A stage IV cancer
survivor does *not* have to say, "Oh, but others have it so much worse, so
I'll buck up."

I *thought* I said that when we, jet-lagged cancer survivors with all
the physical and mental scars and limitations that go with that, are run
ragged with an arbitrary schedule of twelve or more hours a day of volunteer work and lectures and tours, with no breaks, while sleeping on
three inches of foam balanced on wooden crates, sharing bathrooms
that require us to dispose of toilet paper in a trash receptacle, and show-
ers (when we were lucky enough to get one) with water we have to be
careful to spit out, *we* are allowed to complain and we should be heard.
The standard for a legitimate complaint is not that no one anywhere
in the world possibly has it worse than you do. We do not have to say,
"Oh, but those kids in the shantytowns have it so much worse than we
do, so we'll just be grateful." Not when it would be so easy to fix it by,
say, giving us an hour of downtime one afternoon. Or scheduling a walk
instead of a lecture.

I *know* I said, "Don't brush off our concerns by saying 'India is hard'
when you are *making* it hard. The living conditions are hard. Fine, I get
that. But the schedule does not have to be *insane*. You cannot put a six-
week schedule into a two-week one and impose it on *cancer survivors!*"

But what they all *heard* was me yelling at a stage IV cancer survivor
that she shouldn't complain and that everyone else should just keep their
damn feelings to themselves. Or better yet, avoid having them, thank
you very much. It's also possible I said I felt like a prisoner, and not a
U.S. prisoner, because those prisoners have rights.

The group fell into a stunned silence.

I made Terri cry, and I made everyone else hate me. I deserved that.
Terri did not.

Just when I thought the trip couldn't get any worse, I officially made myself a pariah.

————————

The next day, following lunch, Terri asked if she could speak with me privately. I was being called to the principal's office and I felt it. I was chagrined, concerned, and simultaneously defiant. I may not have expressed it in the best way possible, but my complaints were legitimate. The schedule was too much.

So before dinner, I sat in the courtyard, talking to Terri. She thought I'd offended members of our group, and I assured her I hadn't meant to. But, she went on to say, she thought I was affecting people and pointed out that I had a strong personality.

If I had been in a better mood, I would have laughed at this. It's something I've heard my entire life. My *entire* life. I was apparently a three-year-old with a strong personality. And yet I never know what people expect me to do with that information, and asking, "What do you expect me to do with that information?" only seems to solidify their observation.

"I don't see how I'm possibly affecting anybody else. I'm hardly around anyone, except at Mother Teresa's, and we're pretty busy there."

"You are. You're part of the group, and everybody can see that you are unhappy. I was afraid to talk to you. I think the others might be afraid too."

I thought I was mostly alone because I'd missed the opportunity to really get to know anyone in our group due to the room assignments and a schedule that didn't lend itself to leisurely conversations. But somehow, apparently, I'd frightened a group of cancer survivors.

"Look, I stand by what I said about this schedule. But I'm also having a great deal of personal difficulty right now." I took a deep breath. I thought but didn't say, *I'd like to just leave it at that, if I could.*

Terri's already large blue eyes widened and then narrowed as she tilted her head. "I'm sorry."

One look of sympathy was all it took. The tears began to flow. "My dog was diagnosed with terminal cancer before I left. The dog in the book." Terri had read my memoir just after it came out. I suspect that played a role in her selecting me for the trip. A selection she was clearly regretting now. "He means everything to me. He was a huge part of my cancer recovery and now… It's just hard to be here."

"I didn't know."

"I know. And even in the best of circumstances, I need quiet time. Time to write, to think, to just be in my own head. And I can't get that here. Not ever. It's impossible. So right now, all of it, it feels like I'm being tortured. It's just too much." I looked away. "So, yeah, I understand that I may look angry and unapproachable."

Terri shifted sideways. "I was thinking maybe you shouldn't go this weekend. Maybe this weekend would be a good time for you to be alone."

The weekend trip was to Agra to see the Taj Mahal.

Why would I fly all the way to India and not see the Taj Mahal? I stared at the ground, dumbfounded.

Then, no longer crying, I looked up at Terri. "I've thought about leaving the whole trip several times, believe me. But I made a commitment and I'll stick it out. The Taj Mahal is a highlight of the trip. I don't think it's fair to ask me not to go."

"I'm not telling you that you can't go. I'm asking you to think about it."

"I will think about it."

I would *not* think about it. I was *not* missing the Taj Mahal. Not after everything else.

We were both quiet for a few moments.

"Here's the thing. If you decide to go, I need you to not make fun of things. No snippy comments, no sarcasm. I know you don't like the touchy-feely stuff, but you can't affect the others."

"I will think about that too," I said. And I half meant it.

At dinner, Terri informed us all that the late-night group meetings would be voluntary. She had postponed the exercise that involved writing down something we wanted to let go of in our life and then burning that slip of paper. It was to have occurred the night of my outburst, and now instead, they'd be lighting it up that night. Notice I said "they"? Right. I was the only member of the group who chose not to attend. So much for my "influence."

By not attending, I got the chance to IM with Chris. My two main coping mechanisms in life are talking things through with Chris and sarcasm (these thing overlap, not coincidentally). I was miserably unhappy, generally wishing I was home with Chris and Seamus, with only Mother Teresa's Home for the Destitute and Dying as my respite and solace, ironically. I considered booking an early flight home.

Again, Chris talked me out of it by being supportive, assuring me that Seamus was doing well, and that the two of them would be fine if I stayed and made adjustments to get through the trip, like I'd started to do by staying in that evening. He was supportive whether I got on the plane home or stayed and worked through it.

Although, I can see where it will be hard to visit the Taj with one arm tied behind your back. Possibly both.

I responded, What?

If she wants you not to crack jokes or use sarcasm, she's basically removing a large chunk of you, and certainly one of your finest honed weapons.

I smiled. I couldn't even be insulted by this. And suddenly, going home seemed like quitting. I wasn't a quitter. Cancer had taught me that much.

When Terri returned to our apartment that night, I told her I was going, but I couldn't guarantee I would smile through it all. Likely I'd just be quiet. But I was going.

"Fair enough," she said.

I hoped I could do it, but I had my doubts.

Chapter 9

IN THE POND OF WONDER

ONE MORE NIGHT ON MY FOAM-ON-WOOD-CRATE BED AND I DID not wake on a positive note. On the bus to Agra, we were handed name tags. Only they said things like "In the Moment," "Confident," "Peaceful," and "Amazed." I'm amazed. I mean, yes, amazed at the name tags, but also, my tag said "Amazed." These were, we're told, the words we each used in our interviews when asked how we wanted to feel when we came to India. I wanted to be amazed. Now I just wanted to be alone (and that would have been a name tag I could embrace). I'd had a hard enough time remembering actual names, and now I'm supposed to remember to call someone "Present." And Terri wanted me to do this without laughing. Or scoffing.

One of our local guides was handsome and charming, with a brilliant white smile flashing from underneath his *Raiders of the Lost Ark*-style hat. His name was Shakti. He asked us to call him Shaz, pronounced like Chaz. But then Terri explained the name game to him (though she likely didn't call it a game), and he was christened "Happy." Another guide joined us later, and when we learned he had college degrees in Indian history, architecture, sociology, and anthropology (and I hoped cuisine as well), he was dubbed "Wisdom." I refrained from calling foul—if "Wisdom" is a feeling, I would have claimed it as my own. Given any opportunity to avoid a feeling, I will take it. If his tag could read "Wisdom," couldn't mine just read "Sarcasm"?

In a rare stroke of luck, I was assigned a hotel room with Lina. I had chatted with Lina a bit and observed that she had both an enviable camera and an artistic eye. She also loved coffee as much as I did, thus she was willing to slip away from the crowd for either the perfect shot or cup. I liked her, though she probably felt she'd drawn the short end of the roommate stick. Poor girl also had the raging head cold that had been making its way through our group but, in keeping with the custom, had avoided me.

We awoke at five in the morning to be at the Taj Mahal for the sunrise. The Taj is known for, among other things, the magnificent way the sunlight reflects off the marble walls and reflecting pools. Dawn is considered the perfect time to view this Wonder of the World, and having come that far, even I was willing to wake at that godforsaken hour to see it.

The large white bus drove us through the darkness—Agra is not a pretty city and it was early on a Sunday morning, so we did not miss much. When the bus stopped to let us all off, the Taj Mahal was nowhere to be seen. We were standing in the middle of a deserted, dirty street. Then we all saw the horse-drawn carriages approach, brightly festooned with ribbons and flowers. Terri was smiling widely. The carriages were for us.

I rode with Terri, thinking, *I'm in a horse-drawn carriage being taken to the Taj Mahal!* I concentrated on being in the moment, ignoring that the poor horse was far too thin (as was the driver) and the streets were filthy. I appreciated her efforts—the carriage ride, her choice to ride with me, and making the effort to check in to see how I was doing.

We lined up outside the gates of the Taj, not the only group to have decided sunrise was the time to see this monument. There were stray dogs in the street, lying at the gate, sleeping alongside the road. They were not begging and they did not look hungry. They simply looked like they too were waiting to see this wonder. I resisted the urge to pet them.

Though the sun rose while we waited in line to enter, the light was still beautiful—bright without being blinding, with subtle pink and lavender just barely visible. So naturally, everyone stopped and gasped shortly after entering through the front building and landing on the plaza terrace overlooking the Taj. The massive shrine to love was there before us in all its breathtaking glory. Only, so was the crowd, jostling, bumping, and posing for pictures. They handed each other cameras and posed—each in the same, traditional way, just off to the side with the white wonder of the world in the background, gleaming. My group did the same; they handed each other cameras and posed, taking each other's pictures. But not mine. I was still *persona non grata*, and I was still not doing a thing about it.

I am not adept at those teenage-girl selfie photos, and I was not about to hold my arm out and turn the camera on myself to try. I sensed that handing my camera to a stranger was not a good idea. Instead, I raised my camera in an attempt to take advantage of my height and just take a photo over the heads of the happy, snappy tourists. Wisdom took hold of my arm.

"Come with me. Come this way." He led me through the crowd and cleared a space, moving people aside politely but firmly. To my surprise, everyone obliged. At the front, just at the edge of the balcony, he said, "Kneel here for your photo."

I thanked him and knelt, careful not to slip on the damp tile. When I looked up, I was stunned by a moment of perfect peace and beauty.

There was a dog, golden and white, bigger than a beagle but not by much. It was one of the dogs I had seen in front of the gate and wanted to pet. The dog was bent down, his two front paws dangling in the reflecting pool. He was sipping from the pond that stretches a long vertical line from the Taj to the plaza where I was standing, the better to capture the magnificent reflection of this world wonder. And it does. The reflection was perfect. From where I was kneeling, I could see the Taj Mahal twice—the real thing and its full reflection in the smooth clear water, with only the slightest ripple where the dog's tongue met the water. The blue-pink sky, gleaming white marble, dark orange terra-cotta tiles, green grass, violet flowers, and a golden dog were all I saw. I heard nothing. It was a moment of such complete tranquillity I thought I was imagining it. I turned only briefly to look at the people crowded around me, yet far, far away from where I was. No one was looking at the dog. *Did anyone else see him? Was he real?* I was glad I was kneeling. I was thankful for Wisdom. I was breathing deeply for the first time in days. I stayed focused on the dog in the simple act of drinking water. I felt peace. I felt joy.

I was amazed.

I managed a few photos before the dog finished his morning drink, looked up, turned, and went about his day. I won't need the photos to remember that moment always, but I'm glad I have them. It's how I know that moment was real. I knew also that moment was a sign. And I knew I needed to figure out what it meant.

I roamed the grounds of the Taj alone at first and then, briefly, with one of our group, who kept up her steady stream of chatter, as she had, best I could tell, the entire trip. But now, I smiled, appreciative of her enthusiasm. It was indeed unbelievable that we were here. To go from a cancer diagnosis and grueling treatment that itself threatens one's life, to have endured such an utter loss of control and, for a time, one's own destiny, it was indeed a spectacular feat to now be standing on the other side of the world in front of this gleaming, world-renowned monument. It was, indeed.

Once inside the palace, she and I separated, each roaming off to something we were drawn to. I took hundreds of photos that day, most of the architecture but plenty of the people as well. During my first week in India, I had been approached from time to time by young girls asking to take my picture. I get this—I'm blond and five feet ten inches tall; to them, I'm different. The girls usually stood with me, smiling but not touching. I'd always ask to take their photos too, particularly if they or their family members were dressed in the traditional saris in the turquoise, violet, mandarin, emerald, or fuchsia colors I loved. This time, as I walked around the vast courtyards and gardens of the Taj Mahal, I was stopped for photos by many more people. Perhaps my face had softened. I had, maybe, the smallest bit of a smile.

A family of seven adults and two children approached me. A man I guessed to be the patriarch asked if they could take a picture of me with their baby—a boy in purple clothing with a red bindi on his forehead. I nodded, and a younger man came toward me holding the child, who was probably ten months old or so. I panicked, thinking he was going to hand the child to me. (I'm awkward at best with babies.) But instead he stood next to me. Then he motioned to my camera and then to a woman in their group whom I presumed was his wife and the mother of the child. This is when I noticed I was the only one with a camera.

They wanted me to take a photo with my own camera? Why?

The family was gathered behind the man's wife, looking at us, the photo subjects. My mind raced. Was this an elaborate scam to steal my camera? If I handed my camera over, would it be gone forever, along with the hundreds of photos I'd just taken? *I'd lose the photos of my golden dog!* I hesitated, looking at their smiling faces. If it was a scam, it was indeed an elaborate one. And if it was not, well, I'd have another beautiful photo to remember this day. I handed her my camera.

She took the photo and then another. She laughed and nodded and handed the camera back to me. The husband asked, in half hand motions, half broken English ("we see"), if they could see the photo. I popped open the screen and showed them the photo taken moments before. The family gathered around and smiled their approval. We all nodded and, hands in prayer position, said our *namastes*.

Later I asked Wisdom (who else would I ask?) what the photo request was about. He said it was a sign of respect and a story for them—the blond American they met at the Taj. Or for the baby, a story they would share as he grew up. The Hindu culture is very respectful of visitors; this much we had seen and learned. This was one more way of showing that. Since I was so obviously a visitor, they were, in a sense, acknowledging that I was special.

What a very kind thing to do. Especially on that day.

In our hotel room, following breakfast, we had an hour to rest or pack or shower before we needed to meet downstairs for two more stops and the long bus ride back to Delhi. Lina and I opted to rest in our side-by-side twin beds, the height of luxury compared to where we'd been sleeping. Maybe it was exhaustion, the lingering thrill of the Taj, or the sudden comfort of soft beds, but Lina talked to me. I asked her if she was married. She laughed joyfully and pointed out that I had missed the "letting go" burning ceremony two nights before. What she was letting go of, sending up into smoke, was her marriage. She told me her husband had an affair and she'd filed for divorce recently. I remembered then that in the group therapy session before I'd made my outburst, Lina had said she was enjoying the trip because she didn't have to think about anything. Her schedule was set, her meals were made for her and served regularly, and there was no time to think. For her this was a reprieve. I had been shocked, but now I understood why. It's always perspective, isn't it?

I shared with her that my first husband had cheated on me twice (that I know of; I'm sure there were more, but it loses significance after two). One of his mistresses was named Lina. This Lina's eyes flew wide open and she let out a hearty laugh.

"Get out! Are you kidding me? Was she Italian?" she said.

"Yes, she was. So you'll forgive me if I've called you Deena before. I have a mental block about your name."

She laughed again. "You can call me anything you want. I totally understand."

We talked for so long we had to throw our things back in our overnight bags in a rush and still were late getting downstairs. But at least I wasn't alone. I had a friend. I had shared a feeling. Maybe two (anger is a feeling, right?).

As we toured additional sites that day, I made more of an effort to talk with my fellow travelers and to join with the group. Though, even in my new lighter mood, I was enjoying being alone with my thoughts. Seeking to stay in that peaceful space I'd found, I now watched more closely for the dogs, and the monkeys, the cows, the goats, and even the birds.

It occurred to me that the animals were in no better or worse condition than the people. If we were in a particularly poverty-stricken place, the dogs were more likely to be thin, hungry, and sick or injured, or both. At one temple there was a particularly aggressive baby goat. She danced and pawed at the ground to the laughter of the crowd but began to butt her head at the legs of bystanders when no food followed the laughter. It was hard not to be reminded of the small acrobatic girl who performed, grinning, flipping, and dancing, outside our car window a few days before on our way home from Mother Teresa's. We had been told not to hand out money—that it wouldn't help the child and would only encourage the rings of adults who "own" these children and force them to work this way (and indeed, she should have been in school—it was noon on a weekday). When we did not proffer money, she'd approached the car, yelling and banging on the window, going from adorable and amusing to threatening and frightening in one quick moment.

In the impoverished villages too, there were more disfigured beggars, more piles of trash, larger crowds of humans, and smaller shanty shacks (but always clean; miraculously clean lean-tos and shacks, thatched huts and tents). In less impoverished areas, the dogs and other animals, like the humans, seemed content, not starving, and, if not healthy, at least not visibly sick or injured. And, I realized now, in the neighborhood we were living in, middle-class by India's standards, I had seen purebred dogs—a Chow, a poodle, and to my great happiness, a beagle—being walked on leashes in parks, not roaming the streets eating from trash or the handouts given, it seemed regularly, outside restaurants or on street corners.

The symmetry—the equality of people and the animals as sentient beings with souls—appealed greatly to me. Before arriving in Delhi, I had thought I would be horrified by the condition of the animals. I expected to see sick, injured, and even dead animals. I had expected the dogs would be begging and that I would want to rescue each and every one and instead would feel my heart break over and over again at my helplessness. That was not the case. The animals did not strike me as unhappy or in any danger—at least not any more than a pedestrian in Delhi (and in my case, perhaps far less so, as I was not getting the hang of dashing across streets). And the dogs did not beg (and in that regard, I had to note, their manners were much better than a certain beagle, though clearly it was my indulgence that created his behavior, not a true need for food). The cows, of course, got special privileges; they are indeed sacred. We had even been told to follow a cow crossing the street; it would be the safest way across. That was true, but only if the cow went in the direction one wanted. But it seemed all animals were respected as sentient beings. I took comfort in that.

The bus ride home from Agra took more than five hours, much of the time spent not moving at all, stuck in a long line of traffic with young boys waving at us from the streets and children posing for the photos we were taking from the bus window. Again, I watched for the animals. Over and over I noticed that people set out piles of vegetables for the cows, and occasionally poured kibble and food scraps out in piles for the dogs. These dogs were not pets, but it seemed they belonged. They knew where and when to expect food. I realized then that the dog at the Taj pond probably waited every morning for the gates to open. Every morning he trotted in for his drink and perhaps a roll on the dew-dropped lush grass on the grounds before starting his day on the streets. The Taj was home to him and the other dogs I'd seen outside the gates. His place in the universe.

It was nearly midnight when we arrived back at CVV home base. I had not slept on the bus, though at least my thoughts were now restful. I changed clothes quickly, trying not to wake my roommates. I crawled into bed and quickly fell asleep.

When I woke in the middle of the night, I had an email message from Chris.

Seamus was improving daily, Chris assured me, and it was then I remembered reading in my *Traveler's Tales: India* book that dogs at a location were a sign of positivity. Maybe that would be true now in my own life.

Armed with that hope, and with the calm brought to me by the golden dog, I set out to salvage my second week in India from the ruin I'd wrought in my first. Groups would never be my thing, so I made efforts to get to know my fellow participants individually. By running out shopping with one of them, I learned she feared dogs and had never traveled far from home, let alone without any family. And I knew then, though she'd been joking and popular with everyone throughout the trip, how very difficult this all must have been for her being in a land where dogs run wild and the culture is so very different from ours. I had dinner out with a small group, and together we were late to the evening wrap-up session. Though the anger at a late arrival was palpable, this time I made amends by joining the conversation. I shared a story of a friendship I'd lost when I went through cancer. I defused the anger rather than stoking the fires, and I realized I missed the friend of whom I spoke. I tried to help another participant by trading volunteer placements for a day—she had wanted to go to Mother Teresa's and instead was sent to teach at a school. Although the trade didn't work out (Mother Teresa's does not allow a one-day volunteer), I was sent to the school for a day and learned I could, in fact, deal with children. I knew that going in—there was a dog sleeping on a cart outside the school when I arrived.

Chapter 10

WALK BESIDE ME

I WANTED TO RUN FROM BAGGAGE CLAIM, LADEN WITH MY SUITCASES and packages, to Chris waiting in the car at curbside pickup, but I couldn't. On my last day in India I sprained my ankle—I don't even know how, but I guess it was inevitable with the roads and potholes and uneven terrain—but the injury and twenty hours of air travel had swollen my ankle to the size of my thigh (not small, if you were wondering). But I knew Seamus was in the car with Chris, and I needed to see him—alive and happy. Chris had texted me a photo of Seamus in his crate in the backseat of Chris's car, along with a note: We can't wait to see you. I couldn't wait either. Nor could I move more than inches at a time without pain shooting up my leg.

When Chris saw me, he jumped out of the car and took the bags from me.

"What happened?"

"I have no idea. It started yesterday. Or two days ago now, I guess." I opened the car door.

Seamus wagged his tail quickly, thumping the side of the crate. He greeted me with an enthusiastic howl. I opened the crate door and kissed his head, petting him and breathing him in. He was thinner, but not by much, and his energy seemed better than when I had left. Chris had not been deceiving me with his middle-of-the-night emails. Seamus was doing better. I closed the crate door.

"Sorry, Moose. We'll get home and cuddle like mad." I took my place in the passenger seat while Chris finished loading my luggage.

"You have no idea how glad I am to see you," he said.

I kissed him. "I'm glad to see you too. It's been a very long two weeks."

"Tell me about it. Every minute for two weeks, I've worried about keeping this dog alive. I promised you he'd be here when you got back and I had to make that happen."

"Were there problems?"

"No. Just in my imagination. If he sneezed, I panicked. When he slept, I worried he wouldn't wake up. When he was awake, I worried he wasn't sleeping enough. Let's just say it was a stressful two weeks."

"Agreed. Very, very much agreed." I reached across and rested my hand on his thigh. Seamus's tail tapped against the crate wall. I was exhausted and injured, but I was home.

Since Seamus was supposed to be kept calm, and I was recovering from…well, from India…we spent the next several days on the couch watching documentaries. (Okay, Seamus may have slept.)

The movies I'd been stockpiling were documentaries about food. Not "foodie" travel documentaries—not at all. No, these were films about where our food comes from—the abuse and torture of the animals that are the food "products" we eat. I'd watched *Forks Over Knives* at the suggestion of Julieanna, my plant-based diet guru, and now I moved on to *Vegucated*; *Food, Inc.*; and others. Each was progressively more explicit about the horrors inflicted on these animals during their short lives and at the moment of death, which was, I now knew, no short, quick "moment" as we'd all like to believe.

Considering what I was watching—and when I wasn't watching I was reading—it's a wonder I didn't pet the fur right off the poor dog in a frenzy of love and protection. In my post-India state, knowing that my trip had been rescued by the vision of a dog, I contemplated more deeply my feelings about animals. I'd always felt a strong connection to all animals, but most of my focus had been on dogs. But now I was confronted with the subject of the animals we eat and how they suffer. I contemplated becoming completely vegan, but I was unsure where to start, and I had a dying dog home with me that took most of my focus and energy.

After each documentary, I turned off the television to look away from the images of dead pigs left to rot on piles of garbage, no more consideration given to what had been live, sentient beings than was given to the paper cups and rags in the piles below them. I had to look away from the "fryers"—chickens bred and held captive with their bodies pumped so full of growth hormones that they grow rapidly to a size their legs can't support, leaving them crippled and in pain in the few short months they are allowed to live. I had to look away from the breeding sows kept for years in gestation crates so tiny they cannot turn around, covered in their own waste, breathing noxious fumes. I looked away from the former "family farmer," now unable to compete against the large agri-business farm, going against her very soul by turning her own farm into a corporate-controlled factory farm, forcing her to treat "her" animals in a way so horrid that filming isn't permitted because she'll lose the farm if she allows it. I had to look away from it all. And yet I could not. I'd start another documentary or pick up another book until I couldn't take it anymore.

I held Seamus close and let my tears fall into his fur—tears for him, for the cows, for the pigs, the chickens, the turkeys. I got up and poured myself a glass of wine, choosing to overlook that alcohol is a depressant and that was the last thing I needed then. Further into the bottle, I was crying for all of mankind, for what we'd become and berating myself for having been duped all these years, for not knowing where my food came from. I would do better. I had to.

Before I left for India, I had been having headaches and what I thought was probably anxiety attacks—waking up in the middle of the night, my temples pulsing, nightmares vaguely recalled, and my brain seemingly vibrating. In India, the insomnia and a bit of the shaking brain continued, I assumed because of exhaustion and perhaps the grief that was quickly enveloping me. Once I was home, I thought it would all stop. It soon became clear that my choice of "entertainment" was not helping. My nightmares became more violent.

When I was in treatment for breast cancer, I had nightmares that typically involved me losing control—sitting in the backseat of a car, unable to reach the steering wheel or brake to control the spinning, speeding vehicle; or the tried-and-true nightmare of showing up at school completely unprepared for the test to be taken and unable to find the room; and sometimes, of course, I was naked or half-dressed in these dreams. But the animal nightmares were worse because it wasn't only me suffering. It was everyone around me. I'd be screaming at people to look at what was happening—the dog in the middle of the road with traffic swerving around it, the baby pigs squealing in pain as they were picked up by large bulldozers and thrown into mass graves—but no one saw what I saw. No one heard me. I'd wake, frightened, distraught, and unable to sleep for hours. Seamus followed me to the library and we'd sit together in the recliner. He'd fall back asleep and I'd read.

I read *Main Street Vegan: Everything You Need to Know to Eat Healthfully and Live Compassionately in the Real World* by Victoria Moran because that title was exactly what I wanted. Tell me how to do this in *the real world*. Tell me about compassion, because at that moment, I felt like hurting people (who, I don't know…whoever was responsible for abusing and torturing those poor farm animals). I liked her take on being vegan—she too has a partner who is not vegan, and she makes no apologies for that. Her approach was much less "in my face" about the abuse of the animals, so I relaxed into the book.

> Decide, then, that you can do this, because you can. You learned how to drive a car, program the DVR, and use your iGadgets; compared to those accomplishments, going vegan is a piece of Wacky Cake... The biggest obstacle most would-be vegans face is feeling different from other people, but you can change how you see that by replacing "different" with "pioneering."

At three in the morning, this resonated with me. *Pioneering!* Yes, I *can* do this! I can be a pioneer and save all of those cows and chickens and those adorable little piglets! Although, actually, I never have learned how to program the DVR…

The following week, Chris and I both took Seamus for his next chemo appointment, and I was able to speak to the doctor myself. She was kind, tender with Seamus and with me. Since returning from India, I'd felt calmer about what I knew was inevitable. We would lose Seamus. But I was determined to give him as much time and as much quality of life as I could. I thought often of the dog at the Taj Mahal, so quiet and dignified, and somehow so natural there before the Monument to Love that is the Taj. But that did not make hearing that my own dog's disease was terminal any easier. I sat, tears rolling down my face, as Chris rubbed my back and choked back his own tears. Seamus was returned to us, his left leg sporting a bright purple bandage from where the IV had been inserted and the chemo pumped into him. This scene had been so oft repeated, with him, with me, and now with him again, that I wondered if chemotherapy, doctor's offices, and IVs would forever be a part of my life.

Our next stop was the holistic pet food shop, PetStaurant. I'd become friends with Kelle—"Mom" to Bogart from the Beagle Freedom Project—after meeting her at our Words, Wine, and Wags event, and she had referred me to Marc and his shop. Marc, she told me, was a genius with supplements and holistic diets that fight cancer.

When I called Marc and explained Seamus's situation, he asked me what my goal was.

"I want to give him as much time as possible. I want as much quality of life as possible."

"You know this is incurable, right?" he said.

"Yes. I know."

"Okay. Because I don't want to lead you on. I don't want you thinking we can cure cancer with food or supplements."

I was relieved to hear him say that. While I was more open and certainly more interested in food and natural supplements for improving health, I had not come so far as to abandon Western medicine altogether, nor did I believe we could eliminate all disease simply by eating better. If he had promised to cure cancer with dog food, I would not have listened to anything more he had to say. I would have thought he was a nut. Instead, I listened to him. He disagreed with chemo for Seamus and suggested we stop it. The chemo, he said, would lessen his quality of life. Chemo was hard on the body.

I knew this, of course. Firsthand and from watching Seamus the first time, I knew this, but I also believed that chemo had saved Seamus the first time and had quite possibly saved me, so I had made an appointment to see Marc after the second chemo appointment. The vet had agreed that after three chemo rounds, we'd be able to tell if it was helping. We'd be in a better place to know whether to continue. I wanted to hear what Marc had to say; maybe traditional and holistic medicines would tell us to stop.

Marc's shop was only ten minutes from the cancer center in Los Angeles. It was small but well stocked. He greeted us immediately and bent down to pet Seamus, who was straining at his leash to get at the food—any of it.

"He seems to have good energy," Marc said.

"He does. He loves his food," Chris said.

"That's a good sign." Marc stood up again. "So tell me about his diagnosis."

I began to tell him. When my voice cracked and the tears started again, Chris took over. Marc listened carefully, periodically handing Seamus a treat and petting his domed head.

"This is hard," Marc said. "But there are some things we can do. Definitely, I'd stop the chemo. And we'll add supplements—enzymes, colostrums, and probiotics."

I looked up. I remembered my online acquaintance, not-old-man River. He'd suggested the very same thing. *What if I had listened to him then? Was this all my fault?*

"Okay. Yes. We'll do that. Do you have those things?" I said.

"Absolutely. And can you make a raw diet for him?"

"We feed him The Honest Kitchen."

"That's a very good food. But let me show you something better in this case." He showed me the frozen containers of his own raw diet for dogs, prepared by hand with a menu that sounded like it came from a Michelin-starred restaurant. Then he gave me a list of foods to add to Seamus's diet wherever I could. Many of them were the foods I'd been adding to my own diet: broccoli, spinach, cabbage, bok choy, red and yellow bell peppers.

We bought the supplements, loaded up on the frozen raw diet

containers, and selected several packages of treats that were also on the "approved" list. I wanted Seamus to have a good quality of life, and to a beagle, food *is* quality of life.

The next morning, before I made myself a kale smoothie, I made Seamus's breakfast. I reached for the containers we'd brought home from Marc's store and read the labels: lamb, pheasant, quail, Cornish game hen, Angus beef. The ingredients were quite literally the stuff of my nightmares. And yet, suddenly, I could only make myself feel vaguely guilty over these animals. The documentaries I watched, the reading I'd done—that was enough to keep me on the plant-based diet without being tempted to cheat. If I thought about adding cheese or having a burger, all I had to do was think of the animals and the moment passed. But now, all I cared about was giving Seamus every possible moment of life. Did this make me a hypocrite? Probably. Or perhaps I had much more to consider about the cycle of life and the food chain. I don't know. I just knew I wanted the best for Seamus. Selfish? Yes. Perhaps.

I remembered a hilarious comment we heard while traveling a couple of years back when Chris led wine tours in the South of France. A couple on this particular trip with us was vegan, though that hadn't been mentioned in advance. Our French friends who helped make the arrangements for the group scrambled to get the meals taken care of. Rachel, who is American but married to a Frenchman and living in rural Southern France, called the owner of the restaurant where we had a twelve-course meal with wine pairings arranged. This meal had been the highlight of trips past, and there was nothing vegan about it. We heard only Rachel's side of the phone conversation, and it was clear she was having trouble explaining the concept of "vegan" to this Frenchwoman. Suddenly Rachel burst out laughing. She shared the conversation with us, describing the Frenchwoman's frustration, which had culminated in the totally French, exasperated exclamation, "But they will eat *foie gras*, no?"

Right. They don't eat animals or animal products, but if you force-feed and torture the animal, then rip its organs out and serve them— sure, *that* they will eat. It was such an impossibly French statement, we had to laugh. (And no, our guests did not eat *foie gras*, but they did have a delicious meal. The French prepare vegetables really well also.) But I felt like that French restaurateur now. When it came to my little cancer-fighting beagle, I'd be scooping up the livers, bones, and body parts of various animals and serving them with a side of veggies. I couldn't see *not* doing it.

I pureed vegetables and mixed in a little cottage cheese and coconut oil, as Marc had suggested. Seamus turned his nose up at it. I can't say I blame him. I mixed it with the Angus beef and bok choy container, and Seamus consumed every last morsel, though I'm fairly certain he was a tad disappointed I messed with the perfection of his beef. I put the vegetable puree in the empty beef container and stored it in the refrigerator for later use. *It's good for him,* I thought, *and if it supplements the animal product, I can perhaps assuage a little guilt.*

Seamus ate his gourmet meals for another week, devouring each one and happily requesting more with his usual head-thrown-back howl at me, followed by an appalled look at his empty bowl. I wanted to take this as a sign he was doing well and this was the right diet for him. But the truth was, he was in chemotherapy. He had terminal cancer.

I returned to *Main Street Vegan* to read the section on whether dogs can eat a vegan diet. The author gives an enthusiastic "yes" to this question, and her daughter keeps her own dogs on a vegan diet. I could not find enough support in other books or online for switching a dog to a vegan diet—particularly not a dog in the end stage of life, battling terminal cancer. Torn, I stuck with the diet Marc had prescribed (and Seamus loved).

The annual Walk with the Animals event, benefiting the Mary S. Roberts Pet Adoption Center, occurred that same week. We debated whether to take Seamus. I'd adopted Seamus from this very place, and I'd served on their board of directors for over twenty years. I'd gone every year since the event started, missing only the 2009 event when I was in chemotherapy and too tired to go. Seamus, however, did not seem tired. And since I was again scheduled to be the co-emcee of the event, as I had been for the last several years, we decided we'd all go, but Chris would not take Seamus on the long walk. Instead he'd sit at our booth that came with my sponsorship. We'd donated the booth to Beagle Freedom Project, but Chris had a spot where he sat selling my books for me as well. Seamus helped draw folks to the booth, and during breaks from my emcee duties, I was able to talk more with Shannon, the founder of BFP, whom I hadn't seen since our Words, Wine, and Wags fund-raiser for them two months earlier.

There were a lot of animal and animal-rights issues swarming about in my head then, but I had not forgotten about the beagles in the laboratories. I had not forgotten Bogart or Comet or the thousands of dogs subjected to painful testing for things like mascara and shampoo. There was no way I *could* forget those dogs.

"I've been thinking about Beagle Freedom Project a lot since I heard you talk. I feel so naive that I didn't know they tested on beagles," I said.

"Most people don't know. I didn't realize the extent of it until I looked into it. Seventy thousand beagles a year. That's when I knew I had to do something," Shannon said.

"It's astounding. I'm so glad you are doing it. And I want to help. I just haven't quite figured out how yet. Except, of course, donations."

"You help by helping us spread the word. Like you, most people don't know. They don't know how many products are unnecessarily tested on animals. They don't know they can help by simply being careful to shop cruelty-free."

"I'm paying more attention to that now myself."

"Good for you."

"And I would seriously love to adopt one of the Beagle Freedom Project dogs one day." I looked over at Seamus. He was noticeably thinner but still happily greeted the many folks who stopped by to see him. He was well-known at this event, since he was usually on stage with me every year, but since the book came out with his adorable face on the cover, he was even more popular. "We just have our hands full now with Seamus." I could feel the tears welling up and my throat closing—not good for my emcee duties.

"I know," she said. "I know. But when you're ready, when the time comes, we'd be happy to have you adopt."

"Thanks." I picked up the material they were handing out, put on my sunglasses, and returned to the stage. Chris and I had long ago agreed—in the midst of our worst struggles with Seamus's separation anxiety—that when we next adopted, we'd get two dogs so they had each other on the days we couldn't take them with us to work. I determined then that one of those would be a Beagle Freedom Project dog. I just didn't mention that to Chris.

Later at the event, I saw Dr. Davis, who, as the referring vet, had been kept up-to-date on Seamus's prognosis and treatment by the cancer center. He'd already visited with Seamus and Chris.

"He looks good," he said.

"Chris? Or Seamus?"

"Both. Both seemed in good spirits."

"Yeah, I think Seamus is doing well. We took him to a holistic nutriti—"

"You did *not* put him on a vegan diet, did you?"

"Wow. Feel strongly about that? No. I didn't. I thought about—"

"No. I will smack you."

"Okay. Good to know. Violent, but good to know. I didn't find enough support for a vegan diet for a dog. Especially under these circumstances."

"That's because there isn't support."

I decided not to share what support I had found. I wasn't switching Seamus's diet now. I'd save the discussion for another day. Another dog.

Chris, Seamus, and I returned home, where all three of us took a good, long nap.

The following day was St. Patrick's Day. Since we didn't know Seamus's actual birthday or even his age for certain, we'd dubbed March 17 his birthday—fitting for a dog named Seamus with a whiskey howl and wearing a green collar. We gave him several new squeak toys—his favorite—and a fan of the book had mailed him two bully sticks. We'd never given him bully sticks before, but judging by his response, we should have. He took both and disappeared into the courtyard. Late into the evening, we saw him relaxing on the chaise lounge chair, still chewing on one of the sticks.

The following night, when Chris and Seamus arrived home from his wine shop, Chris mentioned that he thought Seamus's breathing had changed. It was hard not to panic, but Seamus ate dinner quickly and happily, so we thought perhaps just rest was needed. When we all went to bed, though, Seamus was restless. I heard him turning and adjusting in his bed repeatedly. Eventually, he fell asleep and I did too, but as was becoming customary, I woke a few hours later. I heard Seamus breathing hard and irregularly as he turned and fidgeted in his bed. I rose from my bed and went to him. He was sitting up, panting. I sat by his bed and petted him. He leaned into my hand.

Something was wrong. Something was definitely wrong. I moved into the library so I could turn a light on without waking Chris. Seamus followed me, as I knew he would. During my days in chemotherapy, there were many nights I couldn't sleep and instead quietly went to the library and sat in the recliner reading. Seamus always followed me and hopped up into my lap, keeping me company, just as he'd been doing lately as my insomnia and nightmares returned. This time I knew he wouldn't be able to hop up onto the chair. I sat on the floor with him. His breathing was shallow and he seemed tired but unwilling to lie down. He leaned up against me and I leaned up against the chair, petting and soothing him until at last we both fell asleep. When I awoke at five in the morning, Seamus had returned to his bed. I allowed myself to think he was better, and I returned to my own bed.

I slept until eight. Chris had gotten up and fed Seamus, and Seamus had eaten and had drunk water. We took this as another good sign, and when Seamus went outside to do his business, we hoped that too boded well. But there was no mistaking that his breathing was not right. He needed to go see Dr. Davis. I called to tell them we were bringing him in. Chris drove Seamus to the appointment while I went to my first of three client appointments scheduled that day.

I called Chris as soon as my appointment ended.

"Dr. Davis said there was fluid on Seamus's lungs. He kept him there to drain the fluid, which should provide some relief and ease his breathing."

"Okay, that's good. So he can do something about it?"

"Yeah, he can. I told him to go ahead. Seamus is with him now, and I'm headed back to work."

"I can pick him up whenever he's ready."

In only twenty minutes, Dr. Davis called me.

"I started to drain the fluid." I could hear the sadness in Dr. Davis's voice. I began to cry before he even finished his sentence. "Unfortunately, it's blood," he said.

"What does that mean?" I knew, of course, that it wasn't good, but I wanted hope. Again, there was that moment of pushing away the inevitable—the brain trying to hold the pain back from the heart.

"It means I can't stop it. Most likely one of the tumors burst."

I tried to catch my breath…to form a sentence. "How long?"

"I'm sorry, Teresa. I really am. But I think it's time."

No. It couldn't be time. He was supposed to have months. It had barely been one month. I wasn't ready. I'd never be ready. But not now. Not today. "Today?"

"He's suffering. He's only okay right now because I gave him a sedative. But I hate to see the little guy like this."

"Can we have an evening with him?"

"I'm sorry. I wouldn't suggest it. I really wouldn't. His lungs are filling with blood."

I don't know how I thought it would happen, but this wasn't it. He was going to beat the odds. I'd allowed myself to think that, but now… *Now. Oh god. Now this. It was time.* Through my tears, I choked out all I could. "I have to call Chris. We'll be there. I'm coming."

I closed my office door and called Chris. He immediately closed his shop and agreed to meet me at Dr. Davis's. I left my office, telling my assistant only that my appointments for the day needed to be canceled and I wouldn't be back. "Family emergency. I won't be in tomorrow either." I couldn't imagine I'd be back in all week. Or ever. I couldn't imagine the next moments, let alone anything past that.

Chris and I both sat on the floor where they'd spread out a blanket. Seamus was carried in and gently laid on the blanket. It was easy to see he'd worsened in only a couple of hours. He was having difficulty breathing and looked frightened, though I could tell he was relieved to see us. We both stroked his fur and kissed his face. They left us with him and told us to let them know when we were ready.

We'd never, ever be ready. How could anyone be ready for this?

"You are the best dog ever, buddy. We love you the most," Chris said, and he kissed the dome of Seamus's head.

I could barely breathe. I held my face against Seamus's and breathed him in. I took short, deep breaths as the tears streamed down my face and onto Seamus. Chris rested his hand on my back. "I can't believe this. I can't do this. It's too awful," I said between sobs, sucking in air.

"I know, baby. I know. But we have to let him go. We said we wouldn't let him suffer."

"It's so soon. I wanted more time."

"I know."

It was painful to watch Seamus struggle to breathe, and I knew it was the last gift we could give him. The last thing we could do for him was to let him go, peacefully and with us holding him. We could give him peace and dignity at the end.

That was all we could do.

We let him go. A large piece of my heart went with him.

Chapter 11

A GOOD DOG

I WAS IMMOBILIZED BY MY GRIEF, AND ONLY MY ANGER MOVED ME. So I went with it. I went all-in with the anger. The changes I'd made in our lives had failed us. Seamus was gone. Nothing mattered. Nothing saved him from cancer, and nothing would save me. Anger seeped out of me.

By day, I couldn't stop thinking of myself as a coward and a hypocrite who couldn't save her own beagle and had for years been the cause of millions of animals dying gruesome deaths following painful, horrific lives in factory farms. (Yes, I was responsible for *millions*! Grief doesn't have to make sense.) At night, it was the farm animals that haunted my sleep.

When I thought of farms, if I ever did think of farms before, I thought Old MacDonald had a cow. Maybe two, or twenty. Or even a hundred. E-I-E-I-idiot. How did I think these romanticized versions of farms could possibly produce and care for the three hundred million cows, one billion (*billion!*) pigs, and fifty billion (*billion!*) chickens slaughtered and consumed annually in the United States alone? Every year. Old MacDonald would need an unfathomable number of cows, and he wouldn't be letting the animals live freely and naturally and then humanely and carefully *slaughtering* them (and I could not, still cannot, get the word "slaughter" out of my mind) right there on the sunny, green farm. That was not happening. That would be impossible in these numbers.

When I was eating cows, pigs, and chickens, I can only assume my brain had done what it did when I was a child and I was being moved back and forth between public and private Catholic school. Rather than question the inconsistency between the theory of evolution and the…um…theory of Adam and Eve (both of which, after all, had been *taught* to me), I simply decided that Adam and Eve had been banished to Earth as apes and had to start all over again in the evolutionary process. This story I told myself allowed me to not question authority and dogma. Good thing there wasn't a test at either school.

But I was a *kid* then. I'm not a kid now, and somehow I had clung to this idealized Fisher-Price farm version of food production. We all know the animals die, right? We're just not supposed to think about that part, let alone how they live during the short period before they are slaughtered.

Admittedly, science wasn't my strong suit in school (or did you figure that out from my evolution idea?), but I'd had enough biology to know how and why the female of a species got pregnant, and how and why she produced milk. But in the same way I created Ape Eve, I must have decided that female cows just magically produced milk to fill my glass, to make my beloved cheese, yogurt, ice cream, and sour cream, and still had plenty left to feed her baby. You know, the one or two she had every few years when she felt like it or met a cute bull.

In order to not question authority or the dogma I'd been fed ("happy cows!"), that's what I needed to believe. There was no rape rack (a dairy industry term, not mine) to keep Bessie pregnant with injected sperm taken from a male cow in what could only be described as bestiality, no calf was ripped from her at birth, still wet and crying for its mama. Bessie was not standing in her own feces, let alone the feces of thousands of other cows on a feedlot with her. Bessie was not pumped full of genetically engineered growth hormones so she would produce the maximum amount of milk, no matter how uncomfortable or sore that made her udders as they subjected her to a mechanized milking machine three times a day, all while crying, distraught and forlorn for her stolen calf. *Not on my imaginary farm! No sirree.* And Bessie's baby boy was not shoved in a crate, unable to move, fed a diet lacking in iron so he would be anemic and pale, and then slaughtered at three to eighteen weeks old so he could then be given his first and only name: veal.

In the farm that existed in my head, and from all I was reading and seeing in documentaries, maybe only in my head, Bessie lives to twenty or twenty-five years old and dies in her sleep on a grassy knoll in full sunshine.

Not so in my vividly real nightmares.

At four in the morning, two days after Seamus died, I woke from one of these nightmares and slipped out of bed.

"Are you okay?" Chris said.

I put my robe on and sat back down on the bed. "Sorry I woke you. I'm having nightmares."

Chris sat up in bed and reached over to rub my back. "About Seamus?"

"No. About cows. About what I read."

"I'm going to regret this, but what did you read?"

"I read how they're killed: They're shot in the head with a bolt, which doesn't always kill them. Then they're shackled, hung upside down… and sometimes…often…they're not dead yet. They're stabbed… in the throat—"

"Okay, stop. That's awful."

"It is awful. They're awake. Alive. In my dream, but in real life too…when they're skinned…alive. Hacked apart—"

"Stop it. Seriously. Stop."

"It doesn't stop. They're slaughtering them in an assembly line. There are so many they can't possibly pay attention to individual animals—to whether they've done their 'work' properly. It's just a gruesome man-made assembly line of torture. I can't get it out of my head."

Chris was no longer rubbing my back. "Yeah, you're kind of ruining steaks for me."

I turned to look at him and he was smiling hopefully. I realized he was, if somewhat misguidedly, again trying to humor me off a ledge. The problem was, I'd already jumped.

"It *should* ruin steaks for you. It should ruin steaks for everybody. It's not just my nightmare. It happens. It's real."

He exhaled heavily. "I understand you are angry. And very upset. I'm sorry."

"I am. I'm furious. I guess this is the anger stage of grief."

"You're going to stay at that stage a lot longer if you keep thinking about all of this animal stuff."

"It's only been two days. Besides, this world is pretty majorly screwed up. There's a lot to stay angry about. What we do to animals is…it's…it's unconscionable. And I can't believe I've participated all these years, like some mindless idiot, and all the while calling myself an animal lover."

"It's not like you're killing the animals."

"I ate the animals. Animals were being tortured and killed for me. For my plate. It's hard to overlook that cause and effect."

"I think you'd feel better if you at least slept. Maybe stop reading and inflicting all that on yourself. At least for a bit."

I could hear the concern in his voice, along with the frustration of not being able to help. I paused and took a deep breath.

"I can't sleep."

"Because you're terrorizing yourself."

"No." I hesitated, because I knew what I was about to say would be frightening. But my habit is to discuss everything with Chris, and this too had been on my mind. "I'm up reading because of my restless brain syndrome."

"Your what?"

"You're not even going to laugh at that? Restless brain syndrome is not a real thing. It's just a name I made up." It was my turn to deflect with misguided humor.

"It doesn't sound funny. Not at all. Made up the name for what?"

"My brain shakes in my head—not in the 'I can't concentrate' way, but physically. It feels like my brain is vibrating in my head. And it usually happens in the middle of the night, so I get up and read."

"Okay, first, that's really, really not good. And second, maybe read something light and happy. Maybe what you're reading is causing this."

"No, because occasionally it's happened at work. It's been happening since Seamus's diagnosis. And it happened in India. Lord Shiva knows I was not reading in India."

"But what you are reading isn't helping."

"When I stop reading, I think about Seamus. And then I can't breathe. Believe me, if I could find something more positive that I felt like doing, I'd do it."

I left out the part where I should be calling to make my April oncology checkup appointment but couldn't bring myself to do it. "Cancer metastasized to the brain" would just have to wait.

At times, that was the thought that crept into my mind. At other times, "metastasized to my brain" wasn't just creeping—it was what was knocking on and shaking my brain. The dog died, and so would I. It seemed preordained.

I tried a change of tactics on Friday and spent the day in my law office, with the door closed, trying to concentrate on legal work, avoiding Facebook, personal emails, and any communication that might be expressing sympathy for our loss of Seamus. I had shared on my blog that Seamus had passed on. I knew many readers had fallen in love with Seamus from our book, and I knew his death would be painful for them too. But I couldn't handle their expressions of sympathy. It was like hearing over and over again that he had died. That I had failed.

But my office filled with flowers sent by caring friends and strangers alike. My mailbox at work had filled with sympathy cards that I couldn't bring myself to open any more than I could the ones that came to our home. At night I went home, drank more wine, and sobbed in the dark. Chris was at his wine shop until eight p.m. The emptiness of the house weighed on me and crushed me further.

On Saturday morning I went for a walk with Chris, mostly to show him I could, in fact, get out of bed and put one foot in front of the other (though I in no way wanted to). It was disconcerting and desolate to be out walking without Seamus, but the fresh air felt good. And that, or fate, is why that afternoon I decided to finally read the emails and look at my Facebook page for the first time since I let everyone know that Seamus had passed away. I figured I'd respond and sob and fall apart on a day I didn't have to face anyone. I made myself a cup of coffee and sat down at the computer, alone in the quiet. I went to Facebook first, but not to my messages or notifications. I eased myself in by just scrolling through my page.

In only a few minutes time, I saw her face. She was staring up at me (at the camera, but at me, it seemed) from behind bars where she was seated on a cement floor. The posting, from Anne, a Facebook friend who also loves beagles, mentioned that this beagle's time was up and she was sitting in a high-kill Los Angeles shelter. She needed to get out right away, but she had a highly contagious kennel cough and needed to be in a home with no other dogs. Could anybody help? the post asked. I kept looking at the wide-eyed adorable little dog. How could she look so happy even from inside a cage sitting on a cold cement floor? I moved away from the photo—I had enough beagle sadness in my life. I had enough animal sadness. I'd been confronted with enough pain. But I continued to come back to her and that beautiful face. And soon, friends were cross-posting her picture, networking for her rescue, so I was seeing her face over and over again. Her smiling, happy, beagle face.

We had no dogs in our home.

I'd been watching what these ladies did—the way they networked and pulled together to rescue beagles all over Southern California. They were an informal group who came together on the Beaglefest Facebook page, and many members became friends "in real life." They scanned shelter postings for beagles needing rescue, posted the pictures and information, raised funds for the adoption fees and any medical needs (and, it seemed, there were always medical needs due to the condition of the shelter or, just as frequently, the negligence of the dog's prior owner), transported the dogs where needed, fostered them, and finally, if all went well, found the dogs their forever homes. It was impressive and meaningful and, at times, distressing work. My involvement had been through monetary donations or, occasionally, paving the way for the rescued dog to be given a place at my local pet adoption center—one which now regularly had a beagle available for adoption, thanks to these group efforts.

We have no dog in our home.

It's too soon.

I could barely get up and get myself dressed to face a day without Seamus, and I was wallowing in the horrors of what I was reading, so how was I going to take care of a sick, needy foster dog? I went back to the Facebook page showing the beagle in the prison kennel, her big soulful eyes looking right into the camera. Despite having been at this miserable municipal shelter and who knows what condition before that, she looked like she was smiling. As if she was saying, "Hey there. Come get me. Let's be friends."

We had no dog in our home.

I emailed Chris at work.

> Would it be insane to foster a beagle for a few days? There's a beagle that needs a foster home, but she has kennel cough. She needs to go to a home with no other dogs. Sadly, that's us.

I was crying as I typed. Maybe that meant I wasn't ready. But Chris responded quickly.

> It might be a good idea. It might help you. I'm okay with it if you think you are.

I'd always thought I would foster beagles, any dog, really, when I could. I'd been involved enough to know that the foster system saves lives. When an animal needs out of a shelter and a rescue group doesn't have room, or, in this dog's case, there was a medical reason the dog couldn't go to the rescue organization, a foster is crucial. I knew I wanted to foster. I just wasn't sure about the timing.

> I don't know if I'm ready or not. I want to help her. And we can help. It's only for a few days, maybe a week I think.

I sent Chris her photo.

> She's adorable. I think it would be good for you. I'm in if you're in.

I shouldn't have been surprised. Chris was spectacular with Seamus, and he grew to love and care for him every bit as much as I did. And

normally, other than when it came to animals, Chris was a more emotional person than I was. I took his consent as a sign I hadn't lost my
mind. This was a rational thing to do.

> Okay, I'm going to tell them we can take her for a few days.
> There may be a beagle here when you get home tonight.

Anne and Janet worked together to put a plan in place. Kindly,
they asked several times if it wasn't too soon for me. When I assured
them I thought it would be good for me and the dog both, they found
a sponsoring rescue group. Anne would spring the dog from the shelter the next day, paying the ninety-dollar adoption fee herself. She
would drive the dog fifty miles east to Janet, who would bring the dog,
a humidifier, antibiotics, and a collar and leash to me. I'd foster the
cute girl for a few days or a week, however long it took for the cough
to clear up so she was adoptable. The plan came together before I fully
realized what I'd done. Whatever I had done, it felt right.

There is no dog in our home.

But there soon will be.

On Sunday, Chris and I waited, anxious for our new arrival. I alter-
nated between excitement at helping to rescue a beautiful beagle, fear
that it was too soon—that I'd made a hasty and bad decision—and
guilt. Guilt that I was cheating on Seamus with…

"She doesn't have a name," I said, the realization dawning on me.

"Veronica or Betty?" Chris said. He was an Archie comics fan and
had once named a car Veronica.

"Betty," I said at the same time he said, "Veronica."

"Daphne it is," he said.

In my fog, I wasn't entirely clear where that name came from, but I
liked it. Daphne sounded sweet, and it matched that adorable face of
hers, which I could still see in my mind.

Daphne herself arrived soon thereafter. I was surprised to see she
was big, over forty pounds. I was not surprised to see she was dirty and
exhausted. She immediately came to me, smiling, wagging her tail, but
quiet. I petted her rough, dirty coat and she licked my face, just once,

gently. Again, I noticed those eyes—so big and brown and trusting. We let her off the leash and she ambled over to Chris with her tail wagging and tongue hanging to the side.

Chris bent to pet her. "Love that tongue. What a cutie." And on cue, she licked Chris's face too. Twice.

Janet brought in the humidifier, and Daphne simply lay on the rug while Janet explained the medications and humidifier to clear up the kennel cough. As we talked, the realization that I would be responsible for this dog began to sink in. I needed to care for *this* dog. This dog was not Seamus. I hadn't picked up or put away any of Seamus's toys. His beds were still where they'd always been—one downstairs by the couch, one in the laundry room, and one upstairs in our bedroom. His smell, at least from a dog's point of view, had to be everywhere. Did Daphne know this? Did it bother her? I looked more closely at her, already asleep on our floor. Her coloring was the usual brown, black, and white tricolor of beagles, with the black saddle. But she had adorable brown confetti spots on the whites of her paws and legs. And her paws were big. She was big. Much bigger than she should be, which I thought was unusual for a dog who'd been a stray and in a shelter for two weeks. Just then she rose and walked over to Chris on the couch. Chris patted the blanket on the couch next to him, and she nimbly jumped up and snuggled in next to him, resting her head on his leg. Whatever she smelled, it wasn't bothering her. Anything was better than where she'd just been.

"This dog is adorable," Chris said.

"She is pretty cute. Anne and I spent time loving on her when she brought her to me. She's very friendly. Just a happy little dog," Janet said.

She's a good dog, and she's cute. But she's a foster dog. We'll help her, and maybe she'll help me. But it's too soon. I can't imagine being attached to another dog.

"Can you see the lump on her chest?" Janet said.

A lump. They'd told me she had a growth—something that had to be removed. That, to me, somehow was different from a lump. My heart froze.

"A lump?" I said.

"I don't know if it's anything, but when we take her in to have her spayed, we should have that removed too."

Chris petted Daphne on her back and side and soon enough she rolled onto her back for belly rubs. The lump was clear and obvious— about three-fourths of an inch in diameter and protruding from her chest nearly an inch. I did not like the look of that lump. Lumps, on dogs or on humans, in my experience were never good. I'd had enough lumps.

Chapter 12

A PLACE IN THE SUN

This lump was not my problem, I told myself. And then I told myself that again. And again. My job was to nurse this beagle through her kennel cough so the rescue group could take her, have her spayed, deal with that lump, and find a good, loving home for her. We could do that much. I wouldn't think about the lump. I couldn't.

I slept downstairs on the couch with Daphne in Seamus's bed next to me and near the humidifier. Since we didn't know if she was house-broken or could use a doggie door, I needed to be able to let her outside quickly. The way I'd been sleeping, a night on the couch was hardly going to matter.

Around two in the morning, Daphne got up, walked out the doggie door, and went to the dirt area outside where Seamus had always gone to do his business. She returned, easily slipping back through the doggie door, and hopped right on up next to me on the couch. Well, really more on me than next to me. I slid over, turned on my side, and made room as she curled up, pressed against my stomach. She was fast asleep before I even had time to consider whether allowing her on the couch was a good idea. I rubbed her belly and kissed the top of her smelly head.

I awoke to her face in mine and an immediate lick to my cheek. I stroked her head and she moved closer, pressing her body against mine. She still had not made any noise—strange after having a beagle as vocal as Seamus had been. But, true to the beagle breed, she was adept at expressing herself. She was thankful for us; that was apparent. She was also dirty; that too was unmistakable. She, my clothes, and the blankets would all need a good washing as soon as we got her over that cough and the risk of pneumonia.

I rose from the couch and went to the kitchen to make my coffee.

Daphne followed me, swaying her tail so joyously her whole rear end moved with it. Once I got my coffee ready, I went to the refrigerator to get one of the PetStaurant containers out for Daphne: Angus beef with wheatgrass, broccoli, carrots, kelp, and pear, infused with flaxseed, acai berry, and burdock. It's a safe bet she had not been eating that well where she'd been. I realized then, though, that I didn't have a bowl for her. I couldn't use Seamus's bowl. It was Seamus's bowl. It was still there on the floor where Seamus ate. I put the container on the counter, much to Daphne's dismay, and went to the laundry room to search the cupboard for an extra dog bowl. Daphne followed me, swinging her butt back and forth, her tail a metronome keeping the beat.

I found a ceramic bowl with fake dog-themed wine labels around the side and "Bone Dry" on the inside bottom, no doubt a gift from someone who knew my love of dogs and wine. I brought the bowl back to the kitchen and dumped the entire Angus beef dinner into it for her. She was chubby, yes, but I suspected she could do with a hearty, nutritious, quality meal. She had not eaten the kibble dinner we'd offered the night before, and we chalked it up to nerves, the kennel cough, and all the traveling she'd done that day. She'd turned down treats as well, unheard of beagle behavior in my experience.

"Here you go, baby girl." I set the bowl down. "I think you'll like this."

She answered me by devouring the meal and then, in true beagle fashion, looking up to ask for more. The beagle eyes are always asking for more—more food, more love, more walking, more fun. Her thick tail thumped back and forth, and again, her back half followed. She practically twisted into a complete "O," her rear end swinging around near her nose. And then back to the other side.

Chris came downstairs then, and Daphne hurried to him. I saw from my rear vantage point that her excited walk had the same sway to it. Girl could shake it.

"Daphne, you're a little doodlebutt," I said.

Chris laughed. "What did you call her?"

"She's Daphne Doodlebutt. Look at that butt go."

Daphne raced back over to me in the kitchen while Chris watched the "doodles" and laughed. "It fits."

"It does."

I should have known then that once a dog has not only a name, but also a nickname, she's staying. But I didn't know that then; my grief still shrouded my thoughts. Daphne Doodlebutt was adorable, but she was a foster dog. I could not cheat on Seamus.

I went upstairs to take a shower. When I came back downstairs, I couldn't find Daphne. I looked in the living room, in Seamus's bed in the family room, in the other bed in the laundry room. She wasn't there. I shouted upstairs to Chris.

"Is she upstairs with you?"

"No. She hasn't come upstairs."

I raced out to our front courtyard. It's not that big; surely I'd see a forty-pound beagle. But I didn't. She wasn't at the gate, on the chaise, or on the patio. There was no beagle to be found. Just as the panic began to swell, just as I thought I'd lost my foster beagle in under twelve hours, I heard a noise. *Swish. Thump. Swish. Thump.*

I turned in the direction of the sound and saw a beagle tail swing out from the climbing jasmine that covered the air-conditioning unit enclosure. Then a beagle head peeked up. She was lying in the jasmine, half buried. She'd burrowed into the vines, no doubt how she found safety and slept as a stray. It *did* look comfortable.

"Baby girl, you don't have to do this anymore. Come on inside."

Her tail swished and thumped, but other than that, she didn't move. I looked around. Well, it was a soft bed she'd found, the sun was shining, and she had access to the house if she wanted it. No reason not to just let her be. I rubbed her head and she licked my hand.

"Okay, sweetie. You do what makes you comfortable."

For the next two days we fed and cuddled Daphne and diligently administered antibiotics. I brushed her coat and rubbed her down with pet wipes so she both smelled and looked better. She went to work with Chris during the day and slept on the couch with me at night, the humming humidifier nearby. Occasionally, we still found her burrowed into the jasmine, but at least now we knew where to look for her. She slept soundly, snoring contentedly, day and night. She would wake up once or twice during the night and either drink some water or head out the doggie door to do her business outside. Then she'd come back to the couch, lick my face, jump up, and snuggle in next to me. I'd rub her belly and she'd again lick my face. But quickly, she (if not I) was back asleep, snoring loudly.

Hourly, it seemed, she was improving, looking healthier, gaining energy and certainly appetite. But still, she never barked. There was never the patented beagle "*AAARRROOOOOOOOOOO*," never a whine or a growl. Just the snoring. Loud snoring. Very loud snoring. And the cough persisted, as kennel cough can do. In talking more with Janet, it seemed we'd keep her longer than a few days. The cough was going to take some time to clear up. I assured Janet that I did not mind keeping Daphne longer. I didn't mind at all.

I did, however, need to take her to see a vet. She could hang around, but that cough really needed to be gone. I made an appointment with Dr. Lawrence, since Dr. Davis was on vacation. I'd never met Dr. Lawrence, and it had been just over a week since we were at the same clinic with Seamus for the last time and I had left sobbing and distraught. I entered with great trepidation. Daphne, on the other hand, trotted in fully prepared to make new friends.

The staff greeted me with knowing, concerned looks, but I could see they were all thinking, "*You have another beagle already?*" I mentioned, perhaps far too many times than was necessary, that I was just fostering this one. She belonged to the rescue group. My loyalty to Seamus was indisputable.

In the exam, though the lump was not my problem, I pointed it out to Dr. Lawrence. He was down on the floor, petting Daphne and laughingly accepting her "kisses" as she slathered his face with her tongue.

"I see that. It's probably nothing. Maybe just a fatty lump. We should remove it when we spay her." He rubbed her belly. "I love hounds. She's a perfect beagle specimen. What a sweetheart. We had a beagle growing up. My parents love beagles too."

Yes, she was a sweetheart, and I was glad he liked her, but I was focused on the lump. Seamus had many fatty lumps during his life. I knew this was not a fatty lump. I pointed to the other abnormality I'd noticed. Daphne had a deformed toe on her back left foot. There was a lump on the side and the toenail grew up and curved back toward her, rather than down to the ground. It didn't seem to bother her, but it wasn't right either.

"That may be an old injury. But if it's not bothering her, just keep an eye on it and keep the nail trimmed down. If my parents lived closer, I'd be talking to them about adopting this girl. What a great dog." Daphne again rewarded him with several full face licks. She certainly knew how to win people over. The doctor was much more concerned with her cuteness than her abnormalities.

I made a note to tell the rescue group about the nail, and I pretended not to notice that I'd reacted badly to the thought of someone else adopting her, that the possibility of saying good-bye to Daphne stung me as though he were taking my own dog away from me. She was only my foster dog, but I hadn't thought about what it would be like to let her go and have an empty house again until the doctor mentioned adoption of Daphne. I'd forgotten the other part of fostering—the letting go.

As a courtesy to the rescue group, Dr. Lawrence did not charge me for the exam. He gave me the new antibiotics and said to check back in a week. If the cough was cleared up, we could schedule the spay and lump removal surgery.

So she'd be with us another week. Or so. I was not disturbed by this news.

I paid for the antibiotics at the front desk, handed Daphne a dog treat, and turned to leave.

"Just a second, Teresa," the office manager said. "Hang on."

I stopped and waited as she came around to the reception area. She put her hand on my arm and quietly said, "We have Seamus's remains. Did you want to take those now?"

I shook my head and rushed out the door. I immediately felt bad for leaving "him," but I couldn't bring myself to deal with his remains yet— I'd come back for them…for him. I knew I'd fall apart all over again if I took the remains then, and I wouldn't be able to care for Daphne or myself. In the car, I let Daphne lick away my tears. It was good to have her there with me then or I may never have pulled it together enough to drive home.

That night Chris sat on the couch between Daphne and me, rubbing Daphne's belly with his left hand as she sighed contentedly. Soon, his right hand was rubbing my bare leg, keeping time with his left hand. I smiled, thinking he didn't realize what he was doing.

"You realize you're rubbing me too, right?"

"Yeah. I was just thinking I've got Chubby and Stubbly by me."

For the first time possibly ever, I was hoping I was stubbly. And I realized, for the first time since I'd returned from India, I was smiling.

"Thanks a lot."

"I'm just kidding. I was just thinking how nice this is."

"It is nice."

"She's a great dog."

"She is."

"So you know we're keeping her, right?"

I turned to look at him. "No. We're fostering her."

"Why wouldn't we keep her? She's sweet as could be, housebroken, quiet, and she loves us. She's the most low-maintenance dog ever."

"It's too soon."

"It's not. She's here already. She's attached to us. I'm attached to her. You know we're getting another dog sooner or later. Is it just that you can't have a normal, problem-free dog?" He said this with a smile, but I was no longer smiling myself.

With that protruding lump and that toe, I wasn't sure she was a problem-free dog. But it didn't matter.

"It's just too soon. It hasn't even been two weeks." My tears ended our conversation and I left the room.

I couldn't get it out of my head that somehow this was unfair to Seamus. It was like dating immediately after the death of a spouse. It may help the pain, but it seems disrespectful to the deceased's memory. And would one be in any condition to make an appropriate choice?

A few nights later, we were back on the couch, sipping wine and watching a movie. I saw Daphne through the French doors. She trotted across the patio, her usual cheerful self. But there was something in her mouth. Something long and brown. Fearing she had a mouse or a lizard, I got up to check. Daphne turned to look at me, wagging her tail in her full-throttle Doodlebutt way. She came to my side without dropping what she had in her mouth. When I bent to look closer, I realized what she had and tears welled up again.

Daphne was holding one of the two bully sticks that had been sent to Seamus. Seamus had gleefully chewed the first of them while stretched out on the courtyard chaise lounge on his birthday, and we never knew what had happened to the other. Seamus was never a digger, so we assumed it was just in his toy box somewhere. But, it seemed, he'd buried this second one in the yard. And Daphne had found it. She trotted away from me, hopped up on the same lounge chair, and began contentedly gnawing on the stick, her tail still wagging.

And then I knew. There were two bully sticks for a reason. Seamus had enjoyed one and left another for the next beagle. The bully stick baton had been passed. Daphne Doodlebutt was ours, lump and all.

I went back in the house. "Okay. We're keeping her."

"Really? Yay!" Chris got up and hugged me, then went outside to Daphne. "You're all ours, Doodlebutt." She thumped her tail repeatedly, but she did not let go of the bully stick.

"But there's just one thing," I said as I joined them on the patio. "Remember we said we'd have two dogs next?"

"Uh-oh." He smiled. "No, I remember. I'm guessing you already have a dog in mind."

"I still want to adopt one of the Beagle Freedom Project dogs too. Maybe Comet is still available."

He was still petting Daphne, as happy as a kid with a new puppy. "Comet would be perfect. I'm good with that. Two dogs is a good idea. Just not, you know, twenty."

"Fair enough. I'll call Shannon."

Chris, Daphne, and I stayed outside on the chaise lounge enjoying a warm spring evening under the stars—our first night as a family.

Thank you, Seamus.

Chapter 13

A SHOT IN THE DARK

To no one's surprise, I threw myself into the rescue of this dog: brushing her, feeding her, giving her the antibiotics and all the supplements I had left over from my attempts to make Seamus immortal. Daphne needed to get well and get that lump removed, and I needed to make that happen.

She improved each day. And she was enjoying the PetStaurant foods we still had left while also losing weight. She (and I) no longer slept on the couch with the humidifier. Instead, she wedged herself between Chris and me on our bed, certain to be leaning up against one of us, usually me. We accommodated her by contorting our bodies in ways known only to dog lovers, though new to us. Seamus never slept on the bed with us. We would have let him, but he had no interest. He'd be on the bed with us when we were reading or watching television, but once we turned the lights off, he'd jump off the bed and retreat to his own monogrammed, cushioned bed with a selection of blankets. On the rare occasion that he stayed on the bed once the lights were out, the moment Chris or I moved he would loudly exhale and *harrumph* off the bed, disappointed in our lack of civility. But Daphne couldn't be disturbed over the sound of her own snoring. There was no way she was voluntarily leaving our bed.

Chris and I were both happy to have Daphne close by. I thought it was probably a good thing she was so different from Seamus—sleeping on the bed, her silence, the complete adoration of us (Seamus was generally on the receiving end of adoration and preferred it that way), and her looks. Where Seamus was red, mottled, slim, muscular, and mischievous in appearance, Daphne Doodlebutt was sweet, plump, standard tricolored, and with the more traditional square beagle head. There was something about her coloring that made me think of cows. It was not the obvious weight issue. Maybe it was all the white on her, or maybe it was her big, round eyes and long eyelashes. It didn't matter. She was her own beagle, and she was ours. She was not a replacement for Seamus, and we would not expect her to be like Seamus; that wouldn't be fair to any of us. We'd help her recover from all she'd been through, and she'd help ease our pain. This was my plan for my new family.

I took Daphne to see Dr. Davis, hoping she was well enough for her spay surgery and determined to get that lump removed. Once we got through that, we could get on to adopting Comet, but not before then. I didn't think it would be a good idea to adopt another dog when Daphne would be recovering from surgery, but I also didn't want Daphne to get used to being the only (spoiled) dog and start protecting her turf. This much we had also learned from Seamus. Daphne's sleeping on the bed was only the beginning, and we knew we'd have to correct that soon too.

Dr. Davis finished his exam. "There's still a little of the cough left. I'm on vacation next week, but I think we can schedule the surgery for the week after."

"We're headed up to Paso Robles for a long weekend. Will she be okay with us and around other dogs?"

"She's not contagious anymore, and by then this will be gone. As long as she doesn't come into heat, you'll be fine. Let's schedule it for when you get back."

"Oh god, I hadn't even thought about her heat. It's been so long since I've had a girl dog. Yeah, let's hope she doesn't come into heat."

"There's one other thing I'd like to do when she's under."

I'm sure my face dropped like a basset hound's. Dr. Davis was a friend and had been my vet forever, but after all I'd been through with Seamus, "one other thing" scared me. Doctors should be forever banned from beginning news with "and one more thing."

"When we do the surgery, I'd like to do an X-ray of her torso."

"Okaaaaaaaaaay. Why?"

"Feel this," he said, placing his hand on her right side just below the rib cage.

I put my fingers where his had been and felt around. Eventually, I found what he was feeling. "A hard bump? Feels like a BB or something."

"That's what I'm afraid of. I think she may have been shot."

Shot?

I was stunned. Though I shouldn't have been. She'd been found as a stray on the streets of a perilous section of East Los Angeles. *People* get shot there. But Daphne was housebroken and heavyset. She did not look like she'd been a stray on the streets for long. In fact, the only sign that she had not been reasonably well taken care of was that she hadn't been spayed and her nipples suggested she'd had at least a few litters of puppies. Anne, Janet, and I all assumed she'd been used by a backyard breeder at worst, or maybe just belonged to a family who didn't know enough to spay their dog. But *shot?*

"People disgust me. Yes, go ahead. X-ray her. Let's find out what it is and if there is anything we need to do."

That night Chris and I retreated to our hot tub, as we did frequently to discuss our day, our week, or, more and more frequently, our dog. Seamus used to wait for us out on the couch inside the house—the couch with the cashmere throw he preferred. Daphne wanted to be closer to us, so she sat on one of the patio chairs, paws hanging over the edge, head resting on her paws, and those big caramel eyes watching our every move. When we looked at her, her tail thumped. It was hard not to love a dog who so enthusiastically loved you back.

Chris reacted to the news from Daphne's checkup the same way I did. The same as any caring human being would.

"What the hell?" He looked over at Daphne. "Poor girl." She thumped her tail.

"I know. It makes me sick. Why are people so cruel to animals?"

"Why are people cruel in general? Wait…forget I said that. Don't start."

"Very funny. No lectures. I'm focused on Daphne now."

Chris turned to look at Daphne. "Thanks, girl!" Then he turned back to me. "Hopefully, if it is a BB or something like that, Dr. Davis can remove it. On the brighter side, it's okay to take her to Paso Robles with us, right? Because it would be weird to go to Wine 4 Paws without a dog."

"As long as she doesn't come into heat, we're fine on that point."

"Heat? I hadn't thought about that."

"I know. But I think we'll be fine. Only there was more bad news today."

Now it was Chris's turn to have the sad basset hound face. "We can't go to Paso?"

"No, we can go. But I heard from Shannon today. Comet already got adopted. He's not available anymore."

"Oh no. I loved that little guy!"

"I know. I did too. But the good news is there are another six dogs still needing homes. So we have six to choose from. I thought maybe on our way home from Paso we could stop and visit each of them, since they're all in the L.A. area."

"Visit six dogs in one day? You'll want all of them!" Chris was laughing, but I'm sure he was actually worried this would be the case. In all fairness, his concerns were legitimate. Only our homeowner's association rules would prevent me from adopting all six. Common sense eludes me where beagles are concerned.

"I thought we'd let Daphne decide."

Chris laughed. Daphne thumped her tail. "So she's like the Bachelorette choosing her mate? She's the Beaglerette?"

"Actually, that's pretty funny. So yes, we'll play it out like that. The most exciting AAAARRRROOOOOOOSE ceremony ever!"

"She'll have to figure out who's in it for the right reasons. Who's not here to make friends."

"And some of the dogs are in the same foster home, so some will get group dates and some will get private dates."

"Will there be a fantasy suite?"

"Probably not until she's spayed!" We continued with the *Bachelor* parodies far longer than I'm willing to admit.

Later, I emailed Shannon at Beagle Freedom Project, and she too jumped right into our Beaglerette game. She immediately emailed the network of foster families caring for the available dogs.

But a funny thing started to happen. The foster families, faced with the reality that their baby might be going to a new home, suddenly realized they couldn't part with their new family members. The six available bachelors dropped to five, then four, and then three as their foster families committed to adopting them. I had to laugh. We understood foster failure. We hadn't been able to part with Daphne. Chris hadn't even made it forty-eight hours as a foster and he wanted to fail. I only made it as long as I did because I was consumed by my heartache.

Two days later, Shannon came through with more good news. Comet remained available for adoption after all. His pending adoption didn't work out. She asked if we wanted to meet Comet as well. *Uh, yeah!* I didn't even ask what hadn't worked out. I just knew we wanted to see Comet again.

All total, Daphne Doodlebutt would have four beagle bachelors to choose from, and we'd have a busy day driving back from Paso Robles.

I posted a blog about each of our available beagle bachelors.

There was handsome Rizzo, rescued from a lab in the Midwest only a few weeks prior. His rugged, handsome face and white markings complemented our Beaglerette's looks.

And there was Lenny—rescued from a lab in San Diego, California, full of energy, fond of tug-of-war, and a shameless flirt.

Ricki, also from a Midwest laboratory, was the sweet, shy, and reserved one who loved attention but proceeded cautiously, unlike our Beaglerette, who went full throttle into all life's adventures (doodlebutt swinging behind her).

And finally, there was Comet—sweet little Comet—rescued in December, lover of all people, dogs, and toys, fond of cuddles but frightened of cars.

As expected (or feared, if you're Chris), I fell in love with every one of these dogs just from hearing their stories. I was far more enthusiastic than any *Bachelorette* show contestant has ever been. I just hoped our results were better than the show's.

Arranging the dates so Daphne could fall in love too proved more difficult. And she was uninterested in my many attempts to read the stories to her, let alone my attempts to have her view the photos on the website. We scheduled a date with Comet's foster mom, who invited us to stop by her workplace where he joined her most days. Befitting a *Bachelorette* star, Daphne's date hung out at a Mercedes-Benz dealership.

Next we made a date with Rizzo—an "at home," meet-the-parents kind of date. Daphne liked the idea of meeting a family man. Er, well, I hoped she liked it. I sure did.

Ricki and Lenny, though, seemed to be playing hard to get. Just about when I was ready to give up, an email arrived from their foster parents—they'd decided Ricki and Lenny were family. The boys had found a loving home and were staying put.

Foster failure was now an epidemic. Our Beagle Bachelorette game had just begun and already we were down to the final two. We'd be at the final *AAAARRROOOOOSE* ceremony in no time. But, as Chris was quick to point out, the decision and our drive home both now appeared much easier.

Maybe.

———•◦•———

Two nights before we left for Paso Robles, I was home alone with Daphne, a book, and a bottle of wine. Seamus had been gone nearly three weeks. I'd kept myself preoccupied as much as possible. But now it was quiet, and I was alone with Daphne. She was ours, and though her surgery was pending, she was indeed low maintenance. There was nothing to keep me out of my own head.

I settled into the couch with Daphne by my side. After the first glass of wine, I was hungry, and I helped myself to a kale and broccoli cole-slaw I'd made earlier. It was delicious and filling.

I sat back down on the couch with my second glass of wine, but instead of reading, I turned on the television. This, like that second glass of wine, was a mistake. Every commercial seemed to feature a burger, steaks, or barbecued animal of one kind or another. I guzzled my wine. This was never going to change. This world was entrenched in dominating and using animals. I now saw a dead cow and not the juicy, mouth-watering burger the advertisers thought they were showing me. But it was like seeing an illusion—I was the only one who saw the cow ("I see dead animals").

When a commercial came on that showed a dairy cow following

a little girl (along with the human mother) to her first day of school, crying and upset to say good-bye, I wanted to throw my wine at the television. What about the cow's own baby? The one torn from her at birth? Were we not supposed to think of that separation? No, we weren't. And was I the only one who saw the absurdity of that school-age child drinking the milk of the cow mother when we'd all gasp in shock if she was drinking her *own* mother's milk? It was just so ludicrous. My life would be easier if I just went back to that naive bubble, unseeing and uncaring but still able to think of myself as an animal lover.

After finishing the second glass of wine, though, I started to see what everyone else saw—I saw the thick juicy burger, covered in creamy, delicious (if unnaturally orange) cheese, grilled onions, and Thousand Island dressing dripping from the sides. *Dang it! It looks good! Tasty even.* My kale-slaw was paling by comparison. I poured a third glass of logic-loosener and dived headfirst into my Pinot pity party. I was naive. Stupid. Ridiculous. *As though broccoli could fight off cancer. Kale was what, better than chemo?* Soon, I was telling myself, berating myself, that none of it mattered. *The animals suffer and no one cares. The dog died, and so will I! None of it matters. Nothing I do matters!* I rose from the couch and headed to the kitchen with a suddenly ravenous hunger. *I may as well have a burger. And throw on some cheese. Slather on the mayo! Maybe add a fried egg! What difference does it make? There's nothing I can do about any of it! I will eat away the pain! Because it all looks delicious!* (The burger...not the pain.)

I opened the refrigerator door and stared in.

I'd been on the plant-based diet—or, as Chris called it, a "member of the cult of kale"—for nearly a year at that point. And although Chris had not joined me, he too was certainly eating better. He even started to enjoy my creative blends of kale, celery, green apple, lemon juice, apple cider vinegar, coconut water, and chia seed smoothies. Okay, maybe "enjoy" is too strong of a word. Let's go with "drink." He began to drink my kale smoothies. After three months of having kale smoothies for breakfast with me, Chris had lost fifteen pounds. The result was that there wasn't a lot in the refrigerator for a suddenly lapsed vegan to chow down on.

There was celery, apples, almond butter, pita bread, and hummus. I had kale chips and flaxseed "tortilla" chips in the cupboard for a favorite crunchy snack. But bacon? *Not there.* A roast beef sandwich? *No deli meat at all.* An omelet? Always good with wine. *No eggs. Fine. A grilled cheese sandwich it is.* The one thing Chris continued to buy regularly was cheese. I reached for the cheese and bread and then the butter. I set them on the kitchen counter and closed the refrigerator door. I was a foster failure and now I'd be a vegan failure too. Failure was my middle name.

Thump. Thump. Thump.

I looked down. Daphne was at my feet doing her doodlebutt swing, her tail thumping the counter. She'd followed me to the kitchen on beagle autopilot. She looked up at me, perfectly ready to share, oblivious to my failures.

I exhaled.

While Daphne may have enthusiastically approved of my food choices in that moment, seeing her innocent face and her little cow-markings body stopped me cold. I knew enough, even in my wine-soaked anguish, to know the suffering that went into that cheese and butter. I'd allowed myself to read way too much about it to ever look at cheese the same way. Dairy cows suffer longer and live more miserable lives than even the "meat" cattle. At least the cows raised for their meat have some freedom of movement and semblance of "normal" before they are put out of their misery (by slaughter, to be clear; they're not getting massages on the range).

The sandwich lost its appeal. I was angry at cancer. Angry at the loss of my companion and cohort in cancer fighting. But eating a product wrought from the suffering of other animals was not going to alleviate my pain, no matter how much television and our culture in general glorified animal products. My pain was mine to bear, and I had no right to inflict it on others.

This was as close as I'd come to giving up my plant-based diet, and it wasn't hard to figure out my grief was playing a role in that. I looked down at Daphne, still waiting hopefully at my feet. "Doodlebutt, your mom needs a support group for this. You're going to be my sponsor. Every time I think about straying off this path, I'm just going to look at you."

She wagged her tail but looked back toward the refrigerator.

"Perhaps I'm choosing an unreliable sponsor." She was focused only on the hope of a sandwich and not listening to me at all. I laughed. "That's okay. You'll do just fine, baby girl. We're together for a reason."

I put the cheese, the butter, and the bread away.

I put the wine away too.

Chapter 14

THE DOG DAYS OF
WINE COUNTRY

Paso Robles was rapidly becoming Chris's and my favorite town. We'd been going regularly for a few years, enjoying the wide-open spaces, vineyards and orchards, the hot days and cool evenings, the funky and chic restaurants, the art, and of course the wine, which Chris featured prominently both in his store and the online website. We'd taken Seamus last year, so now I was happy we'd be taking our little Doodlebutt too—our version of the family vacation.

We left late on Friday night, after Chris closed up his wine shop. We stopped in Buellton to stay the night at a dog-friendly Motel 6. The room was small, clean, and serviceable, just as we'd expected and all we needed. Since we weren't sure how Daphne might react in yet another unfamiliar room without a doggie door, we preferred to be prepared. At least with a cheap room, the damage, if any, wouldn't break the vacation budget.

We needn't have worried. Just as Daphne easily leapt into the car to leave with us, she hopped up onto the hotel bed, snuggled in between us, and commenced deep, rumbling, contented snoring in three seconds flat. It was as if she was born to be with us: she so easily fit in.

In the morning, I took her outside for a visit to the closest tree, then came back into our room and made her breakfast. I had my coffee in bed while Chris slept a bit longer. Then Daphne jumped back up on the bed and snuggled in next to me. I rubbed her belly with my left hand while holding my coffee cup with the right, slowly waking, equally as content as the dog. Soon, though, the bed was shaking and my left arm felt a piercing grip. Daphne had stood, embraced the entirety of my left arm, and was madly humping away. I had to set my coffee down before it spilled.

"Daphne, no!"

Chris was awake. And laughing. "I guess she's gotten pretty comfortable."

"Yeah, we've got to get her spayed, stat."

"Isn't that supposed to be a problem with male dogs?"

"No one told Daphne." The dog sat next to me, staring up lovingly.

"She's got a major girl crush going on."

"She does. I'm kind of proud of that. Violated, but proud."

Later that morning we made our way to Paso Robles and stopped at the first winery of our Wine 4 Paws weekend. Wine 4 Paws is an annual fund-raiser for the Woods Humane Society. Many wineries welcome dogs, donate the tasting room fees or a portion of their sales, and host a variety of events for humans and canines alike. I was scheduled to sign books at one of our favorite tasting rooms downtown, Parrish Family Vineyard, but we had time to make a few stops at other wineries first. At the first tasting room, a photographer was present. What better place for our first family portrait than a winery? The photographer had set up a nice little scene using an old vineyard truck in front of a barn. Daphne hopped up into the front seat and posed perfectly. I think she thought the truck was going to drive us all away, and once again she was making sure to come along.

Chris and I both laughed at her enthusiasm. Seamus would have been howling and far too busy stealing the photographer's lunch, which she'd left on a plate on a low wall to our left, to have ever sat for this. We have several "pet pictures with Santa" where Seamus is howling at Santa, and one particularly memorable one where he is blowing a raspberry at Santa. But Daphne posed like a pro, smiling her doggy smile, tongue hanging out the side of her mouth, and looking right at the camera.

"God, I love how easy this dog is," Chris said.

"I know. Although apparently she thinks I'm the one that's easy."

I adored the photo we got. Chris's hand was even covering the lump on Daphne's chest that was best left unseen. Chris had amusingly begun to call the lump her "control knob" because she was such a well-behaved dog, but for my part, I just wish I could unsee the actual lump on this sweet dog. I forced the thought out of my head.

We took our photo and the bottle of wine we'd bought and headed to our car. Suddenly, we were brought up short by a thundering, unfamiliar noise.

"*BAAARRROOOOOOOOO!*" Daphne strained against her leash.

"What the heck?" I said.

Chris and I both looked in the direction Daphne pulled. It wasn't the first time we'd heard her bark, but it was close. She'd barked once or twice when we were out walking her and another dog passed by, but it was more of a yip: maybe a hello, maybe a warning shot. This was an unmistakable howl. Sure enough, another visitor had arrived at the winery, and their large spaniel-type dog had just leapt out of their car. Daphne was howling as if it were her job to evict the trespasser. Her howl was more of a bark than Seamus's had been, and certainly louder, but it was still the legendary, carrying-across-the-fields, bloodcurdling beagle howl. This was a hunting dog's howl when they'd spotted their prey.

"I've noticed she only howls at dogs bigger than her," Chris said.

"Really? So maybe it's a defensive thing? Whatever it is, that's a loud bark."

"Yeah, that's definitely loud." Chris pulled back on Daphne's leash. "No."

Daphne looked up at him, tail wagging.

Oh, good, she listens to us. How novel, I thought. But then…

"*BAARRRROOOOOO!*"

"Okay, let's just get her in the car."

Once in the car, Daphne morphed back into her usual calm, happy-go-lucky-gal persona. I gave her some water, and she lapped it up and then licked my face in her "Thanks, Mom" way.

"Baby dog, let's not make a habit of that, okay? Other dogs exist. You'll need to get used to that."

She moved over and tried to mount my arm again.

"Okay, this has got to stop!" I took her two grabby front paws and moved her off me.

We parked in front of the Parrish Family Vineyard tasting room. This would be my first signing without Seamus. I'd already given a few talks, which were difficult enough. I'd struggled mightily trying to find a scene from the book I'd be able to read without breaking down, only then to be caught completely off guard when I had to decide, on the spot, whether to use the past or present tense when I spoke of him. But those talks took place in venues where no one expected Seamus to be with me. This time I was at a dog event with dogs abundantly present. I was once again thankful to have Daphne by my side to ease the pain of this transition.

There was a labradoodle in the tasting room. A big goofy labradoodle who danced around and immediately assumed the play position alongside the bar stool and facing Daphne.

Daphne went off again. *BAAARRROOOOOOOOOOOOOO!* Only this time, the hackles on her back went up. Chris and I looked wide-eyed at each other and then both immediately yelled, "No!"

Daphne stood her ground, unfazed. I moved between her and the playful labradoodle and said, "No," once again, more firmly (and less hysterically, since the surprise had now worn off). She seemed to listen but wanted nothing to do with the exuberant pup, so we escorted her back outside. *Sure, me she wants to hump, but the cute labradoodle she ignores.*

The Parrish folks had set up a table for me on the front patio, complete with a little bowl of water for Daphne. We set up my books, a sign, and a donation jar for Woods Humane Society and settled in with a glass of their crisp sauvignon blanc, which would definitely also help me through. This was how to do a book signing.

It didn't take long before Daphne howled again and strained at her leash. We turned in the direction of her howl and saw our friends, Juliana and her husband, who just happened to be named Seamus (and whom we therefore jokingly called "human Seamus"), walking down the street toward us. I met Juliana through the same Beaglefest group that helped me adopt Daphne. Juliana had a beagle named Maizy. On the Beaglefest Facebook page, there were frequent posts by the members about our mischievous beagles and their never-ending antics. When I posted about my comical Seamus, Juliana naturally got a laugh out of it since her husband shared the moniker. I once posted my plans to take my Seamus to Paso Robles (the year previously, for the same event) and asked for dog travel tips from others. Juliana gamely posted that she loves to take her Seamus to Paso Robles as well, and what worked for "human Seamus" (fresh air, great restaurants, friendly winemakers) could surprisingly also be applied to "beagle Seamus." From there she and I learned we had more than just beagles in common, including a love of travel and wine, particularly those from Paso Robles and California's central coast. And Juliana and human Seamus were vegetarians.

"So maybe it's not just dogs bigger than she is that she howls at," I said.

"She's howling at Juliana and Seamus?" Chris said.

"I think she's howling at Maizy."

Chris bent down to pet and calm Daphne. "Doodlebutt, no. You can't howl at other beagles! That's never going to work out." Our talking to our dog in full sentences was also unlikely to work out, but we were as undeterred as Daphne.

We could barely say hello to our friends over the bossy howls of our beagle, who seemed to be screaming at Maizy to stay away. Maizy, in true beagle fashion, howled back but clearly only in defense. Human Seamus suggested he and Chris take "the girls" for a walk together so they would get to know (and like) each other. He meant the beagles; Juliana was joining me for a glass of wine, and we already liked each other.

The walk eased some of the anxiety out of Daphne, but at each new winery we went to that afternoon and evening, when we got out of our cars, Daphne started in again at Maizy as though she was seeing her for the first time. "*BAARRRRROOOO!! You're still here?? These are my people! MY people!*" She was embarrassingly rude. And loud.

Juliana noticed that both of our girls were wearing purple collars and purple leads. I'd given all of my dogs "signature colors" for their wardrobes and even their toys sometimes, and once I realized that Chris had named Daphne after the *Scooby-Doo* character who always wears purple, well, the decision was easy. Daphne's signature color was purple.

"Maizy's signature color is purple! Maybe that's what Daphne is upset about! You know how women can be with their outfits out in public," Juliana said. And that's when we noticed she and I were both wearing turquoise.

I laughed. It was gracious of her to laugh off our dog's antisocial behavior, but I was getting concerned. We were forty-eight hours away from introducing our Beaglerette to the lucky bachelors. Was she going to howl and snarl at them too? Had I adopted yet another dog that wouldn't tolerate competition from a fellow canine?

We went to a barbecue party at Dubost Winery that evening. To my relief, Maizy and Daphne seemed to have settled their differences—or at least resolved to ignore each other, though poor, sweet Maizy really looked like she just wanted a nice friendly game of chase, if only Daphne would stop with the noise.

Fine, I'd take ignoring the other dog, cute as she was. It was better than the howling. But then I had a new worry.

The Dubosts' pigtailed, blue-eyed, chubby-cheeked, four-year-old granddaughter took an immediate liking to Daphne and came hurrying to our table. In the split second it took for the little girl to hurl herself at Daphne, I realized I had no idea how Daphne responded to kids. The girl swung her arms around Daphne's neck and put her face right up against Daphne's, cheek to cheek. A pair of big, bright blue eyes and a set of caramel-brown eyes stared up at me with matching expressions of love. Daphne didn't move a bit—except for her tail. Her tail wagged enthusiastically. The little girl petted and hugged and talked to Daphne (mostly professing her love) off and on for the entire evening. None of it was too much for Daphne; she gleefully soaked it all in, and she never howled at Maizy. Well, that night anyway.

Okay, so Daphne wasn't a perfect dog. She's maybe not crazy about other dogs, but she certainly loved children. And she was smart enough to hide her one bad habit until we were crazy in love with her. Clever. And after all, that's one of the traits I'd always loved about beagles—the clever part, not the loud part.

On Monday morning we left Paso Robles for Los Angeles and our Beaglerette's big day. She'd meet Comet first and then Rizzo. Such a momentous occasion required some special spoiling, so we shared our breakfast with her and stopped at Avila Beach on our way down the coast. For all we knew, this was Daphne's first time on a beach. Her ears flapped in the wind as she ran, tongue flopping out the side of her mouth, eyes wide in excitement, loving every moment. Since it was Monday morning and still cool out, we had the beach almost entirely to ourselves. There was one other man and his dog, and we were pleased to see that Daphne only barked a couple of times. She was too happy to be bothered by this lone intruder far down the beach. She did not bark at or chase the seagulls either, so I allowed myself to think she'd already become more socialized in our three days away.

I must have taken a thousand photos. It was so beautiful to see this former shelter dog, who so clearly wanted only to be loved, happy, and exuberant in the wind and sun. Everything about Daphne said "joy" on that beach as she ran, played, and constantly looked back at us or ran straight to one or the other of us, licked our faces, and ran to play again (cue the melodramatic "walk on the beach alone contemplating love" scenes from any of the *Bachelorette* shows). We would have stayed all day, especially since the beach is my favorite place too, but there were some handsome bachelors waiting on our girl, and I, for one, couldn't wait to meet them.

Chapter 15

SNIFFING THINGS OUT

WE PULLED INTO THE PARKING LOT OF THE MERCEDES DEALERSHIP where Vanessa, Comet's foster mom, worked. I got out of the car and looked up at the building, my hand still on the open car door. What if Daphne didn't like him? What if he didn't like her? What if Vanessa didn't like us? Daphne barked from the backseat. I turned my attention back to her, opening her crate and attaching her leash.

"Ready?" Chris said.

"Yeah. Though I'm freakishly nervous about this."

As we headed toward the gleaming glass showroom and office building, I saw Vanessa walk out with Comet. She held him close, yet he didn't fuss in the least. I wasn't used to a beagle that enjoyed being held. Seamus couldn't stand to lose control of a situation for any length of time and thus struggled and howled when anyone attempted to pick him up. Daphne came to us weighing forty-two pounds, so that limited my efforts to pick her up. But as she slimmed down and I tried occasionally to pick her up , it was clear she didn't like it, though her method for avoiding it was to go limp and roll over onto her back when we moved toward her. Chris had begun calling her the "Flopsicle" for the way she sort of melted down to the floor.

Vanessa motioned for us to head over to a large grassy area in the parking lot (it was Mercedes after all). She put Comet down on the grass. He was every bit as cute as I remembered him. So tiny, especially next to Daphne, whom we had dubbed "Daphne-esque" in size.

Daphne immediately began to sniff Comet from head to tail—well, actually in the reverse order as dogs will do. Her tail wagged and she didn't howl. A good sign! They each jumped sideways, tails wagging quickly, enticing each other to play. Another good sign! They both peed on the pristine Mercedes grass. Another good sign? Who knew, but it wasn't a bad sign. Vanessa suggested we take them inside to her office, now that the obligatory dog sniff-and-pee greeting was over.

The three humans and two beagles traipsed through the shiny showroom of gleaming, expensive vehicles and went upstairs to Vanessa's spacious office strewn with dog toys. Comet immediately picked up a toy and ran around with it, the dog version of asking to play. To our surprise, Daphne chased after him. We had not seen her play alone or with another dog yet and were beginning to wonder if she knew how. Poor Maizy had tried so hard to get Daphne to chase her, with no luck at all. Comet had only to ask once and they were off and running. My smile widened into a big grin—they were tossing a purple toy. (Dear, sweet Maizy—it was probably like loosening a jar lid. You did all the hard muscle-work and then Comet got the last twist in.)

They chased each other around. Comet, knowing the office layout better, looked nimble and athletic, leaping up and off chairs, turning corners sharply, and zipping around and under tables. Daphne was older but craftier. She quickly figured out how to cut him off and realized her superior strength—once she had a bite of the toy, she yanked it out of his mouth easily. Comet seemed to love the game, nonplussed when he lost a toy. He simply grabbed another and took off again.

I found him adorable. And Daphne seemed to agree. When Comet tired, he jumped up on a chair and lay down. Daphne approached the chair, put her two front paws up, and leaned in to smell Comet. Their noses touched. Vanessa, Chris, and I broke out in a chorus of, "Awww."

Curled up in the chair, he looked like a baby deer. I lifted him up.

I was surprised by his weight. He was so light. Surely he needed to put on more weight. He leaned into me and rested his head on my shoulder. *Perfection!* I was falling in love. Looking over at Daphne and Chris, I could see I was not the only one bitten by the love bug.

"He's so tiny," I said.

"He's gained a couple pounds since he was rescued from the lab. He really wasn't much of an eater at first. But he definitely likes his meals now. Though yeah, he could stand to gain a few more pounds," Vanessa said.

"So odd for a beagle. I guess he wasn't exactly given table scraps and treats at the lab, though."

Chris came and stood next to me, petting Comet's soft head.

"No. Definitely not. They feed them specialized junk dog food that is primarily meant to reduce their bowel movements. I can't imagine the food tastes or smells any good," Vanessa said.

"Seriously? They can't even feed them well while they subject them to all the horrible tests?" I said this, and I meant it, but I still wasn't clear what those tests were. What had been done to Comet in the name of "science"?

We left reluctantly, giving lots of hugs and kisses to Comet. Daphne seemed to genuinely like Comet, evidenced by the complete lack of barking. Date number one had gone very well. Rizzo had his work cut out for him.

Our Beaglerette slept for the forty-minute drive to her next date. I'd call it beauty rest, but not the way she was splayed out and snoring.

Rizzo met us high up in his foster dad's arms, standing in their driveway. Like Comet, Rizzo was calm. Unfortunately, Daphne began howling at him before we even got her out of the car.

Dan, Rizzo's foster dad, greeted us and then put Rizzo on the ground, nose to nose with our Bachelorette. He wagged his tail and she wagged hers. Both of their noses twitched into overdrive.

"I thought it would be a good idea to have them meet out here," Dan said. "But let's take them into the backyard and let them play a bit."

As we approached the backyard, it was easy to see the decision to meet in the front yard was a good one. Dan and his wife had three dogs of their own and were also dog-sitting their daughter's dog. Four small- to medium-sized dogs barked and rushed at the gate to meet the interloper. Daphne was not amused. She backed away from the gate and looked up at us like we'd lost our minds. *We're not going in THERE, are we?*

Dan opened the gate and shooed back the exuberant dogs. Rizzo was clearly used to this mob scene as he slipped into the yard and began a fast run around the circumference of the long, narrow yard, hoping someone, anyone, would chase him. Daphne was having nothing to do with this. She entered and was immediately surrounded by yelping, barking, yapping, jumping balls of fur. She put her tail between her legs and jumped out of the way, then ran over to stand at Chris's legs. And where was her date to rescue her?

Rizzo was still running about, so Dan came to the rescue. He moved the other four dogs into the house, but they all stood at the sliding glass door looking out and barking at a bewildered Daphne and a whizzing, spinning Rizzo. Comet's calm, personal Mercedes date was the better idea, but we could appreciate Rizzo wanting to show his family side. Even if Daphne didn't.

While Chris and I talked with Dan and learned what we could about Rizzo (they'd only been fostering him for a few weeks), the dogs began to play. Daphne finally chased after Rizzo, howling of course, but playing at least. Rizzo was fast. He was also very handsome. Where Comet was all cuteness, with a touch of mischievousness, dark almond eyes, and a saddle of black fur over much of his back, Rizzo was handsome, strong, and square, with a lot of white. Rizzo and Daphne looked like a "couple" whereas Daphne and Comet looked like big sister and little brother. Not that any of that would matter in this selection process. I could anthropomorphize my dog all I wanted, but she was not going to play along.

We tried letting the other dogs out again, if for no other reason than to silence all the noise at the door. But the experiment failed. As soon as the other dogs were back in the yard, Daphne lost all interest in playing with Rizzo. She wanted only to escape.

I, on the other hand, could have played all night with Rizzo. He was such a handsome boy and so stoic, yet merry. He seemed to be a very content dog. And like Comet, he enjoyed being held and swooned over. And I enjoyed swooning over beagles (I'm very good at it).

"This is going to be a tough decision," I said an hour into our drive home.

"You think so? I don't," Chris said.

"Really?"

"It's indisputably Comet."

"But Rizzo is adorable!"

"I totally agree, but we're letting Daphne decide. And to stick with your game, she clearly had more of a *connection* with Comet."

I had to laugh. "Well, that seemed to be true. But she also met Comet first. I think she was exhausted and overwhelmed by the time she met handsome Rizzo."

"It's Comet."

"Do you think we're just being influenced by the fact that Comet met Seamus?"

Because of the passing of the bully stick, I felt that Daphne had an otherworldly connection with Seamus. And, I had to admit, I liked the idea of our new dog at least having met Seamus—as though some of the magic could have passed through their sniffing each other. I'd even settle for the mischief passing (prescient, as it turned out).

"Daphne doesn't know that Comet met Seamus, and Daphne seemed to adore Comet. She didn't even bark at him, for chrissake!"

"That's true. And he may be the only dog at whom she hasn't barked. Right, girl?"

I turned to look at Daphne in the backseat. She was sound asleep, snoring in a way that would never be shown on a real *Bachelorette* show. Except maybe in a blooper reel.

I turned back to face Chris. "But I love Rizzo too. I feel like I'm the Bachelorette: 'I'm in love with two beagles and I have to break one of their hearts.'"

"Okay, you realize the dog doesn't know, right?"

"But I'll know. And the foster parents will know."

"I knew this was a bad idea."

I laughed again. It wasn't a bad idea. I loved both dogs. I loved all beagles. I would have loved all of the Beagle Freedom Project dogs if I'd met them all. Heck, I love all of the beagles on their website and on Facebook. Which is why I was not the best one to make this decision. "You're right. We said Daphne would decide. And Daphne picked Comet."

"Comet it is."

I sat quiet for a moment, but then I used the doctor phrase, "There's just one more thing."

"You want Rizzo to come visit."

"Okay, two things. The other is—you know I can't have a dog named Comet."

"Comet is a cool name. Like a shooting star. It's awesome."

"But that's not what he's named for. He's named for a reindeer. A *Christmas* reindeer. Me having a dog with a Christmas name is asking for trouble. It's all I can do to not ask you to change *your* name."

In case it's not clear, I hate Christmas. Hate that whole time of year. When I think Christmas, I do not think peace on earth or shopping or trees or stockings or prettily wrapped gifts. I think Armageddon and cancer and tragedy, all wrapped up in a black bow shaped like a noose. A Christmas-moniker dog would not do.

"So, Percival?"

"Not just Percival. Percival Ramonce."

Now we were both laughing. Our laughter woke Daphne, and she joined in by thumping her tail.

Nine years earlier, when Chris and I first started our relationship, it was summer. He lived in Los Angeles, and I lived sixty miles east in Riverside. Thus geographically challenged, we had several dates at Angels baseball games in Anaheim. He'd drive east from L.A., I'd drive west from Riverside, and we'd meet at the stadium. Chris frequently wore an Angels jersey to the games. The name on the back of his jersey was "Percival," for Angels pitcher Troy Percival, who just happens to be from Riverside (though Chris did not know he'd be dating a girl from Riverside when he bought the jersey). Chris's parents had Diamond Club tickets, so we'd spend the games in the club enjoying "premium liquors" and gourmet food, even occasionally watching the game. After one game, Chris (in his Percival jersey) and I walked out to the parking lot together and then kissed good-bye before we walked to our separate cars. As I walked alone to my car, two young men who'd also been in the Diamond Club started chatting me up about the game. I was a bit slow on the uptake, but soon I realized one of them was actually flirting with me. I was forty-one years old. Chris was then twenty-nine, and these men were probably his same age if not younger (can we all say "ego boost" together?). The one flirting said, "So are you headed over to The Catch?" (a renowned postgame sports bar) and his buddy playfully punched him in the arm and said, "Dude, she was *just* kissin' on Percival!" The moment had made me smile and laugh (and feel wildly flattered like only a middle-aged woman could).

Of course I had to tell that story to Chris. And he also laughed, mostly because I did not in fact go to The Catch. (Who are we kidding...I was the catch! Well, in that moment anyway.) And from that day on, "kissin' on Percival" became a regular saying between us. Chris had long ago commented that "Percival" needed to be our next dog's name. (And if ever there was a dog that deserved a lifetime of "kissin' on," it's a dog rescued from a testing laboratory.)

Then, sometime later, we were (okay, Chris was) watching college football and there was a player on the University of Texas's team whose first name was "Ramonce." Not Ramon. Not Roman. Not Raymond. Not even Romance. *Ramonce.* For some reason (there may have been margaritas involved), I found this hilarious and a perfect name. We knew someone named Ramon whom we referred to as "Sexy Ramon" (because he is), and this name just seemed to encapsulate that—it was sexy Ramon and romance all in one. We somehow (there may have been margaritas involved) decided that "Percival Ramonce" was an even better name for the next dog. So we could be kissin' on Percival Ramonce. (Maybe we needed to cool it with the margaritas...but it's too late now.) And thus, the name Percival Ramonce was born. And thus the dog, now to be Percival Ramonce Rhyne-Kern, was adopted.

Once I told Shannon which dog we wanted to adopt and she told the foster families, everyone was excited for us to pick up the dog, including me. The Beagle Bachelorette game that played out on my blog also meant the "fans" were waiting to hear which bachelor our Beaglerette had selected. I had visions of playing out the announcement with a photo or even video of the two love beagles together when we brought

Percival home. (In my fantastically delusional mind, the two would cuddle, hold paws, and pose adoringly. Ahem.) The problem was our Bachelorette needed to be spayed first.

The fates (and my love of beagles) once again conspired against my carefully laid plans.

The following weekend, I was attending a vegan restaurant fundraiser for Beagle Freedom Project in Los Angeles. Shannon thought it would be a good idea if Vanessa brought Comet/Percival to me then, as the whole Beagle Freedom Project family could wish the couple well. I understood. It would be hard on Vanessa to let him go, but even harder if we left him with her for a few more weeks. Thus, despite my prior planning and my doubts, I agreed to pick up Comet/Percival at the fund-raiser, and I scheduled Daphne's surgery for the following week. A week would be enough time for them to get used to each other. Wouldn't it? And she wouldn't come into heat in just the next two weeks, would she? No worries there either, I told myself—Comet/Percival had been neutered.

This wasn't the first time I'd been blinded by love. And when it comes to beagles, I'm sure it will not be the last.

My weekend plans were set. Saturday, I'd take Daphne to the Bark for Life American Cancer Society walk in Simi Valley where I would be the grand marshal. The plan had been for Seamus to accompany me, so I was thankful I'd be able to take Daphne with me. After that, we'd head to the BFP fund-raiser and pick up our boy.

But there was another event before then. I'd agreed to volunteer at the National Canine Cancer Foundation booth at the Southern California Pet Expo on Friday. Now that I knew I'd have a new puppy, I had an additional reason for going. Though he was nearly two years old, given his background, Percival was for all intents and purposes a puppy. Percival would need a bowl, a leash, a collar, toys, food, all the accoutrements of being a well-cared-for (some might say spoiled) dog. And ooh, this meant I needed to come up with a signature color for Percival! Red would have been the obvious choice since his name derived from an Angels baseball player. But red had been the signature color of my Richelieu, the beagle who had passed away a few months before I adopted Seamus. Blue, purple, green—all the usual "boy" colors had been given to my prior beagles. But I'd have an entire fairground of booths to help me decide.

As it turned out, picking Percival's signature color was the least difficult thing I'd have to think about at the expo.

I rose much earlier than I like to (which, truth be told, is any time before ten a.m.) and arrived at the fairgrounds on time. Already a long line of families waited to get in. Seeing the numbers of folks there to celebrate animals and maybe even adopt a pet was almost as warming as the French roast coffee I was ridiculously trying to carry while also carrying a stack of my books and my purse and camera. The books got heavier as I made my way across the fairgrounds and into the expo building where the National Canine Cancer Foundation booth was located. Given that all of my concentration was required to not (a) spill coffee, (b) trip, or (c) collapse under the weight of what I foolishly thought I could carry, I didn't pay much attention to the hundreds of booths along my path. I did see, however, that I'd have to take some breaks and go exploring.

This was an animal lover's heaven. Outside they had sections set up for various rescue groups—German shepherds (love them!), bloodhounds (those faces!), boxers (so fun!), English bulldogs (such character!), so many more, and, be still my heart…beagles! Inside the buildings were a variety of booths with various pet food companies, dog and cat toys, pet photography, adorable T-shirts and pet-themed jewelry—basically anything that had anything at all to do with pets was there. I was doing my own little *AAARRRRROOOOOOO* inside my head, but I couldn't stop to shop. I had a job to do and a box to set down.

I took a break after about an hour and a half of working at the booth. There was no way I'd have time to see everything, so a carefully plotted-out plan would have been a good idea, but I was not expecting the expo to be that large or that fascinating. I plunged in and began to roam the aisles. Vanessa told me she'd been feeding Percival a sweet potato and fish kibble, so my one specific goal was to find that brand of dog food. If I changed his diet, I'd need to do it slowly, gradually mixing the old with the new. I also wanted to explore other foods and see if The Honest Kitchen was still the best option. Daphne had been enjoying the many containers of PetStaurant gourmet raw foods, but we'd run through those and soon we'd finish up the last of the supply of The Honest Kitchen. As I did with Seamus, I wanted to give these dogs the best meals I could give them. But I still preferred not to have to cut up animal organs.

What better place to compare food products than an expo with nearly all of them on display?

For Daphne and Percival, I wanted, as I'd been doing for myself (and trying to convince Chris to do), the diet with the greatest health benefits, and given that one in three dogs die from cancer, cancer-fighting ingredients were definitely still going to be a part of that. Daphne was still overweight and probably got that way by living off the doggie equivalent of junk food, the commercial, cheap kibble sold in grocery stores, and then whatever she could forage for herself when she was a stray on the streets of Los Angeles. And Percival had spent all but the last four months of his life confined to a cage, eating a diet that had more to do with reducing his bowel movements than providing him with a quality of life (clearly, that was *not* their concern). So what was the best diet for these two?

I approached one booth that emphasized "natural," "organic," and "holistic" in its signage. These all seemed like good things.

"So, tell me about your food," I said.

"What kind of dog do you have?" she said.

"I have a beagle and I'm about to get another beagle. They're both rescues."

"Good for you!" She moved down the display of dog food samples and stopped in front of a blue package. "Beagles are active dogs, so you'll want something more like this." She handed me the sample.

"Okay. Well, one of them is a bit overweight, and the other is underweight. The underweight one was rescued from a laboratory where he was the victim of animal testing. So I really want to be cautious about what I feed them both—no chemicals or preservatives, and as nutritious as possible."

"Bless your heart. The poor dog. And a beagle you said?"

"Beagles are the dog most commonly used in labs. He's one of the lucky ones to even be released, but he spent eighteen months subjected to testing—no sunlight, no playing on the grass, no toys or treats or love. So we owe him a lot."

She grabbed a handful of samples. "It's all natural. The highest-quality ingredients you'll find." She reached for a box of treats and threw that in the bag too. "You give him our best."

My day continued in much the same way. I took small breaks to visit other dog food booths, and when my time at the National Canine Cancer Foundation booth was over, I roamed over to the other buildings. Everybody had samples they gladly handed out, but other than the usual "fresh, wholesome" advertisement-laden hyperbole, it was hard to determine why one food might prove better than another. I also found that even though I had yet to formally adopt Percival, I was already intent on telling everyone what he'd endured and speaking out on the need to shop cruelty-free. "Just look for products not tested on animals!" I found myself repeating. I found I just as often heard "I had no idea" in response. And this was in an exhibit hall filled with animal lovers. While I felt mildly better about my own naïveté (which apparently loves company), I despaired that animal testing was such a well-kept secret.

I explored still more booths, and it became my turn to say "I had no idea." I was now noticing the emphasis on "toxin-free." *Toxin-free toys? Bowls? Dog beds?* So, there is such a thing as a *toxin-filled* toy, bowl, and bed? Yikes! Where had I been? When did all this happen? *When did owning a dog get so complicated?*

My childhood dog, Tippy, was a shaggy black cockapoo who was given to me by my parents as a Christmas gift when I was six years old. He lived until my last year of law school—seventeen years. Tippy rode horses and motorcycles with us, sat in my pony-drawn carriage in the 4-H parade with me, drank out of plastic bowls, ate commercial kibble from the grocery store, and shared nearly everything I ate as well. For seventeen years.

Much as I had liked living in my naive precancer bubble, eating whatever I'd liked, not exercising, and not looking into reasons I shouldn't be doing either of those things, I much preferred the nostalgic era where dogs lived simple lives unaccosted by toxins. Having witnessed Seamus's battles with cancer, and before him Roxy with her heart murmur, and before her Raz and Richelieu, whose deaths were most likely cancer related, I could no longer ignore the obvious: something has gone terribly wrong in this world, and the results are causing cancer in us and our pets. This seemed simple, obvious, and overwhelming.

I had never considered how dogs are even more susceptible than people to the toxic household products we typically use in our homes until I walked the expo aisles. Seamus slept on the floor, ate food off the floor when I dropped any morsels (which was more frequent than I'd like to discuss), and slept and rolled on the carpets, in the blankets, and on the grass and landscaping in our yard. And now Daphne and Percival would do the same. These were all areas regularly subjected to chemicals and toxins in the name of "cleanliness." Percival had already spent enough time around toxins, and who knew what Daphne had been subjected to. This was definitely something I could do better. I could find better products. I made a note and a promise to myself and to Daphne and Percival.

I walked from booth to booth, picking up brochures, talking to the manufacturers, and buying what seemed legitimate, though I couldn't say what my standard was other than a gut feeling. The only decision I was able to make with any certainty was that Percival's signature color would be orange—the color of the animal anticruelty ribbon.

I bought a book on easy, nutritious meals for dogs written by a man whose dog, diagnosed with cancer, set him out on a journey much like the one I'd been on to discover the best way to feed our beloved dogs. He at least had the good sense to have the book endorsed by a holistic veterinarian. I vowed to do yet more research, though my head spun. I needed to know about a human diet that didn't include animals, a canine diet that did, products that weren't tested on animals, products that wouldn't cause cancer, and products that did not harm the environment in which all animals, including humans, lived.

Yikes.

In a less-contaminated world, this exercise might be simple, but as I was rapidly learning, getting accurate information and finding healthy products was very difficult. Nontoxic and healthy aren't the norm. The norm had spiraled into a terrifying mélange of improperly or insufficiently labeled products that likely caused cancer, harmed people and animals, and destroyed the environment.

I was falling down a rabbit hole, and it seemed the rabbits were being harmed.

Chapter 16

HERE COMES THE BEAGLE

O<small>N</small> S<small>ATURDAY MORNING</small>, D<small>APHNE AND</small> I <small>WERE UP EARLY WITH A BIG</small> day ahead of us. On our drive out, no matter how many times I tried to talk to her about her impending nuptials, she merely stared at me with her cheerful face and thumped her tail. She wasn't nearly as nervous as I was.

I spent the morning chatting with the walk participants, selling a few books, and checking to see that the volunteer walking Daphne wasn't having a difficult time. (I could hear Daphne howling, so I knew she was up to her usual bossy tricks.) When the program started, I joined the crowd at the start line, waiting to be introduced. The master of ceremonies asked for a moment of silence for those who had passed away from cancer. Seamus of course came to mind, and just as quickly tears flooded my eyes. I looked down, closing my eyes tight. It had been a mistake to leave Daphne with the volunteer. I needed her with me. I opened my eyes and scanned the group, but I couldn't spot the volunteer. Nor could I hear Daphne howling any longer.

I heard the emcee introducing me and knew it was too late. I'd be on my own. *I was fine right up until that moment of silence, dang it.* I took the microphone.

I got two sentences out before my voice cracked and the tears tumbled out.

I took a deep breath. "I'm sorry. He only passed away six weeks ago."

Several members of the audience were now also crying. Well, maybe that was normal at a cancer walk, but I really wanted to pull it together.

"*BAAAARRROOOOO!*"

A familiar face made her way through the crowd, doodlebutt in full swing. The volunteer was trying to hold Daphne back, but Daphne was having none of it. She'd heard my voice and was determined to be by my side. I took the leash from the chagrined volunteer.

"It's okay. She knows I need her."

I turned back to the crowd. "This is my new dog, Daphne. She's my foster failure."

The audience applauded, and Daphne's tail wagged even faster.

As the morning went on, I could see a habit forming. We walked. We greeted. I signed books and answered questions and petted Daphne in between, getting and giving the assurances we both needed. What would I ever do without dogs?

We finished up, and I was pleased to note there was a food truck with vegan options at the event. Even though I knew we'd next be at the fundraiser for Beagle Freedom Project and all of the food would be vegan, I thought I might be too excited and anxious to eat there, much as I'd grown to love vegan restaurants and their creativity in making delicious food. I had lunch there in the park, sharing bits with Daphne, naturally.

I'd bonded so quickly with this adorable, agreeable dog. I wondered, briefly, if adding a second dog would be a mistake—if I was, as Chris had pointed out, incapable of simply sharing my life with a low-maintenance dog. I looked down at Daphne, her cow eyes looking up with devotion and adoration…for my veggie sandwich, of course. No, I could not resist this beagle or any other.

"Come on, baby girl. Time to pick up your boy." I gave her the last bite of my sandwich and stood. Daphne followed me to the car, doodle-butting her way across the park.

She hopped into the car and settled in, tongue hanging from the side of her happy face.

And off we went.

The Beagle Freedom Project fund-raiser was at an L.A. hipster dive bar with a vegan food truck in the parking lot. When we arrived, fifteen minutes early, I learned from Shannon that the manager of the bar on duty that day had—inexplicably, at a fund-raiser for dogs—declared the patio a "no dog" zone. It looked like we'd be having a parking lot party. Not an auspicious start for our girl's final rose ceremony.

This came as a surprise for several reasons. One of the things I had grown to love about vegan restaurants was that they are almost always dog-friendly, provided they have a patio. A few months previously, Chris, Seamus, and I met up for lunch with Kelle, Manos, and their beagle, Bogart, at a Los Angeles restaurant appropriately named Café Gratitude. We sat on the patio, and both beagles patiently waited for lunch underneath our table. Neither dog made a noise, except to lap up the bowl of water that had been provided to them. It took only minutes before we heard a woman at the table behind us grumbling to the server that there were dogs nearby.

"Yes, ma'am, we're a dog-friendly restaurant," the server said.

"It's disgusting."

"I'm sorry, are they barking? Have they done something?"

"They're dirty animals. They have no business in a restaurant. I want to speak to your manager."

A nearly identical conversation took place with the manager. He offered to move the family inside. They declined.

"I should be able to enjoy some fresh air without having to be near unsanitary animals," she said.

I was floored. But I wasn't sure whether to laugh or scream in outrage—there was nothing dirty about these pampered, groomed, indoor-living, vaccinated dogs. Seamus got his nails done more often than I did. And here this woman was sitting on a patio next to a very busy Los Angeles boulevard with cars, exhaust, and smog in every breath, accusing our dogs of destroying her "fresh" air.

The manager smiled and repeated, "We are a dog-friendly restaurant."

I loved that. I loved him. *Victory for the dog lovers!*

I motioned for the manager to come to our table.

"We will gladly move farther away from her. I appreciate your defense of dogs, but it will be easier for everyone involved if we move tables as far away as possible."

"You don't have to do that."

"It's okay. We're happy to do it. And thank you."

The meals on the Café Gratitude menu are called things like "I Am Fabulous" (raw summer zucchini noodle lasagna with heirloom tomatoes, basil-hempseed pesto, olive tapenade, wild arugula, baby spinach, sun-dried tomato marinara, cashew ricotta, and almond parmesan) and "I Am Pure" (marinated kale salad with sesame-ginger and garlic-tahini dressing, avocado, sea palm, nori, cucumbers, carrots, cilantro, basil, and green onions topped with teriyaki almonds). I was self-congratulatory in ordering the "I Am Gracious" (hempseed pesto bowl with local brown rice or quinoa, shredded kale, heirloom cherry tomatoes, and almond parmesan drizzled with olive oil and topped with sprouts), though I probably lost points when I asked the server if that woman had ordered "I Am Narcissistic." The server merely gave me a smile that somehow managed to agree with and chastise me simultaneously.

Later, though, I reflected that, in a way, the disgruntled diner's attitude had a certain consistency to it. She hated animals; therefore, she dined neither on them nor with them. While I disagreed with her about animals, I had to hand it to her for not being a hypocrite—unlike when I, like most folks, claimed to be an animal lover while consuming them several times a day.

At any rate, there we were, at a beagle fund-raiser with a bar manager who agreed with my Café Gratitude Narcissist.

Shannon wasn't happy about the sudden "no dogs" decision, understandably. While she worked her cell phone to get ahold of the bar owner, Vanessa and I sat in the parking lot with Percival, Daphne, and a few other Beagle Freedom Project supporters. It was a hot L.A. day, so we convened under the shade of the one tree in the parking lot corner. Daphne and Percival were far more interested in the bushes and the people than each other, but we didn't push it.

Vanessa picked up Percival for a few moments, then she kissed the top of his head and set him back down on the ground. He looked back at her, checking in, and then moved immediately for the bushes along the side of the parking lot.

"That's his thing," she said. "He loves to rub into the bushes."

"Is he nervous?"

"Probably. He just feels comfortable there." She tugged gently on his leash to bring him back toward us. Percival threw himself into reverse. All four legs straightened and he flung all twenty pounds of him backward. Vanessa and I both laughed.

"And that's his other thing. If he doesn't want to go with you, he does that. So you have to be very careful with his harness. I'll give you this one. Every other one I tried he was able to slip out of."

"Good to know."

True to their beagle selves, Daphne and Percival both remained interested in the myriad smells on the tree and bushes—and, no doubt, those emanating from the bar and grill—and ignored each other. We let them sniff about. Soon we were joined by Laurie, another BFP beagle adopter, and Caroline, who, I came to learn, had been present at many of the rescues, including Percival's. To my great happiness, the next to arrive was Rizzo and his family.

I loved and hugged all over Rizzo, though he, like the other two, was more interested in sniffing the bushes. The bushes must have smelled of the grill food the way those beagles were obsessing over them. But then, these were former lab beagles. Every smell was a smorgasbord of freedom. I did get Rizzo to sit in my lap for a bit while I admired his sweet handsomeness. Daphne came over immediately, sniffing at this beast that had crawled into the lap of her mama. She wagged her tail and barked at Rizzo, who wagged his tail and sniffed her back. *Oh sure, now they like each other*. I looked over at Percival, now cuddled up with Caroline. These dogs were just so impossibly cute; I couldn't go wrong either way.

"You've got yourself a real character here. We all just love this dog," Caroline said.

"We love him too. He'll be well cared for and loved, I promise," I said.

Vanessa wiped at her eye with her index finger and then put her sunglasses on. Caroline handed Percival back over to her and she held him close.

Shannon returned to the parking lot. "Just bring the dogs in. The only people in the patio are here for our event. Who's going to complain?"

We moved our parking lot party to the gated patio. Five beagles on a patio with a vegan food fest going on, and humans enjoying cocktails and good company—this was the way to spend an afternoon. The patio had six picnic tables and benches and a small kitchen serving area that was commandeered by the food truck operator. The weather was L.A. beautiful and the bar was serving mai tais and Bloody Marys, which went nicely with the vegan sliders and mac 'n' cheese dishes. (Yes, I had two lunches. That vegan mac 'n' cheese was calling to me!) It was not a bad little reception for our *Bachelorette* couple. The bride, however, spent much of the time under one of the tables—not as a result of too many drinks, like a bride or two I've known, but from her desire for a share of the sliders or sweet potato fries. More than one person obliged her with the slip of a hand under the table. I may have been one of those people.

Percival spent his time lapping up the adoration of his many BFP fans. Caroline held him when Vanessa could let go, and Rizzo's folks visited with Percival for a bit while I held and loved on Rizzo one last time. There were toasts and tears, and inevitably, it was time for the lovebeagles to exit.

Vanessa buried her face in Percival's neck and whispered to him. I felt terrible taking him away and simultaneously awful for leaving Rizzo behind (though Rizzo's family looked well in love with him). Also, though, I was anxious to get Percival and Daphne home to our new life together. I wanted to get to know this dog. I wanted to start kissin' on Percival too.

"You gonna be okay?" I said.

"Yes. Yes. I will. I know this is the best thing for him." Vanessa kissed the top of Percival's head and handed him to me. Caroline put her arm around Vanessa, and no one bothered to choke back the tears.

"Thank you for taking such good care of him. You'll see him again, I promise."

"I know. I know. I'm okay."

I set Percival down on the ground next to Daphne. "We're off."

There were hugs all around, and Vanessa and Caroline followed me to my car. Vanessa reminded me that Percival gets carsick and then handed me a bag with a chew toy, a bag of the food he'd been eating, and a card. Now it was my turn to blink back tears as I drove out of the parking lot, with Percival curled up on a blanket on the seat next to me and Daphne in her crate in the backseat. Both dogs slept the entire sixty-mile drive home. Daphne snored contentedly and Percival breathed deeply.

Their exhausted sleep gave me time to think about the reality of two dogs in the house. I grew up with many animals and as an adult always had two or three beagles. But Seamus had preferred being an only dog. So for the last nine years, in my new life, in this townhome, there had only been one dog. One dog with one giant personality. And now there'd be two. I imagined them running through the house, chasing each other and playing tug-of-war with toys, as they'd done in Vanessa's office. I'd have twice the food bill, twice the vet bills, and Chris would have twice the dogs to walk and twice the poop to pick up (see how I'd negotiated that division of duties?), but we'd both have twice as much beagle-cuddling and cuteness as well.

Once home, I let Daphne out from the crate in the backseat of the car, and she ran through the doggie door and into the house instantly. Percival only raised his head. I thought he'd slept soundly, but the look on his little face said he had not enjoyed the ride. And of course, poor baby had no idea where he was or what would happen to him now. I knelt down next to him.

"It's okay, little guy. You're home now. This is your home and you're safe."

His dark eyes stared at me, but he didn't move.

"Come on, baby, it's okay. You can get out of the car now."

No movement.

Oh, this poor baby. I picked him up off the seat and held him close to me. I held him until I felt him relax and lean his head into my shoulder. Then I set him down on the ground in the garage. "Here you go, baby. It's okay. Shake it off. You're home now."

He stood, frozen in place. I walked ahead, calling to him. "Come on, Percival. Comet…let's go in the house. Come on, baby."

He looked up at me but did not move.

Daphne came running back into the garage to see what was taking so long. She raced over to Percival, ran around him howling, and headed back to the house. Percival followed her.

Okay, that will do.

I followed them both out of the garage and saw Daphne's rear end slip through the doggie door into the house. Percival paused only briefly and then followed her through. *Brave boy!*

Once inside, though, he froze up again. He stood, just inside the house, staring straight ahead at the laundry room wall. *Whoa…different scene. How'd that happen?*

Daphne sniffed him and then headed into the family room, and again Percival followed. Both dogs joined me on the couch for a bit of cuddling, but soon they were tearing around the house chasing each other. And when Percival discovered the canvas box of squeaky toys, well, it hardly mattered if I was around. He pulled out each toy, delicately at first and then frantically, as if they'd disappear if he didn't touch them all. He carried them one by one to the dining room and piled them up under the table.

The spring day was still bright and warm outside, so Daphne periodically went to the front courtyard for sunbathing. Eventually, Percival followed her, carrying a purple monkey squeak toy in his mouth. He hesitated only slightly before pushing his head through the doggie door flap, and after three or four successful journeys in and out, he eventually lost the look of "*I walk through walls!*" excitement. But he remained ecstatic to be able to run outside anytime he wanted, and he did it often, as if to check that the fresh air and sunshine were still available. I was equally happy that he'd easily adapted to the doggie door, since I hoped the next thing Daphne would teach him was to head out to the plants and trees to do his business.

Vanessa had told us Percival was trained to go on a pee pad but didn't necessarily know to go outside all the time. She didn't have a doggie door. This meant I'd be back to sleeping on the couch with a beagle, making sure he went outside if he got up in the middle of the night. That was okay with me, though. He was such a cute little guy, and I knew Chris and Daphne would be fine in our bed. Daphne would get a little time alone with her "dad," and that would make her happy too. It would also make Chris happy. Chris adored Daphne, but we'd both noticed that Daphne seemed to prefer me. She loved Chris, but she went nuts when I came home each night and would insist on fierce cuddling for a good ten minutes. I rubbed her belly, petted her head, and held her close while she leaned into me and licked my face. It usually only stopped when she grabbed my arm with her front paws and earnestly humped away, something she did only to me. And she looked lovingly into my eyes every time. (Yes, I stopped her, but only after I stopped laughing. You have no idea how serious she was about this.)

I prepared dinner for both dogs and put Daphne's bowl out in the courtyard and Percival's in the kitchen. Daphne, I knew, would finish her dinner in less than two minutes, but I wasn't sure about Percival, so I closed the laundry room door, preventing Daphne from coming back in the house until Percival had finished eating. I did not need to risk a food aggression fight on our first night. Daphne stared through the French doors forlornly while Percival sniffed at his dinner. Then he walked away, back to the dining room and his stash of toys.

I picked up a bit of the food—the fish and sweet potato kibble Vanessa had given me, mixed with The Honest Kitchen mix I was giving Daphne—and handed it to Percival. He sniffed, then licked gently. His eyes lit up and he gobbled up the rest of what I had in my hand and easily followed me into the kitchen. But when I pointed to the bowl he just looked at me. He wagged his tail, staring at my hand as though more should appear. And so it did. I picked up another messy handful and he ate it. Then I did it again, but tried to lower my hand to the bowl as he ate. As soon as my hand was near the bowl, Percival stopped eating. What the heck? Was he afraid of a stainless steel bowl? Maybe it reminded him of his cage? Equipment at the lab? I finished feeding him by hand. Whatever the problem was, it wasn't his appetite.

When Chris came home, Percival stood unmoving again in the dining room. Chris bent down and called to him, and though he had yet to come when I called him, Percival went bounding over to Chris. Chris picked him up and Percival immediately leaned into him.

"Huh. He hasn't been that relaxed with me," I said.

"He remembers me, I think."

Daphne danced anxiously at Chris's feet, barking up at Percival, so I called her over to me on the couch. She snuggled in next to me, and though we'd been home a couple of hours at that point, she once again demanded her belly rubs and then made her amorous moves, seeming even more forceful with her "attention."

When it was time for bed, Chris got Daphne to follow him upstairs. Percival hopped up onto the couch with me immediately. He was thrilled with the sleeping arrangements. I tried to adjust so he could curl up at my feet, but he preferred standing on me. I turned sideways and tried to maneuver him into a dog-human version of spooning, but he was having none of it. That was not enough human contact. I knew Vanessa had him in her life for four months and clearly loved him. Still, it was astounding to see (and feel) how much human companionship this dog wanted. One would think he'd be terrified of humans. But then again, it was humans, and mostly female humans, who'd given him his freedom—this new life.

I turned over to sleep on my back and Percival climbed onto my stomach, his face over mine. He stared down at me, wagging his tail. Eventually he lay down stretched out on me. This was his own version of spooning—one where the spoons were stacked on top of each other. Good thing one of the spoons only weighed twenty pounds. We settled into sleep.

In the early morning hours, Percival yelped and jerked awake. The yelp was strained, hoarse—the horrid result of the debarking. He was shaking. I sat up and held him. I stroked his soft fur and talked to him.

"It's okay, baby. You're safe. It's okay."

He searched the room and then me with his gaze, figuring out where he was and if he was safe. I could only imagine how frightening this was for him. After all he'd been through at the laboratory—his life spent in a cage, his contact with other beings only resulting in pain—then finally, he's safely in a home for the first time, enjoying a soft bed, toys, human love, and suddenly he's moved again. What would this new place be like? What would he experience now? It had to be terrifying for him.

I held him and talked to him. It was twenty minutes before he relaxed. Then he hopped off the couch and went to the laundry room

for a long drink of water. He slipped out the doggie door into our courtyard and just stood in the moonlight, as if reassuring himself he was still
free. I suspected we'd be reassuring him of that for some time to come.

Chapter 17

NAKED TO A DOGFIGHT

In the morning the sun streamed through the French doors from the courtyard. Percival did not wake. He was sleeping soundly, though silently, much more quietly than Daphne Doodlebutt and her thunderous snores. I unwrapped myself from the semiproper spooning position we'd maneuvered into during the night and made my way to the kitchen to make coffee. Hearing me, Daphne made her way downstairs. I saw her happy face and then her doodlebutt tail wag as she passed through the short hallway and into the family room, on her way, I assumed, to the laundry room doggie door and outside to the courtyard and her morning business. Had I already had my coffee, had I been thinking, I would have anticipated how the rest of the business agenda would go.

I heard Percival yelp, just as he'd done in the middle of the night. More quickly than I could react, both dogs had gone into fight mode. As I rounded the corner, I could see that Daphne was now on the couch too, in a tangle of tricolored fur and teeth. The cacophony of snarls, growls, deep barks (Daphne), yelps (Percival), and strange hissing (likely Percival) woke Chris and sent him flying down the stairs in just gym shorts (he'd learned from Seamus one did not arrive naked to a dogfight). I'd managed to grab each dog by the collar and separate them, but the snarling had not stopped and my arms did not seem long enough to create a safe zone.

"What the hell happened?" Chris said, taking hold of Daphne's collar and pulling her farther away.

"I think she woke him." I moved my body between the dogs and tried to soothe Percival, while Chris did the same with Daphne. They poked their heads around us and hurled doggie epithets at each other but eventually calmed down. Percival seemed confused and terrified, as he had in the middle of the night, while Daphne seemed likewise confused, but also concerned: "*What's up, little guy? Why do you act like that?!*" They both seemed to be on the defensive.

Eventually we let go of them both and they circled each other, hackles up and sniffing, while we watched and occasionally gave a stern "No" when either snarled or lifted a lip. After a few moments they either tired of the animosity or worked out whatever needed working out. Just as it was hard to know what or who started the fight, it was hard to know what conclusion they'd reached. Daphne went outside while Percival circled on Chris's lap on the couch.

I made my coffee while explaining the night's events to Chris.

"So he has night terrors?" Chris said.

"Yeah. I guess that's what it is. He has a nightmare and wakes up not knowing where he is and he's terrified. I think he's probably having flashbacks to his time in the lab."

"Poor guy. That's so sad."

"I know. I'm guessing he had the problem at Vanessa's house too, originally."

Vanessa confirmed our experience but encouragingly told me the night terrors had all but gone away by the time she'd handed him over to me, so she hadn't remembered to mention it.

The next day I took Percival with me to work. The traumatized little boy drooled buckets as soon as he saw my car. I put down a blanket and a towel and did my best to explain it would only be a short six-mile drive. But Percival was not speaking English or calculating distance. He'd gone into a fearful place and was panicking. My heart was going to break daily for this dog, I could see that now. But he deserved a happy life as a carefree dog, and we'd get him there eventually, I promised him.

He threw up at mile three.

I parked in the closest available parking space at my office complex and opened the back door to get Percival out. He was standing, his back right leg bracing him against the back of the seat. He didn't move as I clipped his leash on, nor did he turn to look at me. There was no telling where he'd gone in his mind. I picked him up and held him against my chest. He didn't resist, but he didn't lean in either. He was just there. Compliant. Confused. Frightened.

"It's okay, baby. We're here. It's safe." I put my cheek against the dome of his head and held him closer. "You're safe, sweetie."

Maybe I shouldn't have moved him to another place yet. Maybe he needed time to adjust to our house first. But leaving him home alone didn't seem like a good option, and leaving him and Daphne home alone together seemed risky, given the morning's events. Maybe I should have taken another day off work, but with Daphne's surgery coming up, there was no way I could afford that.

After a few minutes, he pressed against me, and I felt his tail wagging, bumping up against my rib cage.

"Good boy, Percival. Good boy." I set him down on the ground and grabbed my purse. I closed the car door, locked it, and, holding Percival's leash, turned to head to my office. Percival straightened all four legs and jettisoned himself backward. *Errrrrr. Not so fast, lady. Just because I'm out of that torture chamber on wheels does not mean I'm willingly going wherever you have in mind next. Instead let's visit with these bushes right over here. Yeah, that's it. Bushes. I need bushes! Bushes! Bushes! Bushes!* He tugged me toward the shrubs lining my office building and flung himself into their midst.

This behavior I was familiar with. He'd done this all afternoon at the final rose ceremony. I found it reassuring that he'd returned to his normal, if obstinate, behavior. Note to self: add fifteen minutes to the time it takes to get into the office on mornings when Percival comes with me. I let him sniff around for a bit, but I already knew that with his love of flowers and bushes, he'd stay out there all day. And who could blame him? But these squeak toys, premium foods, and vet bills weren't going to be paid for in flowers and grass. We needed to get to the office. Also, I had vomit to clean out of my car.

I picked up Percival—an unfair but necessary advantage I had—and took him into my office.

Seamus's bed and toys were still there. Daphne had been in a few times and certainly didn't seem to mind the smell of another dog. We had yet to see her play with toys, but I already knew Percival loved toys—the bigger the better. I brought a couple of his favorite toys from Vanessa with us and tossed them into the bed in the corner of my office, in front of my desk. After the *coos* and *oohs* from my paralegal and assistant, Percival settled down in the dog bed, his head resting on Seamus's green and purple squeaky frog, and promptly fell asleep. He didn't wake when I left to clean my car or when I came back in. All his time at work with Vanessa was paying off.

He slept deeply and soundly (though soundlessly) for most of the day. So much so that I worried. I'd never seen a beagle so still. *Should I wake him? Take him outside to potty? Was he okay?* I let him sleep but checked on him regularly, watching to see that he was breathing.

Just when I was beginning to feel the effects of my night on the couch, yawning and nodding off at my desk, Percival woke. His tail wagged enthusiastically, and he grabbed the squeaky frog. He took it out of my office into the main reception area, where he walked around exploring, never dropping the toy. I followed him out and tried to get him to play fetch, but he did not want to release frog. Instead, I petted him and he wagged his tail. Emboldened, I tugged on his toy and he immediately bowed down to play tug-of-war.

Okay, so no night terrors when he woke, and there was nothing wrong with him. He's just a deep sleeper. Perhaps I needed to be careful not to read too much into his every move.

When it was time to go home, Percival backed into a corner the moment I'd grabbed his leash, just as he'd done when I had taken him out to the grassy area of my office complex for an afternoon break. And once again when he realized we were headed toward the car, he threw himself into reverse. In a repeat performance, I had to use my unfair size advantage to pick him up and get him home. He maintained his three-legged stance with the fourth leg braced against the back of the seat for the whole drive home, but he did not get sick. Again, though, it took a few moments for him to come out of his trance and get out of the car once we reached the safety of our garage. When he finally hopped out the back door, he was unsteady and slow.

"Shake it off, buddy, we're home now."

He looked at me but didn't move. I bent down and petted him

until eventually he brought his two front paws up onto my knee, and his face to mine.

"Okay now? Okay, baby? Let's get dinner."

I noticed how slowly he ate—much more slowly than either Daphne or Seamus, or any beagle I'd had before them. Still, he seemed to enjoy it, and he did not need me to hand-feed him. I went upstairs, changed clothes, and came back downstairs. Percival had not followed me as Seamus had always done and Daphne was beginning to do. Percival had instead gone out the doggie door and was sniffing around in the courtyard. Fresh air was a good idea for him. I could see why he'd prefer that. I made myself a salad and sat down on the couch in front of the television. Percival slipped back into the house and sat at my feet. He didn't beg. He didn't try to steal food out of my bowl, yet I still guarded my food—years of being trained by Seamus. Percival just sat by me, happy to be near, uninterested in the food.

I finished dinner, put my salad bowl in the sink, picked up Percival, and sat back down on the couch. He leaned in next to me. And I again cooed at him, told him what a cutie he was, and reassured him he was home and he was safe. We were still sitting together like that when I heard the garage door open. The sound meant nothing yet to Percival. He didn't move. Moments later, Daphne came happily bouncing through the doggie door ahead of Chris. One look in our direction and her face fell: *He's still here?*

She came around to my other side, but her hackles were up and she barked at Percival. He bared his teeth and that was all it took. They went at it across my lap. Chris came through the door to a tangle of fur and my screams. This time he pulled Percival back and I grabbed Daphne.

"What the hell happened?" Chris said.

"They are not Trista and Ryan," I said in reference to the only happy *Bachelorette* couple I knew.

"No, they are not. They're freakin' Jake and Vienna." I was impressed that he could come up with the nastiest breakup in *Bachelor* franchise history just like that, but I also had a snarling dog to control.

It was hard to say which dog was angrier, just as it was hard to say which dog lunged first. I wasn't sure it mattered. I just needed it to stop. The honeymoon was over and it hadn't even started.

And that was not the only honeymoon ending.

Chapter 18

COLD TOFU

Pᴇʀᴄɪᴠᴀʟ's ᴘʀᴇsᴇɴᴄᴇ ʜᴀᴅ ᴀɴ ɪᴍᴍᴇᴅɪᴀᴛᴇ ɪᴍᴘᴀᴄᴛ ᴏɴ ᴍʏ ʟɪғᴇ. I'd been flirting with veganism, but I had not fully committed. I'd started following farm sanctuary and animal rescue groups on Facebook and Twitter, and received several newsletters and even a magazine or two on the vegan lifestyle, but mostly I focused on the plant-based diet aspect. There was no denying a vegan lifestyle made sense for me—it aligned with my belief in myself as an animal lover, and it aligned with my tastes. And frankly I was tired of people mocking my food by pointing out my leather shoes (as though my not changing in one area is reason for them not to make any change at all). But to be honest, I feared people would think I was too weird. And I thought it would be too hard (as though that is an excuse). Now, though, with Percival here in front of me, and Daphne with all she'd suffered through at the hands of humans, I knew it was time.

Vegan isn't just about the food, and I didn't want to be just about the food. Vegan is a lifestyle of compassion. A lifestyle that respects *all* animals. How could that be weird? Just as I'd gone to a plant-based diet "cold tofu," I vowed to now go all-in vegan. I *needed* to be vegan. My days pretending to be an animal lover while contributing to their wretched lives and early deaths were over. I just hoped there was such a thing as a haute hippie.

The easiest and most obvious place for me to start was to eliminate products tested on animals.

Well, I *thought* that much would be easy.

I'd vaguely known "they test on animals," and of course, listening to Shannon and getting to know Beagle Freedom Project and their work, I now also understood "they test on beagles." But I didn't really understand what that meant.

I was acutely aware of why "they" test on beagles. Beagles are very compliant dogs; I knew that firsthand. I could see how their personalities would lead these scientists to choose this breed on which to conduct their experiments, and the realization pained me. Seamus, who unfortunately had been a patient of way too many doctors, had his issues, but veterinarians were universally complimentary of what a great patient he was, of how easily he tolerated whatever needed to be done. And a lot had needed to be done to him. He was a perfect example, in that regard, of the beagle personality. I thought too of Daphne so happily licking the face of the veterinarian she'd just met, and the two strangers who'd rescued her from the shelter. She was happy and comfortable with all of them, though she couldn't have known how much better they were going to make her life. She simply, instinctively, trusted. And Percival! Sweet Percival, free from a lab only four months and yet willing to be picked up, held, petted by a human. By several humans!

So yes, I understood (though vehemently disagreed with) the "why beagles" part, but now, as I prepared for another major lifestyle change, and as I calmed Percival's night terrors, I had to wonder, who are "they" and what are they testing?

I knew from my talks with Shannon at Beagle Freedom Project that we'd never learn specifically what testing had been done on Percival. Beagle Freedom Project rescues the dogs legally, in collaboration with the laboratories. Frequently it's the lab technicians, the ones who care for the dogs and, it seems, come to know them as the loving creatures they are, who reach out to find help for the animals when they know a particular experiment is ending and the otherwise healthy dogs will be euthanized if rescue cannot be arranged. The negotiations between BFP and the labs always include a nondisclosure agreement, at the insistence of the labs. I would never know the name of the lab, let alone the experiments done on Percival. One of the other beagles rescued by BFP was later discovered to have wires running throughout his little body. They had no idea why and never would.

How best to care for these dogs if we don't know what was done? Why did Percival drool and freeze into a trancelike state in a car? Why did the trash can on wheels frighten him so? Why did he stick his paw out so frequently, even sitting with his front leg bent, almost but not quite offering his paw? If I learned about animal testing, I could learn how best to help Percival and I'd learn the numerous reasons I needed to eliminate these products from my life.

I spoke again with Shannon and others active in BFP, gathering as much information as I could. And then I asked Chris to set up the DVD player so when I was ready, all I'd have to do was push Play and I could watch the documentary *Maximum Tolerated Dose*.

"Seriously? More documentaries? Are you sure?" he said.

"No. That's why I just want you to set it up. I'll figure out a good time to fall apart watching it."

"Great. I look forward to that."

Chris took Daphne the next morning, and I stayed home with Percival, ostensibly to work. And I did get a bit of legal work done. But the Play button was calling me. And never was there a more inappropriate term for a button than that one in that moment. There was nothing playful about what happened next.

I held Percival by my side while I listened to the cardiologist, the biologist, and the former lab worker each describe what they did in their past lives, subjecting animals to cruel and inhumane testing. As the doctor described, they'd all been trained in classic western medicine and taught to believe this was necessary—scientifically appropriate, if not ethically. They all quit when they learned that the tests were neither scientifically appropriate nor ethical. I watched the footage of the heavily secured, windowless compound where the research was done. I saw the restraining equipment, the frightened, huddled animals, the steel cages. I wept at the scenes of baby monkeys stolen from their mothers, their arms twisted behind their backs as they were dumped in net bags and shoved into holds at the bottom of the Laotian boats. I listened to the description of the tests: a mouse restrained, unable to turn or scratch, so mosquitoes could feed on her all night long; dogs injected with radioactive material, their hearts cut out and dissected; rats used in a college nutrition study for twelve weeks, then killed only to have the same study conducted again and again, year after year, yielding precisely the same results—and death. Over and over again there was death.

And then the beagles came on the screen. Percival had earlier gotten bored and left my lap for the comfort of the sunshine in our courtyard. I realize a dog doesn't watch television and wouldn't comprehend, but still, I was glad he wasn't in the room to see the screen.

The narrator, an undercover investigator, described a compound of fifteen hundred beagles at any one time, the dogs having been "brought into the world to be used as scientific resources." I looked outside at my own "scientific resource," asleep on a chaise, soaking up the sun and fresh air. The screen turned to footage of beagles—adorable, tricolored, healthy-looking young beagles—huddled together in the corner of a cage down a dark hallway in a facility that looked no cleaner, no happier, and no more "humane" than the poorest municipal animal "shelter" that regularly euthanized thousands of dogs a year, as indeed this facility did too. The cages were barren but for these soulful dogs. Then the film focused on one beagle, her midsection bandaged, a cone around her head, her sad round eyes staring up at the camera, looking a lot like Daphne had in her kennel photo, but without the hope.

She was killed the next day. Along with the other dogs, who'd spent thirty days in a test and were no longer needed.

Chris came home from work to find me under the kitchen sink pulling out every cleaning product and dishwashing liquid we had. (Never mind why we had four bottles of dishwashing liquid; that is not the point!) I spread the products out on the counter, out of a curious beagle's reach and next to my iPad, with the screen showing the website for LeapingBunny.org. Through Beagle Freedom Project's website, I'd found the Leaping Bunny website, and then I found their lists of certified cruelty-free products. I didn't recognize too many of the names, which is what caused me to dive under our kitchen sink to begin to check labels.

"Are you actually cleaning?" Chris said.

"Don't be ridiculous."

"Thought I'd walked into the wrong house for a moment."

"Well, I'm sort of cleaning. I'm cleaning *out* things."

Chris picked up a bottle of a very common household cleaning spray. "Cleaning out cleaning?"

"Something like that. I'm getting rid of everything that was tested on animals."

He raised his eyebrows. "All of this?"

"I'm still checking, but so far, I haven't found a single product here that *isn't* tested on animals."

"It's going to be kind of expensive to replace, isn't it?"

"It will be cheaper than the therapy I will need if I continue to use products from companies that are torturing and killing animals." I dived back under the sink. "Everything! I swear to God, everything in our house is tested on animals."

"Why would they test oven cleaner on a dog?"

I came back out from under the sink, window cleaner in hand. "It's how they learn what would happen if you swallow oven cleaner. As though we don't already know that. So they force the dogs to ingest it in a process known as oral gavage to figure out maximum tolerated dose."

"In case some moron doesn't know not to drink oven cleaner or keep it somewhere so their kid doesn't drink it?"

"Exactly. Or shampoo, bleach, laundry detergent, soap, you name it. It's all so stupid and unnecessary. It's not even required by law. It's done out of habit—ease—laziness on the part of the labs and scientists who even get grant money—our freakin' tax dollars—for this kind of crap. And many of the animals die, of course. That's how we learn the 'maximum.' And sometimes they do the procedure wrong and the liquid gets into the animal's—*the beagle's*—lungs and they kill the poor dog. I mean, they call it 'euthanize' but that's not euthanasia!" I was flinging my arms in the air, still holding the window cleaner, and Chris was exaggeratedly, slowly backing away from me in mock horror. Or maybe it was real. "That's torture and killing. And I'm not going to participate in it anymore. Not to mention this shit is all toxic anyway. I should have thrown it all out long ago."

"Well, it's not like we were using it."

I looked over at him and saw he was smiling, a hopeful, teasing twinkle in his eye. Once again he was trying to back me off from the cliff he and I both knew I was running toward. This time it worked. I was exhausted and emotionally spent, but I could not argue the point that neither of us was exactly fastidious about a clean house. We had a housekeeper, and sometimes that was the only way we were able to find our sink and countertops.

"Well, now we definitely won't be using it." I threw the window cleaner into the trash bag. "Remember when I said I was going to a plant-based diet and you asked if I meant vegan?"

"Vaguely."

"I mean vegan now."

Chris moved to the refrigerator and pulled out a bottle of wine. "I'll just leave you be."

"Good idea."

In the morning, I woke early and with the same resolve. I went back online, this time to determine whether my cosmetic products were tested on animals. *All* of them were tested on animals. My foundation, my mascara, lipstick, shampoo, conditioner, toothpaste, deodorant…*all* of them. I was appalled. I now knew they weren't testing the products by lengthening the beagles' lashes and making sure they smelled pretty. Percival, like Seamus before him and so many other beagles, had gorgeously black-lined eyes that made him look like he was wearing heavy eyeliner, but that hadn't been drawn on him in a lab as some sort of "test." That's not what they were doing. The beagles were either ingesting it or inhaling the chemicals. And dogs don't even sweat, so how and why are they testing deodorant on a dog? *Were they even making these poor dogs ingest deodorant?*

The site listed "cruelty-free" companies, and as I searched those to find the products I should be buying, it struck me as ridiculous that a company had to note and proudly proclaim "cruelty-free." "Cruelty-free" was worth noting, because "cruelty" was the norm? Like "low-fat" was worth noting because "fat" is the norm in our foods. Suddenly, it all seemed so very backward.

I not only felt like a hypocrite; I also felt duped. How did I not know this? How did this become our acceptable norm? I thought I was a compassionate person, particularly when it came to animals. Yet, here I'd been spending thousands of dollars on one beagle—my beagle—and

I remained oblivious to the thousands of beagles being tested on every year for the duration of their short lives. I had not only failed to realize this, but also I was using the very products tested on these poor dogs.

I grabbed another trash bag.

But throwing out the cosmetics proved more difficult than the cleaning products had been. I'd not become attached to my laundry detergent in the same way I loved my hair care products. I'd not spent as long searching for the perfect window cleaner (I'd spent no time at all) as I had my favorite shade of lipstick. But shiny hair and luscious lavender lips were not worth animal's lives. My vanity would have to get over it. Over time, I'm sure I could find the right shade of blood-red lipstick that didn't involve actual blood. Which gave me another thought—shouldn't they have to give the products realistic names? Would anyone buy "Beagle Blood Red" or "Pink Bunny Death" lipstick? I *had* bought them—just packaged under misleading and phony names, with no disclosure of the suffering that went into each tube.

But now they were all going in the trash, and I even tried to note and separate which products were in recyclable containers and disposed of those accordingly.

On another website, I ordered cruelty-free makeup, a lip gloss, and some herbal supplements for the beagles. I put my anger to work.

When Chris later woke, I proudly reported my morning's accomplishments to him. He looked bemused and horrified.

"Did you order some tribal drums too?" he said.

"I just care about animals. I'm not going off the deep end. "

"You kind of are. Am I soon going to be living with a hippie in a hemp skirt?"

"Would you rather be dating a hypocrite in high heels?"

He paused and pretended to think. "Can I get back to you on that?"

Chris was joking. I hoped. But he probably saw more clearly what was happening than I did. He'd been watching it build for a year.

Following my early-morning diatribe that had (nearly) ruined steaks for Chris, I had tried to tone things down a notch with him. He had watched some of the documentaries with me, and of course he'd been listening to me as I worked my way through my lifestyle choices. To his credit, he tried and enjoyed many vegan foods with me and was always game to check out vegan restaurants. Once he ran out of kale jokes, he didn't try too hard to come up with new ones, and there are only so many hummus jokes one can make as well. He did not choose to join me in a plant-based diet, but he did begin to search for meats certified as "humanely raised." I didn't want to become the hemp-skirted hippie he feared, but I wondered if his "humanely raised" idea was his Ape Adam—a story he told himself to make his meat-eating lifestyle work. But I refrained from discussing it.

As I was learning about true compassion for all animals, it behooved me to remember to be compassionate to human animals as well. Since Chris was my favorite human on the planet, compassion for his choices seemed a good place to start. After all, I was the one who had changed.

I was, however, losing patience with what others felt free to say to me. The things I heard regularly from otherwise intelligent beings who discovered I had turned vegan gave me almost as many nightmares as my reading had.

"Oh, aren't you worried about broccoli's feelings?" *Yes, because that's a real thing—broccoli has feelings. I'm going to take you very seriously if that's how you start a conversation with me about food. Or anything.*

"I grew up in the Midwest, and let me tell you, cows need to be milked." *Because that makes sense. Evolution or God or some higher (but apparently stupid) power designed an animal that would be entirely dependent on another species to pull on its private parts or it would…explode? And did everyone who grew up in the Midwest (a) live on a farm and (b) then move to California so they can lecture vegans?*

"It's part of the food chain. We're the top of the food chain. It's nature, baby!" *And the hormones and antibiotics we inject into these animals to make them grow faster and fatter so we can slaughter them sooner, that's natural?*

"Look, in the wild, the lion kills the gazelle. Every animal does what it's got to do to eat." *Does the lion confine the gazelle to a crate for most of*

its life before it kills it? Does it keep several gazelle and artificially impreg-
nate them to have a fresh stock always on hand? I mean, it does, right? So
your comparison totally stands up!

"You can't eat cheese?" says the shocked cocktail party attendee.

"I can eat cheese. Just like you can eat kale. I choose not to eat cheese."

"I choose not to eat kale!"

"And I'm not making fun of you or feigning shock."

"That's because I'm normal. Cheese is awesome."

And, oh, the bacon comments. There must not be a carnivore alive who can refrain from exclaiming about the ecstasy of bacon immediately upon finding out someone is vegan.

And where do I go from there? Like a reformed smoker, my tolerance was low and all I wanted to do was explain everything I'd been learning, reading, seeing. I wanted to scream at everyone to wake up to these atrocities that we're all contributing to. But as much as I wanted to, it's not "polite" to explain in a restaurant, at a country club, at someone's dinner table, even in a bar, about the torture endured by the cow that produced that cheese, or the pig that was slaughtered for that strip of fat you now call ecstasy. It's very convenient for agribusiness that the dinner table, indeed anywhere food is served, is a sacrosanct controversy-free zone where one cannot talk about anything crude or gross or disgusting…like where that food came from.

The better argument, and one I only learned of from reading, not from (surprise!) dinner conversations, is just how nearly impossible it is to live without killing *some* animals—and in particular the deaths of rodents and insects when vegetables are farmed with heavy machinery. It makes me wince, and makes me sad, and frustrates me that life does indeed work like that (animals die; humans die), but still…I'm more bothered by the intentional torture and slaughter of animals for our meat than the collateral damage wrought by vegetable gardening. It's one thing to have a rodent die quickly and accidentally in a combine harvester one year into its two-year life expectancy, and quite another to abuse, torture, and then kill a pig six months into its twelve-year life expectancy in a gruesome profit-making routine that is no kinder to the humans working in it than it is the animals.

And now I'd immersed myself in the horror of animal testing too. My frustration and my anger were growing. It was getting harder and harder to remain a polite citizen. Didn't I have a stake in this? If Percival couldn't speak, shouldn't I? It's not polite to talk about the food, but does an animal really need to be tortured for your shampoo? I can talk about that, *right?*

I was sleeping less and less. My brain was shaking more and more. I worried about animal welfare in general and in my living room specifically. And I'd forgotten one important detail in my own life.

I was overdue for my oncology checkup.

Chapter 19

COUCH NIGHTS AND COFFEE MORNINGS

I PUT OFF MAKING MY DOCTOR'S APPOINTMENT IN FAVOR OF FOCUSING on Daphne's. I needed to get her in for the surgery, but I worried about her recovering while she and Percival were each still seemingly hell-bent on being the only dog in our house.

I had spent two more nights on the couch and Chris had resorted to closing our bedroom door, with Daphne inside with him, so that we could avoid the morning confrontations. On the fifth morning, when Daphne came down the stairs and growled at first sight of Percival, Chris spoke up.

"I'm not sure this is going to work."

I tightened my grip on Percival's collar and pulled him closer to me. "It's only been five days. They're still getting used to each other."

"They're not getting used to each other. Not at all. They hate each other."

"It's not hate. Dogs don't hate."

"Whatever it is, it's no love match."

I slumped into the couch. "I know. But we knew it wasn't going to be easy."

"You don't do 'easy' dogs. But it *was* easy with just Daphne."

I had no response. It had been easy with Daphne, but easy wasn't the point. I wanted Percival. I wanted to *help* Percival. I was *compelled* to help Percival.

We let go of both dogs, and after sniffing each other on alert for a minute or two, they happily trotted outside and did their morning business.

"See, there's hope," I said.

I made my morning coffee, wondering if, really, there was hope. I don't ever remember as a child, when our family had many, many pets, having any issues adding in a new one. But then, they were running on an acre or more of land, and there were five family members to give attention, any one of whom was likely to be home. In contrast, Daphne and Percival had traumatic lives before coming to us and now were suburbanites with daily walks and free access to sunshine and fresh air, but in a courtyard that wasn't big enough for a full run. And they were frightened. That was the thing we'd have to remember. They needed stability, love, and a roof over their heads. Didn't we all? They also needed time and patience. *Yeah, me too.*

That night Chris and I arrived home at the same time—he with Daphne and me with Percival. Other than a longer than usual sniffing session with hackles raised by both parties, the dogs did not fight. Each may have curled a lip slightly, and there was definitely some dog dissing going on, but there was no open attack. I liked to think of that as progress and said so to a skeptical Chris. I petted both dogs and handed out treats. Chris got a kiss. Positive reinforcements all around!

The dogs behaved all evening as Chris and I played with them, fed them, and cuddled on the couch with both of them. Since I dearly missed my own bed, and in an effort to ease Chris's concerns (and perhaps because I never learn), I decided to test our luck. I headed upstairs to our bedroom, both dogs following. We all piled onto our bed to watch television, read, and sleep (Chris, me, and the beagles respectively). Daphne stayed next to me, curled up by my side, her head resting on my belly. Percival was next to Chris, splayed out, getting his belly rubbed until he drifted off to sleep. I was in bliss. *This was what I had imagined!*

Over the course of an hour, Percival burrowed under the covers and slept soundly somewhere around Chris's knees. Daphne moved herself down to the bottom of the bed, against my feet but on top of the covers. I fell asleep with my book on my chest. Chris removed and closed my book, turned the light out, and joined us in slumber. One happy little family.

Until… "*AR! AR! AR!*"

Percival's hoarse bark woke us all at two in the morning. Unfortunately, he woke Daphne the quickest, and she pounced on the strange noise coming from under the covers. Percival scrambled to come out from under the weight of Daphne and the dark, strange place he'd found himself in. When he did, he was face-to-face with a frightened and snarling Daphne, who obviously believed the best defense is a good offense. They bared their teeth, white and sharp in the dark night, and lunged for each other. Chris and I each grabbed for whatever we could and pulled them apart.

Chris held and rocked Percival. "It's okay, buddy, you're with us. It's okay. Calm down. Shhh, baby. It's okay."

I held Daphne's collar with one hand and reached for the light with the other. Daphne strained and growled in Percival's direction, her hackles up all the way down her spine. I put both arms around her and held her. "No, Daphne. No."

She barked in response, and Percival shrunk into Chris. I could see from his face he was still disoriented and unsure, still trying to figure out where he was, but seemed to sense that Chris, at least, was safe. I got out of bed and took Daphne with me.

"Back to the couch I go."

"No, you need to sleep. You stay here and I'll take Percival downstairs." Chris stood up and lifted Percival off the bed. "Just watch her while I throw some clothes on."

I held Daphne by the collar while Chris dressed, with a nervous and very still Percival glued to his side.

As he left the room, Chris said, "Still think this is a good idea?"

⸻ · ⸻

I slept better than I had in a few nights, but that was a low bar to clear. I had thirty-five pounds of beagle pressed up against me, leaving only a ten-inch width of a king-sized mattress for me. Still it was more comfortable than the couch. I woke to a beagle snoring in my face and as quickly as my eyes were open, hers were too. She flipped to her back and thumped her tail. "*Belly rubs, please!*" Of course, I obliged. I could see her grin and that doggie look of pure ecstasy and innocence even upside down.

"Baby girl, couldn't you just be this nice and cute for our little Percival too? He's had a tough life and he needs us."

Daphne licked my face and squirmed back and forth on her back. I wished I could take the gesture as an understanding, but it looked a lot more like a no.

I made my way downstairs and Daphne followed right behind me. I had taught Seamus to wait at the top of the stairs until I was all the way down because originally he had this unnerving habit of racing under my legs ahead of me. Not wanting to tumble down the stairs to my death or permanent maiming, I managed to teach Seamus that one bit of manners early on. Daphne did not need that training. She always followed either right next to me but off to the side, or a few steps behind me. She never raced ahead—she wanted to be only where I was, not ahead of me. She barely glanced in Percival's direction as she followed me to the kitchen, doodlebutt in full swing.

Percival tapped his tail against Chris's stomach but did not rise. Chris opened one eye. "Did this couch get smaller?"

"I find that happens around two and then again at four in the morning."

"He's a little dog, but he certainly can take up a lot of space. And he insists on being right on top of me. This was not comfortable."

"I know. Thank you for doing it." I ground the coffee beans and filled the filter. "I'll sleep down here tonight."

"Aren't we kind of young for this separate bedrooms thing?" He sat up, moving Percival off his chest to a space next to him on the couch. Percival leaned back into the crook of Chris's arm. "How many more nights are you planning on doing this?"

I flipped the coffeemaker on and leaned down on the kitchen counter. It was a good question. I hadn't planned on doing this at all. I had a plan (strengthening daily) to stop harming animals. I had a plan to rescue two beagles. I had a plan for a love match and cute little family of four. I did not have a plan for the dogs not getting along. No, my plan had been: *He's cute and he's coming home with me.* That was my plan with Percival just as it had been with Seamus. Once again, I'd thought no further than that.

The coffee dripped—rich, fragrant, and necessary. There were going to be a lot of couch nights and coffee mornings in my immediate future, I could see that now.

"Well, I'm guessing we'll do this at least until Daphne has her surgery and recovers from that," I said.

"Which will be when?"

"Right. Um…she's scheduled for tomorrow."

Chris stopped petting Percival and covered his own face with his hand, then looked up. "Great. So she'll be on pain meds, stitched up, and in a cone while all this goes on. What could possibly go wrong?" Percival pawed him in the face to redirect his attention.

"Believe me, I know. I've thought of that. But I'm worried about postponing it. I'm worried about that lump, and what if she comes into heat?"

"True. Well, maybe spaying her will mellow her out. And maybe the cone will keep her from fighting."

I grabbed a large white mug from the cupboard and poured coffee into it. "After I drop her off tomorrow morning, I'm going to go get a large crate that she can recover in safely. The kind that it's easier to see out of."

"Another crate? Another hundred bucks?"

"Cheaper than vet bills if they hurt each other."

Daphne gave up on getting any food and trotted over to and out of the doggie door. She hopped up on the retaining wall and walked back into the bushes where she squatted and did her morning business, staring back at us through the glass French doors.

"See that, Percival?" Chris said. "That's what you do." Percival looked at Chris and sniffed his chin, continually tapping his tail. Percival used the doggie door to come and go from outside, something he clearly enjoyed, especially if he could sit in the sun. But he wasn't using the door to go outside to pee. No, for that he used the living room rug (it was a shade of sage green but not at all "grassy.") After the first time, we put pee pads down. Vanessa had trained him to use the pee pads, but we had hoped Daphne would demonstrate for him how to use the outdoors as the pee pad. No such luck. I was slowly inching the pee pads closer to the door, but unfortunately Percival had chosen to start us off in the spot farthest from the outside. And frankly, we had bigger issues to deal with.

We swapped dogs. I sent Percival to work with Chris, hoping a strong dose of all that cuteness would win Chris over, though I wasn't entirely sure Chris thought being batted in the face by a little beagle paw was as cute as I saw it.

At work with me, Daphne was a perfectly well-behaved dog. She slept on the dog bed in my office, basking in the sunlight streaming through my wall of windows and periodically coming over to my chair for a little loving, though inevitably she'd collapse in a puddle of furry affection, wanting her belly rubbed. She did not rush to the door when anyone came or went, and she happily, calmly greeted visitors and my staff. She was as adorable and perfect as Chris had determined she was within twenty-four hours of her arrival.

If only she wasn't out to get the equally adorable Percival.

Chris emailed that Percival was sleeping soundly. Too soundly. He hadn't moved at all. I emailed back.

> Yeah. I know. It's a little spooky, but by late afternoon he's awake and fine.

Chris responded quickly.

> I'll have to trust you on that one. I want to put a mirror in front of his face to see if his breath fogs it, you know, like new parents do for babies?

> Ha. Yes. I know. And that's sweet.

Later Chris emailed that Percival had indeed awakened and then proceeded to chew on the ream of paper left on the floor near the printer.

Oh, right. Vanessa had warned us he chewed paper—magazines, books, and sure, why not a full ream of paper just there for the taking? It's possible I forgot to warn Chris about that habit.

The following morning, Chris left early to take Daphne to Dr. Davis for her surgery. We couldn't give her any breakfast—always difficult with a beagle. I fed Percival after they left and he followed me around the house for a bit before climbing up on our bed and curling up on Chris's pillow. I suspected that's where he'd been all night long, and I was more than a little envious. He looked so sweet, though. Like a little fawn, similar in color, with his long, thin legs tucked up nearly to his nose, and his long eyelashes clearly visible. It was restorative to have a quiet moment alone with Percival.

Chris came home to pick up our precious boy before heading to work. We still didn't think leaving him home alone was wise. We wanted him to get used to us, and we wanted to be there for him if he got frightened. So despite how much he hated car rides, we had decided to keep him with one or the other of us at all times. Fortunately, Chris and I both worked close to home.

I went to my office and anxiously awaited Dr. Davis's call to hear that Daphne had made it through surgery. I would stay home on Friday so I could be with her as she recovered. If Chris and I did not both own our own businesses, I don't know how we would have dealt with the dogs that seemed to find their way into our lives.

Shortly after three p.m., the call came. Daphne did great and I could come pick her up at any time. "Any time" meant "immediately" to me. I wanted to see my baby girl and get her home, comfortable and settled in for hours before Percival came home and any shenanigans started—*shenanigans* being the nicest term I could think of.

I was waiting in the exam room at Dr. Davis's within twenty minutes of the phone call. Dr. Davis came in shortly after.

"Surgery went well. That lump on her side was deeper than I thought, though, so that's got some stitches too. I'm a little concerned about it, so we sent that to biopsy too."

"On her side? I was worried about the one on her chest."

"We took that off too, but that wasn't as deep. So she's got three areas of stitches, and one of them is pretty deep. You'll need to keep her from moving around too much. Crate her if you can."

Oh, I can. I have to. "Okay. But she's good? All went well?"

"Yeah, she's good. Coming out of the anesthesia nicely. But let me show you something." He clipped an X-ray up onto a light board. With his pen he pointed at spots spread throughout her torso. One, two, three, four…ten. Ten spots. My heart, mind, and body froze. *Not more spots on an X-ray!* Of course I was thinking cancer. I tried to focus on what he was pointing at but couldn't. I just stared at him in disbelief.

"She's been shot," he said. "Like I thought."

"*Shot?!*" I'd almost forgotten that he had mentioned this possibility before.

"That's buckshot. It's deep in her torso in all these spots. There may be more in the areas not in the X-ray. Whoever shot her shot from a distance so they're spread out, not all clustered like they would be if the shooter had been close."

"What the hell?"

"I know. Unfortunately, we see this a lot with strays. Somebody may have shot her when she was on the street. Or whoever had her and clearly used her in breeding—that was one big fatty uterus I removed, and you can see she's had a few litters—they may have shot her to get her to leave the property when they were done. Who knows?"

I was seething and my head was reeling. It wasn't cancer, but a human did this intentionally? Inflicted this on a defenseless *dog*? "Did you remove them?"

"No. It would do more damage to dig in there and pull these out. She's built up scar tissue around them by now. Best to just let it be. People and animals survive with bullets and shrapnel embedded in them. It happens, sadly."

Right. Humans were horrible to humans too.

Daphne was brought to me, droopy-eyed and a bit dazed, but still wagging her doodlebutt and happy to see me. She had a cone on her head and a shaved right side, chest, and belly.

I bent down to pet her and she licked my face. "Come on, Doodlebutt. Let's get you home for some serious spoiling."

I drove her home, slowly, careful not to have to brake quickly or turn sharply, while cooing words of comfort in her direction. She slept through it all. Once we were home, I gave her a small amount of food, her pain medication, antibiotics, and a fluffy blanket on top of her bed so she could rest while I assembled the large crate. Once that was done, I moved the blanket into the crate, on top of the cushion, and lured her in with treats. Gate closed and dog settled, we both slept for two hours straight, though I was still on the couch.

I woke in time to let Daphne out, feed her, get her some water, and love on her before Chris and Percival came home and she would have to return to the crate. She was fine with this, as she was clearly groggy still, and the pain medications kept her sleepy enough that not even Percival's arrival could stir her.

For his part, Percival was just happy to be home. He'd gone into his trance and drooled for the car ride home. It seemed he just needed to lie down somewhere familiar. That spot was, of course, the couch next to Chris, who had sat down next to me.

I told Chris what I had learned from Dr. Davis and Daphne's X-ray.

"My head is just spinning with all this cruelty to animals. Everything I'm reading, those documentaries, poor Percival's life in a lab, and now this. It's making me insane."

Chris made an exaggerated face indicating his fear of me, and leaned away. "Really? I hadn't noticed."

"So you have noticed?"

"Noticed that you don't sleep through the night, even before you were on the couch? Noticed you—who never normally cries—are regularly in front of the television in tears? Noticed that you're throwing out everything we own? Noticed that we're eating at hippie restaurants? Noticed that your new BFF is kale, with nutritional yeast as a close second? Noticed that you are obsessed with saving this laboratory beagle, even though that might not be in his, yours, Daphne's, or my best interest? Noticed that even that is not enough, that you have to save every animal on the planet too? No, I had not noticed."

My throat tightened. I got up from the couch. "Now is probably not the best time for this conversation."

"Okay, relax. Fine. You tell me when the best time is."

"Sometime after I get eight hours of sleep." I tried to keep my tone light, but I may have been too tired to muster that.

"That might not be anytime soon if we don't do something about this. You see how that's a bit circular, right?"

"No. I don't." Well, I *did*. But I didn't *want* to.

Percival flung himself across Chris's lap and looked up at him adoringly, as though he'd just seen him for the first time all day. Chris laughed.

Well played, Percival. Well played.

Chapter 20

I DIDN'T KNOW

APHNE'S PAIN MEDICATION AND HER CONFINEMENT TO THE CRATE made the night an easier one. I had a full couch to myself and only woke twice, both times to let her out for some water and her visit to the courtyard bushes. She seemed quite content to return to her crate and snored soundly, which made my falling back asleep somewhat more difficult but not impossible. On Friday, Chris again took Percival to work and I stayed home tending to Daphne, alternating between working and catnapping. Friday night in our exciting household looked a lot like Thursday night. Until about three in the morning.

Daphne woke me, this time not with her snoring but her loud panting. I opened the crate door to let her out, but she came only as far as my hand, which she nudged. I petted her head. "What's the matter, baby girl?"

Her big caramel eyes looked up at me, and I could see she was not just panting but drooling. We'd switched out the plastic cone for an inflatable one that was more comfortable for her, but she looked anything but comfortable. I brought the water bowl over to her and she lapped up a few drinks. Shortly, she was back to panting. I chopped one of her pain pills in half and gave that to her. She took it and came out of the crate gingerly, in case there were other treats to be had. Count on a beagle to look for treats even when sick.

I sat on the floor, leaning up against the couch, and she sat next to me, leaning into me on her left side—the only section with no stitches. Poor baby. I was sure she was uncomfortable, but this was all reminiscent of my last night with Seamus, and I worried there was something far worse going on. I petted her head and her one good side and eventually she seemed to relax. On her own she walked back into the crate and we both returned to sleeping.

By six thirty, though, we were both awake. She was sitting upright again, and the panting had resumed. Though again she walked outside on her own power, drank water, and even ate breakfast, she looked miserable and never stopped panting except to swallow. For a dog usually so happy, this was a bad sign. When Chris woke, he agreed we'd have to take her to see Dr. Davis. While neither of us mentioned it, I could tell he too was reminded of Seamus's last night.

I was torn. I wanted to stay with Daphne and rush her to the vet myself, but I had volunteered to sit at a Beagle Freedom Project booth at Glen Ivy Day Spa resort where they were launching a line of cruelty-free beauty products with a "Beagle Bliss" spa day. A portion of every admission was going to BFP, and they'd asked Shannon to have a few of the beagles present. Of course when I volunteered I hadn't known the sleep schedule I'd be on or that Daphne would need to be rushed to the vet that morning. But I didn't want to let down Beagle Freedom Project.

Once again, I and one dog (Percival) went one direction, and Chris and the other dog (Daphne) went another. Chris promised he'd call the moment he had any news, and I texted Shannon to let her know I'd be late, but I'd be there.

I drove to the resort, eating an apple on the way and trying to reassure Percival that the car ride would be over soon while reassuring myself that Daphne would be fine.

Chris called as I pulled into the spa parking lot. "Is it me, or do I call you with dog diagnoses a lot?"

"That's not even funny. Is she okay?"

"She is now. They gave her a shot for pain. He thinks the postsurgical pain is causing the panting, so we're adjusting her pain meds."

The news was better than what I feared. At least it was something easily managed. But I'd been following the instructions we'd been given, and our poor girl was still in pain. Something so easily controlled, and we'd failed her.

Chris knew where my thoughts would be going, that I'd be blaming myself. "She's fine now. She's relaxed; she's asleep in the crate. We did exactly what we were told."

"I should've known better."

"How? How would you have known better than the vet?"

"I don't know." I felt a wave of exhaustion roll over me. I exhaled. "I'm just so tired of everything going wrong. I'm just tired. Period."

"Yep. I'll turn the hot tub on. We'll talk about that tonight."

That wasn't going to help. I knew what he wanted to talk about, and I was feeling defeated but not yet willing to admit a permanent defeat. These dogs *needed* us.

I reached out to the drooling and fearful beagle beside me and gave him a piece of apple. He licked the apple slice gently, took it in his mouth, and then put it down on the seat. He sniffed at it and looked at me with those dark, almond eyes. *What's this?*

"It's an apple, buddy. It's good for you. Go ahead." I picked up the piece and handed it to him again. This time he chewed it and you could see the joy as "sweet" and "tasty" registered. He wagged his tail and looked at me for more, his eyes now less doubtful and widening to hopeful. I bit off another piece and handed it to him. He sat up, chewing happily. I kissed his face.

"Almost makes it worth a car ride, huh? Okay, buddy, but we've got to get going. You've got fans to meet. Today, you're the face of the anti-cruelty campaign." *And what a face it was.*

I spent the morning letting the guests meet and pet Percival. I showed them the tattooed number inside his ear (1800192) and explained how that was all he had been known by for the first eighteen months of his life while he lived in a cage, the unwilling victim of pharmaceutical testing.

A young woman in shorts and a tank top waiting in line with two friends petted him and put her face next to his. "He's so sweet. How could anyone do that?"

"It's sadly the norm. That's why it's important to shop cruelty-free." She was probably in her early twenties, so I went for the obvious. "Most of the makeup sold in department stores and the big, common drug-store brands are tested on animals. And I don't mean they're putting mascara on the beagles. They drip it in their eyes, force-feed it to them, cause them to inhale the fumes from the chemicals. A lot of painful, unnecessary procedures."

Her eyes widened, as did her friends'. They moved closer and petted Percival. "That's so awful! Why do they need to test makeup on animals?"

"They don't. Animal testing is not required by law. And that's what is important to remember. Plenty of countries and companies have given up animal testing. When you shop, be sure to look for cruelty-free products. They'll say it on the packaging or you can look for the Leaping Bunny logo." I was aware I sounded like a poorly written commercial, but I didn't care. I was new at this evangelizing, but I was earnest.

"I'm going to do that," the young woman said. She was looking right at Percival when she said it, so I had great hope she would follow through.

One of her friends gave the now familiar refrain: "I had no idea."

They began to rattle off the names of several large and popular cosmetic companies, asking if they tested on animals. They all did. I'd been as disappointed as they all looked now.

"There are some very good brands out there that don't test on animals. You just need to do a little research before you shop. Go to Beagle FreedomProject.org and find out more. And I hope you will all shop cruelty-free now that you know. Percival thanks you." To leave them with a smile rather than the stunned looks on their no-longer naive faces, I held up Percival's paw in a wave.

I moved down the line, introducing Percival to more of the spa guests. He seemed to enjoy his newfound fame as he wagged his tail and took in the petting. I hoped that everyone he met that day would remember his sweet beagle face when they made their shopping choices. It took a little more time and effort to shop cruelty-free, but protecting these dogs was worth that. (I bought the Primavera line of skin care products the resort had promoted all day at the event; that much was easy at least.)

Walking Percival around the serene resort grounds gave me a chance to get to know him a bit better. I gave him the lead and let him sniff about wherever he wanted to go. On the rare occasion I tried to dissuade him from heading in a particular direction, he engaged his patented four-paw braking system and flung himself in the opposite direction. Eventually, I'd have to pick him up and move him along. He loved being held, though, so this was a close second to just getting his way. At one point, the direction he wanted to head was toward a small pond and waterfall. I tugged his leash to bring him back onto grass, but he was having none of it. Knowing beagles aren't big fans of water, I gave in and let him walk to the edge of the pond. To my great surprise, he did not stop on the edge. He walked right on into the pond and was wet up to his belly. He turned back to look at me, first with surprise and then pure delight. It was about ninety degrees out and the pond was no doubt refreshing, but if he went much farther, he'd be swimming, and this wasn't a dog spa. I pulled his leash to bring him back out.

"Come on, Percival. That's far enough."

No, it wasn't, apparently. He flung himself backward again and was quickly submerged up to his neck in water. He was now convinced of my point. He scrambled forward and leaped to the safety of the grass in one nimble move. His look was one of excitement, joy, and a bit of uncertainty. He was proud of himself, no doubt. He shook and began rolling about in the grass, creating his own version of an all-body botanical spa scent.

We rejoined the group and Percival posed for many photos while I sat and chatted more with Shannon about the work of Beagle Freedom Project. To my happiness, Rizzo was also there that day. He had not yet been adopted, but it looked like more than one of the spa employees had fallen in love with the sweet boy. I was sure it wouldn't be long until he was adopted too.

I was tired, but I felt good about the day. I hoped we helped spread the word about animal testing, Percival got the chance to be out and about exploring, and Daphne was going to be fine. Chris had texted that she slept comfortably at his wine shop all morning, no panting at all.

But when Chris arrived home that evening, it was obvious he was not feeling fine. He still wanted to head to the hot tub. I agreed, as much because I owed him that as for my tired and achy body.

While we headed to our back patio, Daphne rested in the crate and Percival slept in the dog bed not too far from her. A détente had been reached—at least between the dogs.

I sunk down into the hot, soothing bubbles and closed my eyes. "Just give me a few minutes."

"No hurry. Let me know when you can talk."

Turns out it's not all that relaxing to soak in a hot tub with someone waiting to tell you things you don't want to hear. I sat up.

"Okay. Go."

"Are you going to listen?"

"I'm going to try."

"Fair enough. I have two concerns. First, and not what you're expecting, I'm sure, but have you made the appointment for your checkup?"

"Huh?"

"Don't you go for your oncology checkup in April? April is almost over."

Somehow I had forgotten that since Chris had for years gone to my appointments with me, he knew the schedule as well as I did. I'd been caught. "I haven't made my appointment."

"Don't you think that's kind of important?"

Kind of. Maybe. But what's the rush to find out that my cancer is back too? "I haven't called to schedule it because I don't know when I'd go. What would we do with the dogs?"

Chris leaned forward and put his hands on my knees under water. There wasn't enough steam from the hot tub to block the strained concern on his face. "Which brings me to point two. I think you may have to consider that this is more than we can handle. Maybe we're only meant to have one dog. And maybe we should have stuck with the one easygoing, already housebroken, loves-to-drive-in-cars dog."

"It's only been two weeks."

"It's been a hell of a two weeks."

"He's adjusting. He's already doing better."

"That's only because she's medicated and in a crate. That's not going to last much longer."

"It's not his fault. I'm not going to give up on him. Not now."

"That's what I'm afraid of." Chris let go of my knees and leaned back in the water, running his hand through his thick, salt-and-pepper hair. "You're never going to give up. No matter what happens or how bad it gets, you're going to keep trying to save these dogs, and now cows. And pigs. And chickens. And more beagles. It won't stop. And look, it's already affecting your health."

My head snapped back. "No, it isn't." *Nightmares aren't a health issue, right?*

"Checkups are part of your health. You had cancer, remember? Not the flu."

I had no energy to argue, and no arsenal of facts or logic with which to launch a defensive strike. I knew I needed to make the appointment. I just didn't *want* to.

"Okay, fine. I'll make my appointment. But we're giving the dogs more time. They'll adjust. Can we just take this one day at a time? Just like with Seamus and all his problems? He took time also." Seamus had taken a lot of time. And energy. And dog-sitters. Frankly, I hadn't been sure my relationship with Chris was going to survive Seamus, and we'd ended up a tight-knit family.

"Okay. But you need to keep an open mind too. This may not be the best situation for Percival either."

When we went back in the house and changed out of our wet bathing suits, Chris sat on the couch. Percival immediately leaped into his lap and put his two front paws on Chris's shoulders, looking him right in the face and wagging his tail. Chris petted Percival while I sat on the floor next to Daphne's crate and scratched her behind the ears, reaching my fingers through the bars of the crate side.

My temples were throbbing, my brain was vibrating, and I felt the overwhelming urge to cry—but I had no specific thought in my head, nor the ability to focus on any one thought. There was nothing. I was on empty.

I remained seated, staring through the bars of Daphne's crate.

Chapter 21

YAPPY HOUR

I TOSSED FROM SIDE TO SIDE, BACK TO STOMACH, HOPING TO FIND A position that would relieve the vibrating, pulsating feeling in my head. The back of my skull ached, and when I would start to drift off to sleep, black and red images and violent nightmares of crated and crying animals woke me again.

Unlike the dreams I'd had while in treatment for cancer, my new grisly animal abuse dreams didn't bother with the subtlety of symbolism.

I drifted off to sleep somewhere around three in the morning. Chris and Percival woke me at seven when they came downstairs. I chose not to mention that I hadn't fallen asleep until three. Instead I vowed to pull myself together. For my sake and the sake of the dogs, I had to find a way to calm our lives down.

Daphne had her postsurgery checkup that afternoon. It was hard not to notice how Percival was falling for Chris, though I wondered if Chris realized that. So again, I took Daphne with me and sent Percival off with Chris.

As soon as I got to my office, I called to make the appointment with my oncologist—step one in pulling myself together. *Or at least convincing Chris I'd done so.* The cancer center had an opening the following week. I emailed Kelle and made plans for lunch right after the checkup. Another lesson learned well from Seamus was to always have something to look forward to after these appointments. In his case, it had been green dog bone treats. In my case, I'd find something green to eat at Native Foods Café with Kelle, and I looked forward to talking more with her.

Then I settled in to work, burying myself in my clients' matters, almost feverishly taking control of anything I could gain control over. Though I was tired, it felt good to resume a sense of normal. I had a law office to run, clients who needed me, and, well, bills to pay. Practicing law was something I needed to do.

Daphne slept soundly until the afternoon, when we went to visit Dr. Davis for her checkup. We were in a waiting room in no time at all and just as quickly, Dr. Davis joined us.

"I got the biopsy report back." He stood across the exam table from me, Daphne at our feet. "The lump on her side, the one I was worried about, is clear—just a lipoma." Then he inhaled deeply. "But the one on her chest, I just…I can't even believe it…it was a mast cell tumor."

There would be no step two in my pulling myself together. At least not today.

I sucked in air but still felt unable to breathe. A mast cell tumor was what Seamus had the first time. The time they told me that with surgery and chemotherapy he'd live maybe a year. They were wrong of course, but it was a year of fighting, thousands of dollars of vet bills, constant nerves, heartache, and anxiety. *Holy shit*. Would cancer ever be out of my life? Even as I thought, *Can I do this again?* I knew that I would. In my mind, I was already allocating the funds and figuring out what we'd give up to fit it into our budget.

"Okay. What do I need to do?"

"Well, the good news is that this time I got clean margins. The pathology shows no cancer cells at the edges of the tumor I removed, so that's good. I should have the full report back later this week to see if any further treatment is recommended."

"It's possible there won't be any more treatment?"

"Yes. It's entirely possible. I'll let you know as soon as I get the report."

At home that night, my vow to pull it together already a historical footnote, I raged to Chris. I cursed out cancer with everything I had (and with my Irish ancestry, that's saying a lot).

Chris took over the role of rational adult. "He said he got clear margins. We know how important that is. And you know from before, some dogs get mast cell tumors and surgery is all it takes."

"I'm not that lucky."

"You don't know that. And Daphne is lucky. She's lucky she's with us and it's being taken care of for her. Imagine what would have happened if you hadn't seen her photo that day?"

I paused. There was no *what if I hadn't seen her* scenario in my mind. I'd seen her. We'd rescued her. She was ours. I'd almost forgotten she was supposed to be a temporary foster dog.

"Whatever it is, you know I'm going to fight it, Whatever we need to do."

"Oh, I know. Believe me, I know."

"And I made *my* checkup appointment today. So I'm sure we can all guess how that's going to go."

Chris put his arms around me and drew me close. "I know this has to be scaring you, but it's all going to be okay. It is."

I let the tears flow until my head ached and I had to blow my nose. When I left the couch to get a tissue, Daphne followed me. Percival hopped up and took my place next to Chris.

For the rest of the week, things seemed to improve, at least between the dogs. They did not regularly snarl at each other and had not fought for more than forty-eight hours. We'd begun to joke that it was like those signs in factories, "Over X days with no accidents," only for us it was "incidents." If, however, Chris and I decided to be on the couch together and the dogs joined us, eventually the snarling started (the dogs, not Chris and me). I knew this much was normal for dogs—they'd need to establish their position in our pack. But Daphne seemed intent on Percival's not being in the pack at all, and Percival seemed terrorized and perhaps too aggressive for a simple territory "discussion."

So we instituted a "no dogs on the couch" rule and brought a second dog bed downstairs so they didn't have to share. Neither dog was happy with the solution, but the old lawyer adage that a good settlement is one where neither party is happy seemed to apply here.

Nights were more difficult. After more than a week of sleeping apart with one or the other of us on the couch, we were tired and I desperately wanted to be in our bed. We tried both sleeping in our bed with each dog in their own bed in the room with us, but were quickly woken with the now familiar sounds of a dogfight. We tried leaving Daphne alone in the library with a bed, a blanket, a pillow, and the door closed. She scratched maniacally at the door. We tried leaving Percival in the library instead, but within moments, his habit of shredding paper was once again demonstrated on those poor books on my lower shelves. We brought them both back into the bedroom, but put Daphne in her crate. She howled and growled and snarled through the gate. Apparently even the smell of Percival in the same room with her was enough to send her into a frenzy. I returned to the couch and took Daphne with me. It didn't matter. Again, I was tossing, turning, and futilely attempting to block horrific images from my mind and calm my restless brain. Sleep eluded me no matter where I was.

Finally, on Friday, Dr. Davis called. The pathology report showed clean margins, very low indicators of the myriad other things they test, and reports I couldn't understand. What I did understand was the last part of his statement: "No other treatment is required or recommended." *No other treatment is required.*

"Seriously? No chemo? No additional surgery?"

"No. We'll watch the area of course. And any other bumps or lumps that appear."

"I always watch for bumps and lumps."

"I know you do. So, no different. She's fine. And we'll hope she stays that way."

I called Chris immediately. "I can't even believe we finally got a break."

He laughed. "I'm so happy for Doodlebutt. And yes, we were due a break. So what about Beaglefest this weekend?"

Ah, yes, what *about* Beaglefest this weekend?

We'd attended Beaglefest—an annual gathering of beagle fanatics at a dog park in Huntington Beach—for the past two years, and even attended a Phoenix Beaglefest the week following my first chemo session. I had such plans for this next one, back when I foolishly thought I could simply rescue two dogs and go about my merry way. I'd made reservations at the Shorebreak Hotel—a dog-friendly hotel at the beach close by the park where Beaglefest would be held—so I could bring the dogs and participate in the "yappy hour" at the hotel bar patio the night before. I was relieved enough at the news about Daphne that I could almost…almost…laugh at my naïveté. I had not remembered to cancel my hotel reservations; I hadn't even *thought* about the event.

"Oh. Right. Well… I guess I could go and take just one of the dogs."

"So you and Daphne get to stay in the nice hotel and enjoy yappy hour while Percival and I sit home?"

Good point. And I had so looked forward to this nice mini-vacation. The Shorebreak looked fabulous, and they even had a doggie yappy hour menu. In my (continually delusional) mind, when I made the reservations, all four of us would enjoy appetizers (two of us would have some cocktails) with some fellow beagle lovers, then have dinner and spend a relaxing evening in a luxurious hotel room with a oceanfront view from the balcony, before a room service breakfast followed by heading out to a rambunctious Beaglefest day at the park the next morning. How I had thought this was going to work with not just one, but two, new rescue beagles is beyond me now. It's as if I'd never had dogs before.

"Well, hmm. How about if I go and take Percival for the yappy hour part since he's a bit more social with other dogs, then you and Daphne meet us there after you close up the shop? That way we'll have two cars and if the two maniacs go at each other or they get kicked out of the hotel for snarling, snapping, and growling, one of us can take them home."

"Sounds delightful."

"Doesn't it?"

"No. Not at all. But maybe they'll surprise us."

"And maybe you can bring Daphne's crate in your car. Just in case."

I arrived at the Shorebreak Hotel later than I had planned, but there was no hurrying Percival. He still needed to disembark from the car slowly and take a few moments to shake off the transportation trauma before he returned to his normal, happy self. I walked him over to a small planter with a palm tree in the middle and let him sniff about. The salt air and nearby restaurant smells inundated that famous beagle nose and pulled him out of his car reverie. He sniffed the tree, peed, and turned to face me, wagging his tail. He was ready to go.

"Okay, buddy, let's get checked in and get you to yappy hour!"

The Shorebreak was gorgeous—contemporary and beachy and abundantly dog-friendly. I was not the only one at check-in with a dog, and I immediately noticed that two of the four other dogs in line were also beagles, no doubt also here for the Beaglefest yappy hour, which, it now occurred to me, was sure to be a loud one. Or, forgive me, a howling good time. The hotel clerk offered me a dog bed to take to the room. *Sure, why not!* I had no idea how or where Daphne and Percival would sleep, but an extra bed could not be a bad idea.

I wheeled my suitcase to the elevator, carrying my purse, the dog bed, and Percival's leash. Luckily, he followed along merrily. This would have been a terrible time for one of his four-paw braking moves. When the elevator door opened, I turned to him. Maybe I should pick him up? An elevator had to be a scary thing for any dog, but a dog that had been a science experiment and kept in a small enclosed space for eighteen months? While my concern (okay, let's be real, my panic) built, Percival trotted forward into the elevator, still sniffing about. I followed him in and pushed the button for our floor. He sat and watched as the doors closed.

"Good boy! You brave, good boy! Who's getting appetizers tonight, huh?"

Percival wagged his tail. The doors opened and we exited as though we'd been regular hotel guests. So far, so good. I found our room easily, on the beach side and not far from the elevator, which would be good if we needed to get the dogs outside in a hurry. I slid the card into the key slot and pressed down on the handle. And *that's* when Percival decided a four-pawed reverse was appropriate. The elevator, sure, but apparently he was not going in any ocean-view suite with a heavy door and who knows what behind it. If the door didn't open automatically, no way was he going through it. He pulled backward and I dropped the dog bed, then my purse, and when I saw he was trying to slip out of the harness, I lunged and knocked over my suitcase. The ruckus caused Percival to yelp and jump sideways, his harness now nearly over his head. I squatted down and tried to give some leeway to the leash, to reduce the resistance so he couldn't slip out.

"It's okay, buddy. It's safe. Come here, buddy."

He stopped pulling but did not move forward. I took that opportunity to stand and sweep him up into my arms. I opened the door again and, holding Percival and propping the door open with my rear end, used one arm to pull my luggage and the dog bed into the room.

The room was worth it.

We had a living room area with an eight-foot-long couch and plenty of room. The walls were adorned with gorgeous photographs of the sea, surfers and their boards, and, of course, a sunset. The king-size bed was in a separate room, with a small but inviting balcony with a view of the actual sea, and best of all, the bathroom was spacious, white, and well-equipped with an irresistibly huge, beckoning bathtub. I had not seen a bathtub that large since the one in the townhome I'd rented when I'd first gotten Seamus. The one Chris and I, in our early courtship days, frequently spent romantic candlelight evenings in, champagne in hand (howling Seamus in another room…if he wasn't busy stealing food from the kitchen while we were otherwise occupied). Oh how I missed that tub! Our hot tub was wonderful, but there was something different about an actual bathtub.

"Percival, if you and Daphne could just get along long enough for Chris and me to take a much-needed, long, romantic bath tonight, I'll buy you toys, give you treats, whatever you want all day tomorrow. Think we could work that out, buddy?"

Percival jumped up on the bed and pawed at me. I rubbed his head and he fell over onto the fluffy white comforter, exposing his belly for more rubbing.

"I'm going to just take that as a yes, okay?"

He pawed at my hand for more. Or to, you know, shake on it. I'm sure.

We joined the Beaglefesters on the bar patio. I was so late there were only about ten folks still there, but I'll take a small crowd over a large, noisy one any day. And for Percival, small crowds were probably better as well.

I greeted the group, but as is the case with beagle lovers, it was really all about the dogs. Most of the group had known Seamus and read our story—either in book form or on my blog. And most of them knew of our adoption of Percival. There was great crossover between the Beaglefest group and Beagle Freedom Project supporters. So everyone was excited to meet and start kissin' on Percival. Percival, I was pleased to note, was just as excited to greet the humans. He immediately hopped up on the patio couch and introduced himself.

I love a good happy hour, but I was far more excited to see the doggie menu. It featured chicken stew, bacon strips dipped in yogurt, a grilled burger patty and gravy, and even Skippy-treats with a nondairy ice cream and scoop of peanut butter for doggie dessert—but no canine crudités plate. So adorable! But then I had a moment of anxiety as I was faced with the vegan dog-companion's dilemma. While I searched the human happy hour menu, I also searched my conscience for what to order for Percival. Even though I did not feed them vegan meals, I tried to keep their treats vegan. As I looked around, I could see that my fellow beagle-peeps were feeding their beagles the chicken, the burger, bacon. I could just imagine trying to get Percival to settle for broccoli.

I ordered the pita and hummus for me, and the bacon and yogurt for Percival. I shouldn't have, and I felt horrible immediately after doing it—all I could see was the adorable face of a pig who gave her life. *Her life so that my dog could enjoy a snack at yappy hour in a beachside hotel?* Oh good lord, what had I done? Who was I? I turned in my chair and searched for the already-departed server. *No! My dog would eat broccoli! And carrots!! And sprouts! Bring him sprouts! Wait! Peanut butter and nondairy ice cream is an option!! Why hadn't I ordered that?* Percival must have sensed what was about to happen—how his dining delicacies were about to change—instantly he engaged the braking system and flung himself backward with all of his might. And this time he slipped out of the harness in one easy maneuver. His practicing had paid off. Before I even had time to shout his name or "No!" or any command that he might possibly acknowledge, he turned and bolted, as alarmed by his instantaneous freedom as I was. He ran to the indoor restaurant area and made a beeline for the kitchen, whether out of fear, luck, or that beagle sniffing skill that would always identify the scent of food, I didn't know. And it didn't matter.

I leapt from my chair and chased after him. My long, flowing orange patio dress and gold sandals, while no doubt making quite the flamboyant scene, were not allowing me to gain much ground on the exuberant beagle. The diners, casually but smartly dressed couples out for date night and safely away from the dog cacophony on the patio, all turned and stared, first at the blur of a dog, then at the lunatic woman in bright orange chasing the blur. And if there was ever a time one needed a quick, cute, nonembarrassing name to shout for their dog, this was it. Instead, I was running through the dining area of an elegant oceanside restaurant, on a busy Friday night, shouting, "Percival! Perc-AH-VAL!!!" I may as well have been yelling, "Percival Ramonce, young man, you get back here. You get back here right now. I'm going to count to three!" from my front porch, in a robe, with curlers in my hair and swirling a highball.

Luckily, the maitre d' (yes, of course there was a maitre d', and of course he saw this all happen) headed Percival off at the pass to the kitchen, and though the dog, true to his college-football-based middle name, made a sharp, nimble ninety-degree turn, he was at a loss as to what end zone he could run to. Instead, blessedly, he stopped.

"Percival, stay!" I said, apologizing as I stepped around one table and the bemused diners to get to Percival.

Apparently my command translated to "Please introduce yourself to the diners" in beagle-speak because Percival walked to the closest table and put his two front paws up on the woman's lap to steady himself while he sniffed at her entrée. I can only hope the red in my face was complementary to the orange of my dress.

I grabbed Percival and picked him up. "I'm so sorry."

"Oh, no worries, he's adorable," the very kind, very patient, very wonderful woman said.

I was completely prepared to launch into his lab experiment background to garner sympathy for him (and me) if need be, but this woman was the epitome of laid-back beach cool. *Percival, you are one lucky dog.*

"Thank you. And again, I'm so sorry."

I carried Percival back out to the patio and had one of our group hold him while I tightened his harness. Just as I got the harness set and Percival strapped back into it, the server arrived with my drink (yay!) and Percival's yogurt-dipped bacon (groan).

Forgive me, beautiful pig. And forgive me, every dog trainer in the universe. I gave a strip of bacon to Percival.

Oblivious to my moral dilemma, or perhaps sensing it, he dropped the bacon on the ground and instead turned to play with his new buddy, an adorable female beagle named Daisy. Daisy's sister Jaxie gobbled up the bacon strip.

Chris and Daphne arrived well after yappy hour, but while some of us were still contentedly hanging out on the patio and letting the dogs play. Daphne, naturally, began to bark at the other dogs and sniffed at Percival frantically. She could tell some fun, and perhaps some food, had been enjoyed without her, and clearly this was intolerable. *Against. The. Rules.* She barked.

I took Daphne for a little walk and left Chris to enjoy his cocktail in peace, albeit with Percival standing on his lap. Percival was clearly beside himself with joy at Chris's arrival and had immediately laid claim to him. There was no risk Percival would be running off anywhere now that Chris had arrived. Percival wanted nothing more than to bask in the glory of Chris. And lick his face.

We went to our room around ten that night. We'd had enough cock-tails to not be stressed about navigating a hotel lobby, elevator, and new environs with two rescue beagles we'd had for only weeks. And the dogs seemed content to merely follow us along. All cheer yappy hour!

Chris and Daphne were as thrilled with our room as Percival and I had been. Daphne sniffed about and then very quickly made herself at home on the couch. Much to our surprise, Percival jumped up and joined her. Sure, he was four feet away and it likely only happened because the couch was as long as it was, but still—*they were on the same couch!* I took advantage of the moment.

"Wait till you see this!" I grabbed Chris's hand and led him to the bathroom. "*Look* at that tub!"

"Wow. Wow. I haven't seen a tub like that since your old place!"

"Exactly! So...dare we try?"

We both poked our heads back into the living room. The beagles were asleep. Daphne's snore was loud and deep.

"Oh yeah. We're goin' in," Chris said.

The dogs did not wake as we filled the tub. They did not wake when we opened the bottle of wine that Chris brought with him. They did not wake as we turned out the lights in the room, dimmed the bathroom light, undressed, and slipped into the tub.

As far as we knew, they didn't wake the rest of the night either. Not that we were paying a lot of attention to them...

But once the sun streamed through the windows of our gorgeous room, the beagles were up and ready for breakfast. They used their new-found tolerance of each other to gang up on us. Percival leapt onto Chris's head and began to paw at his face, while Daphne took the more subtle approach of lying down next to me, her head sharing my pillow and her tongue licking my face—urging me to wake. I was so happy they were happy and not fighting that I overlooked my headache and lack of sleep. I got up and got their breakfast out of the bag we'd packed and stored away high up on a shelf in the closet. I fed Daphne in the bathroom and Percival in the living room, shutting the bathroom door between them. No point in testing our luck.

Close to one hundred beagles and nearly twice as many humans converged on the dog park in Huntington Beach in the morning. You could hear the howling from blocks away. *Aaarrrooooooooo!!! Aaarrrooooooooooooooo!!! Aaarrrooooooooooooooooo!!* Daphne joined the fracas from the backseat of my car while Percival concentrated on not vomiting. We found parking several blocks from the park and got the dogs out, together with our blanket and the dogs' water bottle and snacks, and set out toward the festivities.

Beagles with their telltale white-tipped tails swarmed the lawn, with many of them congregating, not at all surprisingly, near the picnic tables and barbecue area. Daphne howled and pulled at her leash, straining to join the melee. Percival was a bit more interested in sniffing the grass and taking his time before meeting the masses. I walked ahead with Daphne while Chris let Percival do his stop-and-smell-the-flowers—or, well, the grass blades—thing.

We found some of our online friends easily (I'd met them at last year's Beaglefest). With others it took hearing the beagle's name to be able to place the human. It was just like going for walks with the dogs in our neighborhood. We may not know our neighbors' names, but we know their dogs' names. One of the best parts of Beaglefest is that no one can be in a bad mood with that many howling clown dogs around. Not even those of us who may have enjoyed yappy hour a bit too much. (I'm not naming names.)

We took Daphne and Percival to the fenced off-leash area, figuring that running a little energy out of them would not be a bad thing. Percival was thrilled to be let loose and, much to our surprise, immediately began to chase and play with the other dogs—beagles, poodles, corgis, shelties, mixed breeds of all sorts, it did not matter. Percival was happy to be free and running wild. And run he did. Daphne, on the other hand, put her nose to the ground and very methodically began to sweep the premises, carefully identifying each and every scent. "*Yep, beagle pee. Yep, that's a poodle. Ooh, dachshund, and that's a pug over here. Yep, yep, lots going on in this yard.*" Chris and I took a seat on a park bench with some friends. Daphne joined us after about twenty minutes of nonstop sniffing. Even a beagle nose needs a break now and then. She hopped up next to me on the bench and surveyed the park from her new vantage point.

We watched for Percival, who seemed blissfully happy to run about. I spotted him in one corner facing two dogs that were crouching in play position. Or at least, I hoped it was play position. Two more dogs ran over, and then a fifth. Percival seemed lost in the dog pile, and I was just about to hurry in Percival's direction, offering aid, when Daphne leapt up, let out a bellowing howl, and ran toward Percival. I watched in amazement as she flung herself between Percival (now backed all the way up against the fence) and the four other dogs and howled. There was no mistaking her message: *Leave him alone! Or you will have me to deal with! Back off, dudes!*

Chris turned to me. "Did you see what just happened?"

"I did! I'm so proud of her!"

"She came to his defense! She's looking out for him!"

"I guess it really is like family. Family can pick on each other but nobody else gets to."

Daphne and Percival together came sprinting back toward us, tongues hanging sideways, eyes wide, and tails wagging. *This is the best time!*

"I think they're going to be fine," I said, petting Daphne while she licked my face.

Chris responded as best he could given the tongue washing Percival was now giving his face. "You may *mmfphtfmmm* be right. We'll *pffmh-phhmmm* see."

Chris was seeing a glimmer of hope, while I was already booking our family Christmas photo, which somehow involved trained beagles, cuddling, smiling, and posing. I don't even like Christmas, but why should that interfere with my hallucinations? If I was going to be having brain issues, at least some of it should be enjoyable.

Chapter 22

A PIECE OF MY MIND

I WAITED ON THE EXAM TABLE IN MY CUSTOMARY AND OH-SO-fashionable paper towel dress. I practiced how I'd mention my restless brain syndrome and considered not saying anything at all. I hadn't had the problem lately, so perhaps it was just stress. Normally, I never like blaming things on stress—it seems like such a cop-out. But hey, I was looking for a cop-out on this one. When the alternative is cancer metastasized to the brain, stress is my friend. Well, maybe my frenemy.

Denise, the physician's assistant, came into the exam room. The further out I got from my diagnosis, the less I saw the oncologist himself. I liked the oncologist just fine, but I was happy to see the PA—I liked her and I liked thinking they weren't as concerned about my health status now. I was no longer a DEFCON 1 patient. Maybe more like a 4.

She did her usual exam and began the list of usual questions. How was I feeling? *Great, I'm good. Things are fine.* Any pains? *Nope. No pain.* Any digestive or bowel issues? *Nope. All good there too.*

"Great. So any complaints in general? Any changes?"

Weeeeeell... "Um. Well. I've been having headaches. Well, not really headaches, more like head vibrations. I call it restless brain syndrome." Her left eyebrow shot up, but I pushed on, hoping that was only because of the name I'd given my symptoms. "It doesn't really hurt; it just feels like my brain is pulsating. I can't concentrate and I can't sleep."

"That's not good."

DEFCON 3.

"No, I know. It doesn't happen all the time, though." Because it's okay if your brain only shakes once in a while, right?

"How often?"

"Uh. Um. Well, maybe a couple of times a week? Usually at night but sometimes at work."

"That's not good." She closed my file. "Let me get the doctor."

DEFCON 2.

"I was afraid you'd say that."

Dr. Glaspy joined us a few minutes later and I repeated my story.

"I don't think this is anything serious. I'm not concerned this is a recurrence of your cancer," he said.

It's not MY cancer! I gave it back! I do not accept it!

The doctor continued, "But it's something we should check out. Just for peace of mind."

He was not the kind of doctor to make a pun, but I heard it that way anyway—*yes, definitely, I want my mind at peace.* The war zone in my head was not really working for me.

"Check it how?"

"I'm going to send you for a brain MRI."

DEFCON 1 had been reached.

"A *brain* MRI?"

Over lunch I explained it to Kelle. At least she got the "peace of mind" pun, though she wasn't really laughing.

"That's pretty terrifying," she said.

"Well, yes and no. I mean, it's not like it hurts or anything."

"Still. It's your brain. That's kind of serious."

"I do use it for a few things."

She laughed. We both paused while the waiter set down our vegan "bac-un" cheeseburgers and sweet potato fries.

"Do you think it could be stress-related?"

"Stress? What stress?" I mimicked a facial twitch.

"Right. Well, it sounds like maybe things haven't been going so well with the dogs. I'm sure that's stressing you out."

She didn't start with my job, or family things, or even my "cancer patient" status. Nope. It was the dogs. She understood what they meant to me. And since she'd had her Bogart for more than a year by then, she understood what it meant to have a Beagle Freedom Project dog too. So at last, I had someone to talk to about Percival.

"Well, it's gotten a lot better. A lot. I think they just need time to adjust. Percival has these horrible night terrors, and it's heartbreaking and frightening. And of course it scares Daphne. But he's getting better with time. How did Bogart adjust when you got him? Did he and Jack get along right away?"

"I'm not a good one to ask. We just got really, really lucky with Bogart. He was easy from the moment he was rescued, so we've never had any issues at all. I know that's not even fair, and Shannon teases me about taking the easiest dog, but it just turned out that way."

"Wanna trade?"

"Oh, you wouldn't trade Percival!"

I took a hearty bite from my burger and contemplated. "No, I would not. He's really adorable, and I love his spirit. But Chris might want to trade."

"No! I can't believe that. From all the pictures you post on Facebook it looks like they're totally in love."

"It might be unrequited love for Percival at this point. He is obsessed with Chris. He'll sit with me and cuddle for a while, but the moment Chris is around, Percival bolts from my lap and launches at Chris. He climbs all over him. It's like he wants to be absorbed by Chris."

"Awww."

"I know. But Chris assures me it's cuter to watch than it is to experience. He may have been scratched more than once. Especially as Percival continues to paw at Chris's face."

We ate in silence for a few moments until Kelle spoke up again. "I'm not forgetting about this brain MRI thing. When is your appointment?"

"I don't have an appointment yet. They've got to get insurance approval first, then we'll schedule."

"If you want, I'll go with you."

I hadn't known Kelle that long, so this was a generous offer. We'd met only months before at the Words, Wine, and Wags benefit Chris, Seamus, and I did for Beagle Freedom Project. It was easy to see we had not only a shared passion for beagles, but also a remarkably similar sense of humor. "No, just meet me for a drink after."

"You're on. I'm always up for that."

"I don't think it's really going to be anything. Things have been better with the dogs and hence better with my brain, so that tells me something. Now, if I could just stop the nightmares and get some sleep, I'll be just fine."

She put her burger down. "Nightmares?"

I put my burger down too. "I told you I'd been watching all these documentaries and reading about factory farming, animal testing, and all the reasons to stay vegan? Like, you know, saving the world and all?"

"I recall."

"Turns out, that's kind of stressful."

"You think? Maybe, I don't know…stop?"

"I know, but I feel like I need to know this. I'd been in denial all this time about what I was eating, about what was happening to literally billions of animals, about what it was doing to my body. And did I tell you I finally watched *Maximum Tolerated Dose*?"

"No, you did not. I can't watch that."

"I can't get the images out of my head."

"And hence the headaches maybe?"

"Well, the nightmares anyway. It was all I could do to refrain from describing to everyone I dine with where their meal came from—what happened to the cow, the pig, the poor chicken they're chowing down on. But now I want to talk about animal testing constantly. I need to tell everyone—even random strangers."

"Oh no, don't become that person. Is Chris vegan with you?"

I'd gotten used to answering this question. Used to it, but not comfortable with it. "He's one-third vegan. He has vegan smoothies for breakfast with me. And he's eating a lot better. A lot. But no, definitely not vegan."

"So you can't really get in the habit of discussing the animals suffering at every meal."

"No. I can't. I want to. But I can't."

"I know people who do that. It's not effective. All it does is alienate everyone from ever dining out with you. And, you know, I've seen a lot of people really burn out from just throwing their all into animal rescue or advocacy—whether it's the people rescuing the beagles, or going into shelters, or protesting circuses. You just have to be really careful to not stress yourself out. I mean, I know it's all horrible. I know this. But you have to watch your own health too."

"I am. I'm vegan!"

"You know what I mean."

I did know what she meant. I *did* want to stop reading about mass-produced and mass-slaughtered animals. I didn't want to read or see images of man's depravity toward animals anymore. But I felt like I had to bear witness. I needed to really, deeply understand the things I'd so blindly ignored in the past. People were regularly asking me if I was "still" vegan. Like it was a fashion trend I'd tried on. And it was, originally. But I knew now I'd stay vegan. And I knew that because I'd painstakingly and painfully educated myself. I'd have nightmares, sure, but I'd stay vegan.

"I do know. But, you know, I've got this cute little beagle at home looking me right in the face and reminding me daily of the horrors humans inflict on animals. I can't look away. None of us should look away."

"Just be kind to yourself," she said.

Back at home, I told Chris about the MRI and my conversation with Kelle. And then the next morning I did something really dumb. I posted my status update to Facebook and mentioned the impending MRI.

This was dumb for two reasons: the first is of course that random strangers (also known as Facebook "friends" I don't know in real life) post medical advice including such useful tidbits as *MRIs cause cancer!*—and the other is that while my father isn't on Facebook, his wife is. She let him know about my referral for an MRI about two-fifths of a second after I posted it. Three-fifths of a second after that my cell phone rang.

"You can't even call your poor ol' dad and tell him you're going in for a checkup? And I need to find out on this Face-thing that you need an MRI?"

My dad was neither poor nor old, but he was sarcastic. "Sorry. Right. Yes, I went for my checkup and everything looks fine, but they want to do the MRI for peace of mind."

"Well, why? There must have been a reason."

Oh. That. *Right.* I explained my restless brain syndrome.

"When did this start?"

"Maybe six months ago?"

"When did you turn vegan?"

I had thought it was odd that my oncologist didn't ask about any change in diet—not even when my weigh-in showed me at least twenty pounds lighter. (I may have gained back a bit of the initial weight I lost. Wine will do that.) But now I didn't want my veganism blamed for anything.

"No, that's been well over a year ago now." *Or, you know, thirteen months ago. That's more than a year.*

"When did you learn Seamus was terminal?"

Tears sprung to my eyes. I knew where my dad was going…that ol' favorite "stress" bully. "February. Three months ago."

"You need magnesium. I'll bet that's what it is."

"Magnesium?"

"Magnesium is a mineral, stress depletes it from your body, and you may not have been getting enough in the first place. When your magnesium gets low, you can suffer from depression and muscle spasms. And insomnia."

A spasm was a good way to describe what my brain had been doing, but "brain spasm" did not sound better than restless brain syndrome. On the other hand, "take magnesium supplement" sounded much, much better than "brain MRI" or "cancer recurrence."

My dad is a chiropractor and has been one for over forty years. He believes in vitamins and supplements, eating right, and holistic health methods. He also paid careful attention when I went through cancer treatments, gave me excellent advice on handling the side effects of chemo, and believed in my surgeon and my oncologist, but closely followed what they were doing. I get my logic from him. My penchant for fainting over the sight of blood or the mention of the word "stit…" I do not get from him. I don't know where that comes from; I just know it isn't going anywhere.

"That's interesting. I did not know that. I've been taking vitamin B_{12} and vitamin D, but I hadn't read that I also needed magnesium."

"Well, have you been under stress lately?"

This was likely a rhetorical question. My dad had held the position of "dad" in my life for, well, my whole life (and the nine-month period immediately preceding it). He excelled at the position. Telling him I was not stressed would have worked about as well as saying it to Chris, who was witnessing my stress on a daily basis. Normally I find discussions of stress to be ludicrous. What adult over the age of, say, twenty-five does not have stress in their lives? Life *is* stressful.

"Maybe a bit of stress, yes."

"Are you still doing yoga?"

I assumed sulking child pose: "No."

"Walking?"

I assumed defensive adult pose: "Sometimes. Maybe. Well, Chris is walking the dogs. He's got them on this dual leash thing I bought at the Pet Expo…" *Deflect! Deflect!* "It's working really well to force them to cooperate with each other. It's helping them bond and they're fighting less."

"You've got to do something to get your stress under control." It's like he didn't even see the bait I threw out! *Puppies! Walking in tandem! With someone else…*

If people I respected—Chris, my dad, Kelle, basically anybody I respected enough to actually talk about the problem with—were all coming to the same conclusion, my logic was going to lead me there as well (gently, ever so gently). Maybe, just maybe, I'd not been handling my stress well. And maybe, just possibly, I'd brought some of it on myself. Being sent for a brain MRI brings a certain clarity to one's life.

Perhaps I'd been approaching my veganism incorrectly. I remembered something I'd said in India: "Stop saying India is hard when you are *making* it hard!" I had to laugh. I'd been so unforgiving and self-righteous then. And yet maybe I had made my own life as a vegan hard. Maybe there was a better way of doing it. A way that perhaps didn't involve nightmares of butchered little piglets.

Maybe I was trying to control too much. To do too much. *I couldn't save Seamus, so by Buddha, I'd save all the world's animals!* Was that what I'd been raging against—what happened to Daphne, to Percival, and the cancer that had taken Seamus before that? And what had I changed?

What good had all my rage brought? It brought me an appointment with an MRI machine.

There had to be a better approach. Something more peaceful.

I recalled another moment in India—my favorite moment in India. That one true moment of utter peace with my golden dog at the Taj Mahal. I, for once, was still—not controlling what would happen, not trying to "help" or change things, not worrying about what had happened to the dog before or what would happen after. I was merely present. I was "in the moment" (with my apologies to whoever on the trip had that "name"). *Huh.* That was never anything I was good at, but if I could have a moment of peace like that again, it would certainly be worth it to try. And it seemed like the place to start was with my own dogs. I could try all I wanted, and all I had the energy for, with every fiber of my being, to change what had happened to both of them and nothing would change the past. Nothing. Better to stay in the present.

They were healthy now, Daphne and Percival. They were on their way to happy. I'd been trying to force this bizarre Beaglerette love story when really, that doesn't even work on the actual show. Chances are the dogs picked up on my anxiety and rage. No wonder Percival so clearly preferred Chris! These were dogs, with different personalities, different backgrounds, and different needs. Maybe if I relaxed, they'd relax. Maybe it was time to let them be. Let them drink from the fountain, so to speak.

I shared my thoughts with Chris.

"So I realize I've been kind of nuts. And I'm thinking that's affecting not just me, but you, the dogs, everybody."

Chris smiled knowingly. "Really?"

"And yes, maybe I was trying to do too much. But I love these dogs. I love you. I want to make it all work, but I'm not going to force it."

"It's getting a lot better—the dogs anyway. Your brain thing, not so much."

"I will admit these might be connected. What I'm thinking is this— let's just leave the dogs be. Let's leave them home together instead of splitting them up and taking them to work with us. Percival hates the car and they both love the sunshine, so why not leave them at home?"

"What if they fight?"

"I don't think they will. We won't be home for them to fight over. Or, more to the point, *you* won't be home to fight over. I don't think Percival is prepared to fight for me. And I can come home at lunch and check on them. You leave at ten thirty. I'll come home at one thirty for lunch. If everything is fine—you know, both dogs alive, no bloodstains or gaping wounds—I'll go back to work."

"Percival will definitely be happier at home."

"We can still take them to work with us later, but let's let them work things out for now."

"Walking them together on the tandem leash you got is really helping, though Percival still wants to stop and smell every grass blade. Daphne just pulls him along."

I laughed. Daphne had slimmed down quite a bit, but she definitely had a weight advantage over little Percival. "Well, that's probably part of the dominance battle. Daphne appears to be winning."

"I think letting the dogs work things out is a good idea. They did great together at Beaglefest. And it will help both of our schedules if we're not chauffeuring the dogs around."

"And I'm going to lay off reading my torture-and-slaughter-of-animals books."

"This makes so much sense."

"I'm going to try a calmer approach."

"Okaaaaaaaay…"

"I'm going to see how others handle being vegan—being an advocate for the animals in a world that doesn't really seem to care much about the animals."

Chris was in the kitchen preparing his dinner—his chicken dinner. He looked down at his plate and back up at me. "How is this different from what you've been doing?"

"There are people who've advocated for animals their whole lives, or at least their adult lives. I have to assume they've been able to find some perspective, some way of living with the knowledge of all the horror without going insane. Or, you know, having brain spasms. So I think I need to go find my people. See how it's done."

"Fascinating."

"To start, I'm going to a vegan cooking competition this weekend. It's at the Animal Advocacy Museum in Pasadena."

"I had no idea there was such a thing."

"A vegan cook-off or an animal advocacy museum?"

"Both, actually."

"Me either. I'm kind of excited about it."

And I was.

Chapter 23

RAW VEGAN

I TALKED MY FRIEND LEELA INTO MEETING ME AT THE EVENT. LEELA was another person I'd met through Beaglefest, and in fact she had organized and been primarily responsible for the one we'd just attended. She too helped rescue dogs, primarily beagles, and was a fanatic about the proper care and feeding of her beagle, Chloe. She was also a former vegan, which intrigued me. I knew a few folks who'd tried out veganism for a short period of time, but none was as much of an animal lover as I knew Leela to be.

The cook-off was scheduled to happen from two to four in the afternoon. I pulled into the parking lot at two thirty. Or at least, I thought I did. There was a banner that read "Animal Advocacy Museum" hanging from the second floor of a two-story building, so this had to be the place, but the first floor and the grounds were a Montessori preschool. Hmmm... I looked around for an entrance to the museum and a parking spot, though it wasn't likely those things would be near each other. There were several cars double-parked, and it was hard to tell if the lot I was in belonged to the school, the museum, or the church on the adjoining lot. I noticed an empty parking spot right in front of the school and quickly took it.

I walked around the building looking for an elevator, stairs, a sign...anything that indicated there was a museum entrance to be found. There was nothing. Chatter was audible, coming from the second floor, so something was going on, but I could not find access to the upstairs, at least not without walking through the playground, and that couldn't be right. I returned to the front of the building, then around to the side, but found no stairs. Finally I dared to venture through the playground and at last found the staircase. Two young men in skinny jeans and flannel shirts, with floppy hair and extensive tattoos, were seated at the top of the stairs. Can someone look vegan? Well, I thought they did, so I headed up the stairs. They moved aside to let me pass, and I noted they were eating macaroni and non-cheese. This must be the place.

A woman behind what I assumed was the check-in podium looked at me but didn't speak.

"Is this the vegan cook-off? For the Animal Advocacy Museum?" I said.

She finally smiled. "Your name?"

So this really was the "museum." A sort of traveling exhibit, I imagine. *Have banner, will travel.* As an author who'd been at many a dog and cancer event with my signs and stacks of books over the prior eight months, I could certainly relate.

I was given five tickets and careful instructions that I could have either a sample size of five different mac 'n' cheese dishes or three slightly larger portions. I was also given a drink ticket.

The museum was in fact one room—one classroom. There were about twenty-five people in attendance, all dressed in some version of L.A. vegan hipster: black and gray tones, faux leather, message T-shirts, hoodies, tattoos, and piercings. I was overdressed and under-pierced. I was also about eight tattoos short of fitting in, and that was if I counted my radiation tattoos. Leela was not among the guests.

I turned my attention to the food table. There were fifteen trays of vegan mac 'n' cheese and not one of them was warm. Fifteen trays of room temperature food for twenty-five people and they were worried about the sample sizes? Nonetheless, I'm a rule follower. And a guest.

I selected five of the trays to sample from. There was no methodology involved—it all looked like mac 'n' cheese and I had no "vegan mac 'n' cheese" baseline from which to work. The only one I knew I wanted to try was the one that included "bacon"—fake bacon, of course. With my sample plate in one hand and a plastic cup of lavender lemonade in the other I searched the room for a seat. Or someone to talk to. Or a clue as to why I thought this would be a good idea. Finding none of the above, I roamed outside. I now understood why the flannel boys had been dining on the staircase.

Sitting on the stairs was neither comfortable nor comforting. I felt ridiculous. I'd dressed for a *museum*—a museum in Pasadena, home of the Norton Simon Museum, the Huntington Gardens and Library, fine dining, and urbane shopping. Pasadena also has quite the hipster scene (from my middle-aged vantage point anyway), and I'd forgotten that part. At least I wore pants, even if I had a flowing top and high heels on. And where the heck was Leela?

I tasted the macaroni. Not bad. Not terribly cheesy, but then, what did I expect for a dish that had no cheese? The samples likely would have been better—much better—warmed up. The lavender lemonade was, however, delicious.

"Hey there!" Leela came bouncing up the stairs. She could bounce up the stairs because she had, wisely, worn leggings, a long cotton top, and tennis shoes. As though she knew where we were going.

"Hey. How'd you know to dress like that? And arrive an hour after it started?"

She laughed. "I told you. I was vegan once. I went to a lot of events like this. It's always casual, on the cheap, and longer than it needs to be."

"Huh. Well, the macaroni and cheese isn't bad, though it's room temperature."

"Gross."

"Well, get your tickets and your samples. You are limited to five."

Now it was Leela's turn to roll her eyes. "Please."

I followed her back in and watched, impressed, as she broke the rules by taking spoonfuls of more than five of the dishes.

"There's room on the floor over there, and that's about it. I'll go stake out a spot for us. Drinks are over in that corner." I pointed to the table across the room. Leela nodded and headed for the drinks.

While seated on the floor waiting for Leela, I had plenty of time to consider the artwork in the museum. Most of it was brightly colored, somewhat childish, and, from all I could tell, had absolutely nothing to do with animals or advocacy. Mostly the works had to do with humans, body parts, and sexuality. There was an entwined nude couple that I tried not to think of as a Klimt rip-off, a male torso in shades of pink (mostly hot), a Van Gogh-esque landscape or two, and several nudes—in groups, alone, or coupled up. All were in bright, unnatural colors. There wasn't a nonhuman animal among them.

Leela returned with her drink and her plate. "So what's happening?"

"Best I can tell, the cooks are heating their dishes one at a time and then bringing the samples to the judges. Those are the judges at the front table."

"And this has been going on for how long?"

"Since I got here. So probably since it started."

"And what's up with the artwork? What is this?"

"I don't… Oh god…"

"What?"

"I can no longer hear anything you say. I'm too distracted by what's hanging above your head."

Leela twisted around to look at the wall above her head, not perhaps the best angle to view the twenty-four-inch-tall blue vagina painting hung there. "Oh my god. Is that what I think it is?"

"It is. It's like Georgia O'Keeffe meets the Picasso blue period. With drugs."

Leela giggled. "What does this have to do with animal advocacy?"

"Um…maybe it's a 'we're all animals' sort of message?"

"Doubtful."

"A stretch, I know." I leaned over to the couple seated on the floor next to us. "Do you know anything about the exhibit? What the connection is to animal advocacy?"

The young woman looked at the walls. "I don't know actually. But I heard the artist is vegan." She smiled.

Okay then. Good to know I had met all the requirements for getting my own art show.

Leela shook her head while I concentrated on not laughing. Maybe this was not going to be as instructive to me as I'd hoped.

A young woman, dressed in all black and looking like a Betty Page pinup wearing bright red lipstick, walked to the front of the room to address the group.

She announced the winners of the mac 'n' cheese contest first—the bacon version won (see, vegans *are* just like regular people!). Then one by one each person stood and reported on upcoming advocacy events. I listened, dumbstruck.

I was already overwhelmed with how my plant-based diet led me to an exploration of a vegan lifestyle, which had opened my eyes to the horrors endured by "farm" animals, and how my love of beagles led me to Beagle Freedom Project, which led me to adopt Percival, which shocked me into an awareness of the cruelties of animal testing. But now as I listened to each impassioned plea, I realized there was so much more. So much more was *wrong*.

The group's main focus was to stop UCLA from testing on animals. UCLA. *My UCLA*? My beloved medical center where I'd met my good and great surgeon, Dr. Karam, where I'd been successfully treated for an aggressive form of breast cancer? Where I went religiously for the annual Festival of Books? *That* UCLA? *They* experiment on animals?

They did. And this group regularly protested outside the campus, in the streets of Westwood.

Someone else stood and talked about the protest at the zoo. Another reported on the upcoming circus protest and the abuses of elephants that had been photographed. Yet another talked about SeaWorld and the upcoming premiere of the film *Blackfish* that would, she said, expose SeaWorld for the animal abusers they were. And still another advocate rose and told of a facility nearby that bred and sold animals to laboratories. They were trying to shut down the facility. I heard about International Elephant Awareness Day—every fifteen minutes an elephant is slaughtered for their tusks. I heard about mock funerals they staged for the animals.

This part of the event lasted perhaps twenty minutes, but it felt like longer. I had not before, in such a compressed period of time, thought about the innumerable ways humans use and abuse animals for our "entertainment." I was moved by the passion of the speakers and yet ambivalent about their approach. I wondered how many commuters, neighbors, pedestrians, upon seeing this group with their signs, their messages, and their justifiable anger, would really see or hear them. Could they change anyone's mind? Wake anyone up? *Could I?*

The young woman who appeared to be in charge took the floor again.

"I know some of you have a hard time with home advocacy, but we're going to talk about it. If you're not ready yet, I understand. But know that it works and it's necessary."

Home advocacy? Signing petitions online? Emailing people from the safety of your home computer? From all the protests and plans I'd heard them discuss, home advocacy seemed like the entry-level activity. Why would someone have a hard time with that?

"When we show up in their neighborhoods, on their streets, and show their neighbors what they do—who these monsters are, when we show them that their neighbor tortures animals and gets paid to do so, it has an effect. Nobody wants to live next door to an animal abuser."

Ooh, that kind of home advocacy. They were showing up outside the homes of the research scientists and protesting their research… or their existence. Like the abortion protestors who went after the doctors personally.

Oh.

I looked over at Leela. She glanced sideways at me.

When the event ended, Leela and I stood in the parking lot.

"So, is this why you're no longer a vegan? Too over the top?" I said.

"No, not at all. I totally agree with all of this," Leela said. "It was the diet part. After being a vegan for about four years, out of the blue I started intensely craving meat…and literally dreaming about it. It wasn't an effort for me to be a vegan—even at Thanksgiving I was happy to just eat side dishes. It was an organic decision to go vegan, and when my whole body started wanting meat, it was also an organic decision to have it again. It was as if it was the best thing I had ever eaten when I ate meat again. A few weeks after having meat again I went to the doctor and my blood work showed that I was seriously anemic, so my craving meat made sense."

"I can honestly say, I have never craved meat. Not before turning vegan and not since," I said.

"Right, so your body is different. But I was also diagnosed with Hashimoto's thyroiditis—an autoimmune thyroid issue—and I then had to avoid soy products. Without soy it limited my vegan options."

"Oh yeah. That would do it. I try to limit soy, but mostly try to find non-GMO soy." I was fascinated by Leela's experience. Still so much to learn.

"I share the ethical concerns of vegans. But I feel I have to look for other alternatives. At first, I decided to become a vegetarian pescatarian. But then a year later I was suffering from heavy metal poisoning with super-dangerous levels of mercury and arsenic. So I then added in meat, along with fish at reduced amounts, and felt much better."

"It's all so complicated! I get overwhelmed. I think that's part of what's got my head spinning."

"It's about finding out what works for you—for your body, for your ethics. I follow the Human Genome Project and related research, and it's clear to me that there is no 'one size fits all' in regard to medications, food, exercise, salt intake, and so many other things. Not all people feel better and physically benefit from a vegan diet, but all people, animals, and the planet benefit from a more natural, responsible, and humane food supply where plants and produce and animal products are concerned."

"Definitely." We moved toward my car.

"So what made you want to come to this?" Leela asked.

"I wanted to meet some vegans. Some advocates. I guess I just wanted to find somebody to talk to about how to handle it all. I'm so horrified with everything I'm learning about the animals in our food production, and it's just so much to deal with that I've worked myself up into nightmares and headaches. I was looking to see how others approach the vegan lifestyle in, I don't know, the real world."

"And how'd that work out?"

"Well, on the one hand, I admire them. I mean, a lot. Their passion. Their willingness to do something. Anything. Everything. And like you said, I agree with pretty much everything they said and everything they stand for. But I'm not sure I agree with their methods. Or that I could participate. This doesn't seem to be *my* real world. I live with a nonvegan. I work with nonvegans. Almost everyone I know, with the exception of the Beagle Freedom Project people, are leather-wearing, bacon-glorifying, cheese-mongering, unapologetic carnivores who buy products without looking for a little bunny symbol. And they go to zoos! If I was doing what these folks are doing, I'd have no friends and no family."

"Right. This is not your tribe."

"My tribe. I like that." I thought about the expression for a moment—a group who lived like I lived. Who could guide me. Help me grow. *That was a tribe, right?* "Yes, I need to find my tribe."

The trouble was I had no idea what my tribe would look like. And as my trip to India had glaringly reminded me, I was terrible in a group.

(Much later I saw a video of this same group in a "home advocacy" protest outside a UCLA vivisector's home. They were peaceful, quiet, and respectful, holding candles and signs and remaining silent, careful not to step on private property. They were also being verbally attacked, insulted, and threatened by the UCLA scientists and their friends, who were behaving abhorrently. The animal advocates remained still and dignified as these "scientists" hurled abuse at them. So I learned I'm not yet worthy of this tribe. I'm not yet brave or strong enough.)

The tribe I did belong to, and had for over twenty years, was the lawyer tribe. My law office was still what paid our bills (medical and veterinarian mostly) and still where I went Monday through Friday (unless a dog needed me) and sometimes on Saturday. I still needed to pay attention to my business.

I went to a legal seminar, and because California lawyers are required to take a certain number of continuing education courses in ethics (*stop laughing!*), I went to a course called "When Good People Do Bad Things." You would think it was a class on marketing your law practice, but it was not. The speaker was a psychologist and a lawyer, and she was discussing how scandals like Enron, WorldCom, and Lehman Brothers happened. Her focus was on how and why so many otherwise good people made such unethical choices. (She was referring to the folks down in the chain of command, not the guys at the top who don't qualify as "good people" to begin with.) She discussed a concept called "cognitive dissonance."

I looked up from my notes. I'd heard this term. I'd heard it in *Maximum Tolerated Dose*, but I didn't quite comprehend what it meant. It's hard to comprehend thoroughly through tears and a blanket held up to my face. But now I could hear. I listened as she described "the presence of incongruent thoughts and actions that frequently result in excessive mental stress and discomfort."

Mental stress? Discomfort? Yeah. I'm listening.

"So the mind makes adjustments. For example, a successful, otherwise honest person working his way up at a major accounting firm is asked to prepare what he knows are fraudulent financial statements. He holds two thoughts in his head. One, he is a good, ethical accountant. Two, preparing fraudulent financial statements is wrong. The action he is being asked to do is incongruent with his beliefs. This is, obviously, stressful to him. Adding to his stress, it's his boss making the request and assuring him it's just this one time. He can either refuse and risk the respect of his boss and quite possibly also risk his job, or he can act to reduce the cognitive dissonance that is causing his stress."

While she spoke, she was drawing a diagram. She drew one circle and wrote inside it "ethical accountant/high standards." She drew a second circle and wrote in it "produces false financial statements." Then she drew two overlapping circles and scribbled harshly, shading in the intersection of the circles. She drew an arrow and wrote "cognitive dissonance."

"There are three ways the dissonance can be reduced. First, he could change his action—not prepare the fraudulent statements. This takes a tremendous amount of courage. Second, he could change his belief—he is *not* an ethical person. Very difficult to do. Or, third, he can justify his behavior so the belief is no longer in conflict: preparing the statements as he's being asked will save thousands and thousands of jobs within the company; by preparing the statements he is being a 'team player'—he's running with the big dogs while helping the little dogs. This is how business works, he tells himself. He rationalizes. Thus, he reduces the dissonance and justifies his behavior. He is, in his now-settled mind, both an ethical person and one who produced an 'incorrect' financial statement—for a 'good' reason."

She drew a third circle and under it wrote "rationalization." Then she listed the ways our accountant had justified his behavior to settle his own cognitive dissonance—why good people do bad things.

Could people see the lightbulb illuminate above my head?

This was my conflicting Adam and Eve versus evolution beliefs, with the childlike rationalization I'd created. This was also my brain in the last year.

Cognitive dissonance was a *much* better term than restless brain syndrome.

I drew my own three circles. Under one I wrote "I love animals." Under the second I wrote "I eat animals" and "I buy products tested on animals." Under the third, the one connecting the first two circles, I wrote, "I need the protein. Meat tastes good. We're the top of the food chain. If I didn't eat them the world would be overrun by cows. I only eat 'humanely raised.' I only eat free-range. And it's only a chicken." Then I crossed out the third circle. I wrote, "I didn't know any better. But now I do."

I also now understood why I heard the kinds of responses to my vegan lifestyle that I heard from so many people, even people I knew to be animal lovers. This is why nonvegans need to mock my eating choices so as not to confront their own. This is why people who call themselves animal lovers won't watch the documentaries about where their food comes from and what happens to the animals. This is why people who buy clothing and toys for their dogs still pay money to be "entertained" by wild animals at zoos, circuses, and marine parks without giving any thought to how their actions contribute to the captivity and abuse of the wild animal. They need to keep their own dissonance at bay. They were protecting themselves. But they were doing so at the expense of the animals.

I was both relieved and horrified to realize this. I understood now what my journey had been about. I had let go of my rationalizations. I had changed my actions and honored my beliefs. And I would continue to do so. But there was still much work to be done, and the efforts needed in the fight for animal rights and respect for all sentient beings seemed so monumental.

Chapter 24

SUPERPOWERS

Things began to get easier at home. Whether because time is the great healer or because my cognitive dissonance had settled itself, I don't know. Perhaps it was both. Our decision to leave the dogs to work it out between themselves during part of the day was paying off. They seemed to have settled into not the love connection I had in mind, but more of a big sister/little brother relationship. Percival taunted and teased Daphne, and Daphne in return both bossed around and protected Percival. There were even signs they might one day play together, although it was also obvious that neither one had much experience in that department. Percival would bow down in play position and Daphne would bark at him. He'd grab a toy and shake it, but when Daphne latched on to the same toy, Percival would simply let go and run off to grab another toy rather than playing the tug-of-war game she had in mind. Then Daphne would drop the toy she'd stolen and return to the couch to sleep it off.

Percival was, however, happy to play alone. He tore through the box of dog toys, disemboweling them one by one. Whenever Seamus had torn apart a toy, he removed the squeaker and the game was over—victory for Seamus, of course. Not so for Percival. He'd tear the squeak out and carry it around, launching the horn, the siren, the gurgle, the hoot, or, most annoyingly, the Christmas carols, at random moments. He'd also shred every last bit of stuffing, leaving mounds of white and green fuzz throughout our living room, the stairs, our bedroom, and—his favorite—the formal dining room. Then he'd carry the "skin" of the toy around with him—bits of brightly colored fabric that no longer resembled the moose, duck, beaver, dog, or squirrel it had once been hanging from his jowls. He even carried the pieces of carnage with him outside to do his business, still holding the toy in his mouth.

Daphne didn't play with toys yet, unless she was taking one away from Percival, which seemed not so much "play" as "showing who's boss." Yet she picked out one toy to carry around herself—a red fire hydrant. She held it in her mouth gently, never chewing or tearing it, just occasionally squeezing it enough that the odd noise we guessed was supposed to be a siren was set off. Then she'd simply use the toy as a pillow. Percival eventually settled on a favorite as well: a formerly round lamb (quite originally named "Lambie") that had been destuffed through the top of her head but otherwise kept enough body parts to still resemble a lamb. This was his favorite toy to carry around, sleep with, and, in a regular offering to express his love, deposit on Chris's face.

Because while the dogs were no longer trying to kill each other, it now seemed Percival was determined to kill Chris. Death by love and obsessive devotion.

The moment Chris came home each night, Percival raced to him and launched himself upward in a projectile rocket of affection. Chris is over six feet tall. The odds of Percival landing one of his kisses on the intended target of Chris's face were slim, but this did not deter his zeal. He flung himself at Chris until Chris sat down on the couch and "accepted" the wild passion display that was Percival. If Daphne dared to reach the couch before Percival, we'd experience the one area where Percival was the boss. He'd use his small, wily size to dive between Chris and Daphne and then use his back paws in unison to buck Daphne aside, while his front paws held either side of Chris's face and he gave Chris a tongue bath as if Chris had used gravy for shaving cream…and then forgot to shave it off. If either Daphne or I tried to interfere or greet Chris ourselves in any way, Percival would again fling all now twenty-three pounds of himself between us and start his gravy-consumption process over, this time with more feeling. If Chris tried to move, Percival swatted him with his paws. Daphne and I contented ourselves with our own cuddles on the couch, so while Percival pawed and licked away, Daphne groaned and tail-thumped in her own contented happiness.

"Oww, Percival!" Chris grabbed Percival's right paw.

"Tell him 'no.' He understands 'no.'"

"No," Chris said. In response, Percival licked Chris's face and pawed him with the left paw. Then both paws together, leaving a mark on Chris's right cheek. "Oww. No, I don't think he does know 'no.'"

"Well, we haven't been using it a lot. But perhaps it's time. He seems obsessed with you."

Percival, hearing that I was trying to converse with his beloved, flopped his entire body across Chris's neck and nibbled on his ear, the better to prevent Chris from hearing anything anyone else had to say.

"You think?" Chris said. And Percival swatted his head. *Me! Pay attention to ME! Only ME!*

I laughed. Daphne thumped her tail. "We've got Thunder Tail and Power Paws."

It was Chris's turn to laugh—through the pain. He repeated the instantaneous nicknames in the voice of a cartoon announcer: "*Thunder Tail! And Power Paws! Engage superpowers!*"

It worked. Daphne's tail thumped harder and faster and Percival reared back to attack Chris's face with both paws as he tried to climb onto Chris's head—the better to enter his brain, I suppose. Chris grabbed him and lifted him back down to his lap. Percival spun around and leapt from the couch, racing to the dining room. Daphne followed him, bellowing her big sister bark: *Slow down! Not in the house!*

I looked at Chris. He was laughing, and though his cheek had a dark pink scratch, he didn't seem to mind. "So. Percival," I said.

"Yes?"

"I think they're okay. I think he can stay."

"You've always thought he could stay."

"I have. But now I think you think that. And really, I don't see how you could say no to him."

"Dang it."

"It's the beagle charm." I smiled. Chris was nearly as susceptible to beagle charm as I was. It was just the one time he got to play the heavy to my emotional marshmallow approach.

"It is. And yes. He's staying."

Percival came tearing back into the room, Daphne in hot pursuit. From five feet away, Percival sprung over me and onto Chris's lap. Daphne, less agile but twice as strong, leapt onto the couch and slammed in next to me, howling her victory in corralling the kid back to us.

Chris looked Percival directly into those dark, almond eyes—easy to do since the dog had again placed his front power paws on each of Chris's shoulders. "Okay, you win, Power Paws. You're family now," Chris said. Percival licked Chris's face in his quick little lizard-lick way and wagged his tail. Daphne turned and looked up at me, big caramel eyes ready to work me over for whatever she wanted, but I could swear there was a little *Oh seriously? I thought you were kidding with this thing* in her look.

The next morning I awoke and went downstairs for my coffee. Daphne and Percival followed me, Percival racing ahead and Daphne staying right by my side. The peeing in the house had gotten better, but our X DAYS SINCE AN INCIDENT sign was not yet ready to be retired, so I was making an effort to get up early and get them both outside immediately. We had a sneaking suspicion it was no longer Percival who insisted on using the pee pad in the living room. He seemed to be regularly and happily going outside. Daphne, on the other hand…well, our girl had been caught midstream in the living room twice. She was probably trying to set him up.

I made my coffee and the dogs' breakfast and waited out the five minutes of morning aerobics while they jumped and danced and encouraged me to call "time" and put their hydrated-enough bowls of food down. I left them to their meal and returned upstairs to my office. Soon after, I was joined by Percival, who approached my chair and pawed at my leg.

"Hi, buddy. You want up?" I sometimes picked him up and let him sit in my lap while I wrote. This time, though, he ran out of the room immediately.

Two minutes later he was back and pawing at my leg again. I turned to pick him up, but he dashed out of the room. Then ran back to look at me still in my chair in the office and dashed out again.

I guessed that he wanted me to follow him. Seamus had behaved similarly when he wanted me to follow him (usually to the kitchen), so I did.

Percival led me to the bedroom, where he danced back and forth in front of the upholstered chest at the foot of our bed. He looked from me to the bed and back again, licking his lips with anxiety.

When it became obvious that most of the dogs' fights occurred on the bed in the middle of the night—not to mention how the two dogs' presence cut into our human cuddle time—Chris devised a method for keeping them off the bed. We allowed them on the bed when lights were on and we were reading or watching television. But when it was "lights out" time, I would take them downstairs for a snack while Chris propped open the lid to the chest. Although both dogs were surely capable of jumping up onto the bed from the side, neither had done so. They had always used the extra step up by leaping first onto the cushioned chest and then the bed. When the lid was up, they couldn't, or didn't, get up onto the bed. Now, though, Percival thought it was time for the lid to come down. He was tired of waiting.

"Are you awake yet?"

"I am," Chris said.

"Are you ready for the Power Paws massage? Because he's dying to get up there."

Chris sat up, covered himself with blankets, and put both hands up in front of his face, like a catcher behind home base. "Okay. Lower the drawbridge."

I barely had the lid down before Percival bounced onto it and sprung onto the bed. In two bounces he was on Chris like he'd just been rescued from a deserted island and Chris was the clean water supply. And he licked him like that was the case as well.

"This is a *mffphffff mmmmhhhffffppphhhh*," Chris said.

"Not sure I know what you're saying. There seems to be a beagle glued to your mouth."

He moved Percival to the side, turned him on his back, and rubbed his belly. "This is a fine way to wake up."

"Sorry. He desperately needed to be with you. He came in to get me to lower the drawbridge twice."

"Well, what Percival wants…"

"Exactly."

I had to admit, I was a little jealous. Chris had frequently commented that Daphne—the world's easiest dog with her calm sweetness and love of cuddles—had, against odds and certainly against type, seemed to prefer me, the less calm and sweet human in the house. And no matter what Chris did, or how many times he pointed out to her that he was the one who first wanted to adopt her, Daphne was a mama's girl. She loved Chris and certainly cuddled with him too, but her preference was obvious. It was not, however, as obvious as Percival's preference. In a mere matter of months, I had gone from the one fighting to keep him and loving him unconditionally to a mere means to an end. And that end was Chris. Chris was the beginning and end of Percival's world. He worshipped him, plain and simple.

When I got out of the shower, I heard Chris singing to Percival and I laughed. Percival had his first theme song.

Seamus had many nicknames and theme songs.

And Daphne had early on picked up an appropriate, classic theme song sung to *New York, New York*, which was simply:

Doo-Doo-Doodlebutt,
Doo-Doo-Doodlebutt,
Start spreading the news…
This beagle's in town…

Mostly we just petted her cute face while singing "Doo-Doo-Doodlebutt, Doo-Doo-Doodlebutt" and she would reward us with thumps from Thunder Tail. Eventually her looks of love were rewarded with a second theme song, this one sung to the tune of the *Chitty-Chitty Bang-Bang* song:

Oh. You. Pretty, pretty Daphne,
Pretty, pretty Daphne,
We love you.

But now Chris had Percival on his back, squeezed between Chris's knees, while he was singing, to the tune of *La Cucaracha*:

Percival Taco!
Percival Taco!
Silly beagle in the bed!

Percival seemed to enjoy it and was gleefully submitting.

"That fits. A dog with this much exuberance needs a quick and bizarre theme song," I said.

"He does." Chris grabbed two of the Power Paws and began a little air dance with them. "Percival Taco! Percival Taco! Crazy, weird, my little dog!"

Yeah. Percival was staying. We all had our idiosyncrasies—dogs and humans alike—but we seemed to be meshing them just fine. We seemed to be completing our family.

It would be really nice if we also found out I wasn't dying.

My headaches, restless brain, and insomnia had stopped, but my brain MRI was scheduled. Even the insurance company thought I needed peace of mind. I considered canceling. I'd been taking the magnesium, vitamins B and D, and even the ginseng, gingko biloba, and valerian extracts my dad had sent. I'd also given myself a break from the intense reading I'd been doing, since I now felt I'd resolved my cognitive dissonance. And the dogs were getting along. So maybe it had been stress all along. Maybe I was fine. Who needed to drive all the way into Los Angeles for an expensive test when a few bottles of supplements and two cute dogs could do the trick?

Apparently I did.

The other fallout to having mindlessly posted on Facebook that I was being referred for a brain MRI was that my friends and family, and even some strangers, couldn't forget that I'd been *referred for a brain MRI*. Seemed everyone took this rather seriously and kept waiting to hear results.

The last time I spent a half hour or so holding still in an MRI tube was the day after I'd been diagnosed with cancer. I'd entertained myself that time by planning out the blog that Chris had suggested and figuring out how to explain to my friends and family that I'd been told two weeks earlier that I had a breast lump that was "highly suspicious of malignancy" (that much I had not put on Facebook). This time, I was determined not to think about the very things that had driven me to brain spasms...or, er...cognitive dissonance. That is, it wouldn't do to think about the cruel treatment of animals that had become the norm in our society and that I had unwittingly contributed to. That would make me cry, and it's hard to hold one's head (let alone brain) still when crying.

I thought instead about what I'd learned about cognitive dissonance and the ways in which people rationalize eating animals. I thought maybe I'd see the other side of the argument. The lawyer in me, heck, the *human* in me, knew there were two sides, minimum, to every story. So what was the other side of the compassionate, vegan lifestyle? What was the argument? Was there a rationalization *for* killing and eating animals that made sense? Was there a right way to do it, as Leela suggested? I'd even picked up a book (of course I did!) specifically to see things from "the other side"—the side of the family farmer (there was no way the factory farm could ever be rationalized, and my days of reading about that had ended). I'd picked up *Folks, This Ain't Normal* by Joel Salatin, the family farmer featured in the documentary *Food, Inc.* and the book *Omnivore's Dilemma*.

Farmer Salatin makes a persuasive and careful argument for the family farm. And he even made me realize there are still some family farms. Food production hasn't all been turned over to agribusiness that treats animals like mere parts in a compassionless production line where only profit matters, not health, not humanity, not even common decency. Heck, he even makes me think that if I knew my eggs, or chicken, or bacon was coming from his farm, I'd eat it. But just as quickly I *see* (in my tube-encased mind) the face of a chicken and a very adorable pig. So, uh, no, I wouldn't eat them. Maybe the egg...if I knew that the chicken, like the chickens my mom had in her backyard, had lived a "normal" life with her beak and feet intact, able to spread her wings, socialize with other chickens, scratch, peck, and do what chickens do, then maybe I'd eat the egg that she laid without a human prompting her to do so, and without hormones or massive dosages of antibiotics. Maybe that egg I could eat. Maybe. And, I was pleased to note, Farmer Salatin railed against the machine that is agribusiness too.

His book made me want to raise chickens. Which I'm sure my homeowner's association would love—as though my insistence on having beagles was not enough to permanently alienate my neighbors.

Maybe I'd find my tribe with him. With the family farmer. I had cheered (in my head) and answered, "Me too! I do!" out loud when I read his statements, like:

> Whatever happened to the scientific precautionary principle? Apparently as a culture we quit paying attention to that principle long ago. We wade into this world of unpronounceable food additives like a bunch of swashbuckling pirates, looking for profits and stuffing our treasure chests with swelling medical and pharmaceutical millions to keep us alive while we destroy ourselves with concocted chemicals. Does anybody besides me think this is crazy?

But he started to lose me as a potential member of his tribe when he seemed to mock vegans and referred to them, to us, as animal *haters*, when nothing could be further from the truth. And he really lost me, an estate planning attorney, when he inaccurately explained our estate tax system—leaving out salient facts—in order to make a point. That, of course, caused me to wonder what other facts he might have been seeing through a different-colored lens than I would use. What other facts had been stretched to make a point or serve a purpose? He'd gotten me thinking, though, I'd give him that.

Maybe if food, including animal products, was produced in the manner Farmer Salatin did on his Polyface Farm, I'd be okay with that. His view was much the same as Leela had explained hers. For me, I doubted I'd ever eat animals again, but maybe I'd be more comfortable that others did eat animals. At least I'd be more comfortable if there was less torture of animals in the world. And maybe I'd wince less every time I looked at a menu that lured people in and fooled them with non-meaningful hyperbole like "grain-fed" or "free-range" labels that meant nothing and were in no way monitored, but allowed people to thoughtlessly eat the remains of tortured, mass-produced, drugged-up animals without guilt. (Or, um, I'm sorry—allowed them to rationalize and settle their cognitive dissonance.) But that just wasn't happening. The vast majority of our food was still borne of torture. So while I liked his ideal, I was not joining his tribe.

He did give me one idea, though.

Once again I plotted from inside an MRI tube. This time it wasn't a blog I was planning. No, this time, I was going to visit a farm. In Los Angeles.

Chapter 25

SANCTUARY

P LANNING MY FARM VISIT WAS PREFERABLE TO THINKING ABOUT MY MRI results. I'd get those results when I got them, and I just couldn't bring myself to worry about it. I was feeling confident that I had my restless brain settled down. I'd confined my reading to books that gave me constructive suggestions, like *Living Cruelty Free: Live a More Compassionate Lifestyle* and Sara Gilbert's *The Imperfect Environmentalist.* (Yes, vegans care about the environment too. We and the animals live in it after all; oh, and yes, *that* Sara Gilbert, the one from *Roseanne* and *The Big Bang Theory,* and, you know, earth.) Most importantly, *Farm Sanctuary* by Gene Baur. Turned out there was a Farm Sanctuary right outside Los Angeles, and not far from The Gentle Barn, which I'd learned about from my vegan Facebook and Twitter friends who, apparently, all learned about it from Ellen DeGeneres. So I'd be going to not just one but two farms outside L.A., but obviously not *too* outside L.A.

I found The Gentle Barn's website and read that they did private tours for four hundred dollars, which I figured wasn't bad if I could get nine other people to join me. Forty dollars per person seemed reasonable. The private tour appealed to me because while I love animals, I abhor humans acting like animals…which they tend to do in crowds.

While the public group tours of The Gentle Barn and the Farm Sanctuary were not likely to involve drinking or revelry or any of those things that make me uncomfortable in large groups, it was likely to involve crowds, since they were open to the public only on Sundays. It was also likely to involve children—what with its emphasis on interaction with animals as a way of teaching children. And truth be told, if I could avoid children that weren't related to me, I'd prefer to—especially when I wanted to learn from and talk to the people who worked at The

Gentle Barn. No way were they going to prefer talking to me over some impressionable, wide-eyed, chubby-cheeked vegan in the making.

Alas, I could not find nine other people willing to drive seventy miles and spend forty dollars getting a tour they could get for ten dollars if we just put up with really short, cute people. Dang these vegans and their compassion for all creatures.

Leela once again agreed to journey on the adventure with me, game to meet the animals herself. Another Beaglefester and vegan, Karal, also met us at The Gentle Barn. And Michelle, an animal-loving, vegan-curious friend from Riverside, agreed to drive out with me. Michelle's sister and, ironically, her two children, also joined us.

The day was filled with nostalgia for me. First, because The Gentle Barn is in Santa Clarita, formerly known to me as "the place out by Magic Mountain." As a kid I lived, for a time, in Sylmar, not too far from Magic Mountain...I mean, Santa Clarita. We lived off a dirt road, rode our horses through pomegranate fields, and had an acre of olive trees where the dogs (and the kids) could run about. When we lived in Sylmar we had horses, dogs, cats, hamsters, and a parrot.

And I hated it.

I believed my preteen self to be a sophisticated city girl, and I'd been dragged out of North Hollywood under protest. North Hollywood was neither sophisticated nor a city (a suburb, sure), but try telling that to a precocious eight-year-old who preferred dresses, libraries, and shopping to...well, to Sylmar. I hated getting dirty (though had no trouble leaving my room a mess) and spent most of my time either earning every possible Girl Scout badge or huddled in the library waiting to be old enough to leave cowboy town for the more glamorous life I knew must exist somewhere. That escape occurred only a few years later when we moved to La Habra Heights and traded olive trees for avocado trees, a dirt road for a paved, winding hilltop road, and a rural lifestyle for a middle-class suburban one. The horses, dogs, cats, hamster, and parrot came with us.

The other reason my day at the farms was nostalgic was that once I arrived at The Gentle Barn, much to my surprise the younger sister of one of my (now long-lost) best friends from junior high also joined us (she had seen my post on Facebook, of course!). Shelley had been the "kid sister" who tagged along or played with us at pool parties, Girl Scout events, or other sixth-grade and junior high outings, when we were so much cooler than anyone an entire eighteen months younger. And, ironically, I would always remember her dad as the chef whose poolside barbecues first made me enjoy steak in a way I never had before (or, now, ever would again). Just one of those random childhood memories I had after all these years, and then up walks Shelley, ready to meet cows with me.

We'd arrived early—very unusual for me—but such was my excitement. Scores of volunteers were also arriving, in their green Gentle Barn–logo'd T-shirt and hoodies. I was impressed with how many there were, but in thinking about it—what a wonderful way to spend a day. I could handle volunteer work that involved petting, talking to, and acting as bouncer and bodyguard to farm animals. I assumed the visitors would be respectful, curious folks who would have the best interests of the animals at heart. Otherwise, why be here? There was a sign out front (and I'd seen the same message on their website) asking that guests not bring any meat, poultry, dairy, or fish onto the premises out of respect for the animals. It was probably too much to ask that guests not wear leather either, but I'd worn my vegan boots and was carrying a vegan purse as well. (Sounds so much better than "faux leather" doesn't it? Right. But it's the same thing. And no, you can't tell.)

They opened the gates promptly at ten and we streamed in with the growing crowd of visitors. Luckily for me (and the animals) The Gentle Barn is on six acres and visitors can disperse to the horse corrals, the cow barn, or the goat paddock before gathering again up a hill to a shaded seating area to meet and hear from the founder, Ellie Laks.

We headed to the cows first.

The volunteer at the gate to the cow area lets in a few people at a time to visit with and pet the four or five cows present. A volunteer stands with each cow to explain their story and, I'm sure, to assure that the visitors are respectful in their approach to the animals. Some of the cows are quite friendly. A large black-and-white cow was lying down, enjoying the sun. She willingly allowed us to stroke her face and her ample body, and she certainly seemed to enjoy a scratch behind the ears. Her caretaker told us her name was Crystal. She'd been taken from her mom and shoved in a veal crate, destined for slaughter at eight weeks old. When The Gentle Barn rescued her she was so weak and sick she could not stand. And now here she was, content in the sun, enjoying human companionship. Again I was struck by the capacity of animals for forgiveness. Just as Percival seems to have left behind his days in a cage, subjected to violent, painful procedures, and now enjoys fresh air, toys, sunshine, and time with his humans (Chris! Mostly Chris!), this cow had recovered enough to trust random strangers who approached her. I took a photo with her.

Another cow—a big, blond female named Buttercup—was not only comfortable letting us pet her, she began to lick our arms and even Karal's face. Cow kisses are to be cherished, and we'd like to flatter ourselves, but it became obvious Buttercup was a fan of the coconut oil we all used as moisturizer (a vegan favorite, so no doubt Buttercup had become accustomed to seeking out the coconut-y vegan visitors). Buttercup had been rescued from a backyard butcher. She was pregnant at the time, but because she'd had so little care, her calf did not survive. However, with time and loving care, Buttercup had become, the volunteer told us, the foster mom to the rescued calves brought to The Gentle Barn.

Staying removed from the groups of humans and even the other cows, but looking a bit curious, was a red-and-white cow named Aretha. I approached her quietly and listened as the volunteer told me about Aretha. She was one of the newer rescues, and her spirit was still broken, though healing. She did not yet trust humans to be kind to her, so I did not reach out my hand to pet her. I just stood near and wished her well, looking in her big, beautiful sad eyes, with maybe just the smallest glimmer of hope.

We visited with the horses next. I bought a bag of carrots and found myself to be very popular with every horse and donkey as a result. My time in Sylmar had at least taught me the proper way to feed a horse without losing any fingers, and I'd also learned how horses, just like dogs, can have very distinct personalities. That was true of these horses as well. Some had been abused, not provided with proper shelter or food or water; some had been beaten, one was rescued from a backyard butcher (yes, butcher…of horses), and two were the babies of an unfortunate mare whose urine was used in the production of Premarin, a drug that women take in menopause and can only be made with the urine of a pregnant mare. The mare is prevented from moving and is hooked up to a catheter during her entire pregnancy. The babies are disposed of. These two, Lazar and his sister Zoe, were the lucky ones— saved and raised by The Gentle Barn. One of the donkeys, now happily taking carrots from all of us and gleefully lowering his head for a scratch behind his ears, had been beaten by his "owner" to near death. Donkeys freeze when frightened or in pain, and rather than understanding that behavior, the man had simply continued to beat Addison, this beautiful donkey now so friendly and full of personality.

The volunteers soon herded the human crowd up a hill to what was referred to as the "upper barnyard" for a group discussion with Ellie. I was interested in this discussion, but did not feel the need to hurry up the hill and grab a front row seat. This was not a day for rushing; this was a day for learning and contemplating. Besides, wherever I sat I could surely see over the heads of the numerous children in attendance.

When I got to the gathering area, I saw that the rush had been as much to grab a seat in the shade as it was to be front and center. I was content with a place in the sun.

Ellie was younger than I had expected, probably in her late thirties, with long brown hair and a smiling, happy demeanor. Being around all of these animals would make me happy too, but as she welcomed us and told the story of founding The Gentle Barn, I realized there was a heartbreaking side to her work too. I imagine that for every story of an animal they save, there were countless stories of the animals they couldn't save, the ones that didn't make it out alive. And even the animals she'd saved, the ones we were seeing in their rehabilitated state, had such cruel beginnings. Was she always this happy? Probably not, but the fact that she could rally herself day after day to stay in the fight for these animals was impressive. I surely had something to learn here.

Ellie told us her story—her lifetime love of animals, which she was not allowed to have as a child. She talked about respect for the animals and encouraged us all to get to know them, to see their personalities, their emotions, and the way they interact with us and each other. And she encouraged us to always respect the animals. I learned that The Gentle Barn works with inter-city kids, at-risk youth, children from group homes and mental health institutes, foster homes and schools, as Ellie said, "to teach them that even though we are all different on the outside, on the inside we are all the same and are deserving of the same rights, respects, and freedom."

The groups of these children were brought to The Gentle Barn to interact with the animals and learn from them. The success of the programs—the rehabilitation of the kids in conjunction with the animals—is no doubt part of what had caught the attention of Ellen DeGeneres and resulted in her featuring Ellie and The Gentle Barn on *The Ellen Show* in an episode that apparently everyone but me had seen. Ellie ended her talk with a gentle, but enthusiastic and persuasive, bid for all to consider a plant-based diet for their health and for the sake of the animals and our environment.

Our group was then free to roam about the upper barnyard to visit with sheep, goats, pigs, chickens, turkeys, and even llamas. I wanted to do that too, but I also wanted to talk with Ellie. I had so many questions, and I'd precipitously decided she'd have the answers—all of them! Leela hung back with me. I put a donation in the jar for a colt, Worthy, who'd had surgery to fix a deformed leg, and I signed his "Get Well" card. Then, when the crowd cleared, I approached Ellie, and abruptly I was shy, awkward, and inarticulate. I was out of my league. She was so impressive and yet so humble, so…*real.*

"Hi. Um, so I have questions," I muttered, ever so eloquently.

"Great! Let's talk!"

For all she knew I was a kook, or a stalker-fan, or about to argue with her, spout off how people need animal protein, how animals are put on this earth to serve us, how bacon is *soooo* delicious, or any of the ridiculous, insulting, and vaguely threatening comments I'd been hearing myself. But still she was completely open to a conversation.

"I'm a breast cancer survivor, and I turned to a plant-based diet a little over a year ago—"

"Good for you!"

"Thank you. And I started reading up on it a lot, and I'm appalled by what we've done to animals, by how our food is produced."

She was still smiling. "I know."

Well, yes, of course she knew. She'd been rescuing the victims of our food production machine for a decade. So where was I going with this? I wanted to say, "How do you handle it all? Aren't you having nightmares? Does your brain spasm too?" But my brain functioned well enough to decide not to sound *immediately* crazy. "I'm still learning a lot. That's why I came here. Besides to visit with the animals. To talk to you."

She motioned to a picnic table. "Let's talk. Have a seat."

She sat on one side and Leela and I on the other. Now was my chance—one-on-one with the leader of a tribe I thought I just might want to be a part of. If only I could be more articulate than, "So what's the answer? What would become of cows and pigs and chickens, and all of them, if we just stopped eating them? Or using them? Don't get me wrong, I think we should stop it all. Absolutely. I hate what I learned we're doing to animals. But then I get stuck. We stop eating them, subjugating them, imprisoning them... Then what? Are cows and pigs just roaming freely? And chickens? Yikes! They seem so defenseless, so... bottom of the food chain."

To Ellie's credit, she remained smiling and open. I'm sure all of her experience with schoolchildren asking (far more intelligent and articulate) questions came in handy.

"Well, first, we wouldn't have so many cows, pigs, and chickens. There are only millions and billions of them because they are mass-produced for slaughter, so if we stopped eating them, they'd stop force-impregnating them."

"And then it would only occur naturally. But still we'd have cows and pigs and chickens."

"Wouldn't that be lovely? They could live like this." She swept her arm out to encompass the upper barnyard, the mountain view, the Eden she'd created.

"Like pets?" I actually liked the idea, and I hoped I sounded like that, but it was hard to picture.

"Probably not like dogs in our houses." She laughed.

"No. Probably not quite like that," I said, though I could recall once visiting a dog rescue that specialized in the giant breeds. The founders ran a rescue on their own ranch with a guesthouse—human-sized, a real house—that functioned as the "doghouse" for about fifteen Great Danes. They came and went, lounged on the couches, ate in the dining room and kitchen, and sunned themselves on the patio. (They did not use the human toilets; I know you are wondering this.) If the Great Danes could live in a house like that, I was sure the chickens and pigs could, if not the cows.

"There'd be enough farm sanctuaries and caring people to handle the animals. And who's to say they couldn't live in the wild? They eat grass."

"Huh. It's a beautiful vision."

"It is."

I was quiet, trying to recall any of the seemingly million questions I thought I had, but the truth was I liked just sitting in her vision, thinking about a world that worked like that—which is what she'd created on those six acres.

"What about eggs?"

"Eggs?"

"Yes. Chickens lay eggs, regardless of human involvement." Suddenly I was less sure of even this basic fact. "Right?"

Her mildly amused tolerance and willingness to openly respond to whatever came out of my mouth continued. "Yep. That they do."

"So if the chickens are free…if they aren't being subjected to any cruelty or manipulated in any way…not suffering…what's wrong with eating eggs? You have chickens here. What happens to those eggs?"

"Oh, I feed them to the dogs."

Ah! Her dogs are not vegan! *Yes! Where was the sign-up sheet for this tribe? Is there a secret handshake? How do I join?*

"But you don't eat them? Just on principle?"

"I don't eat them because I've seen too many laid and they gross me out!" She was laughing now.

Oh, how I adore how down-to-earth and logical this woman is! And I felt free—free to eat the eggs laid by my mother's chickens! My mother and her chickens are in Missouri, and I'm in California, but no matter—the possibility existed! Without guilt! I pressed on.

"And milk? Some say a cow gives plenty of milk and can feed her baby and give us plenty of 'excess' milk for cheese and dairy products." Okay, I still miss cheese a little…so I was hoping, against all that I knew. And Ellie knew too.

"Well, first, they don't do it that way. The mama cows are not allowed to give their milk to the babies, so that should tell you something. If there is enough milk for all, why strip the baby from its mama? And second, the cow is producing extreme amounts of milk because she's been injected with hormones and chemicals and things that are in no way natural. And speaking of unnatural…"

We discussed how the cows are impregnated, and now it would be Leela's turn to have nightmares about bestiality and the "rape rack."

"Horrifying!" Leela said.

"Isn't it?" Ellie said.

"From everything I've read, and had nightmares over, the dairy industry is among the most horrific." I, like many vegetarians I know, was hoping this was not true, hoping she had something better to tell me.

"Absolutely," Ellie said. And now she lost her smile. "If someone held a gun to my head and said I had to eat either meat or dairy, I'd choose meat. We'd be a lot further along as a more compassionate society if we all gave up dairy. The dairy cows have it much, much worse than the meat cows."

Ellie walked Leela and me over to the upper barnyard gate. Most of our group, including my other friends, had spent the last half hour petting and visiting with the animals, and another group would soon be arriving. She asked the volunteer to let us in and allow us to stay however long we needed.

"Thank you so much," I said. And I hugged her. Voluntarily. I am normally not a hugger—not at all. But this woman deserved hugs. This woman radiated "huggable." This woman might be the leader of my new tribe!

I petted a pig. And then another. And another. And one very, very large black-and-white pig. I rested my head on a sleeping pig, and Leela took my photo. I'd frame it and have it on my desk at work if I thought that would be remotely acceptable (and I just might, anyway). The goats and sheep were friendly, moving their faces toward you for a pet or a treat, and the volunteers taught us how to pet a turkey (scratch up under their wings). The llamas were beautiful but distant. My dad had a llama at one time, many years ago when he had acreage up in the mountains, and I remember that llama, like these, was beautiful and regal…until she spit. So I kept my distance. A smaller pen was filled with hay and little "dog" houses, with smaller pigs sleeping in them. These pigs had been rescued from petting zoos, breeders, and, in one case, a well-meaning but ignorant woman who had raised a piglet with such an iron-deficient diet that the poor piggy went blind. Sidney was now healthy and happy, and though still blind, he managed to get around well enough to get his share of pets and scratches and return to his piggy-house shelter when he'd had enough or needed his beauty rest.

If we had not made plans to visit Farm Sanctuary down the road, and if Michelle, her sister, and her sister's kids, had not been waiting for us in the lower barnyard and picnic area for lunch, I'd probably still be there petting pigs and soaking up the serenity. *This* was peace of mind.

We made our way back down the hill to enjoy our vegan pizzas amid the peacocks and shade trees before heading over to Farm Sanctuary.

Animal Acres is the name given to the Farm Sanctuary just outside of Los Angeles. The original Farm Sanctuary is in Watkins Glen, New York, and there's another in Northern California, so I suppose to distinguish them, this one has been dubbed "Animal Acres." And it's fitting because there are, as you'd expect, acres of animals. The facility is more manicured and orderly looking than The Gentle Barn. I think "ranch" instead of "farm"…but maybe that's because there are buildings that look like homes…homes for ranch hands or something of the sort. And there's a long one-story building with a breezeway all along the front that looks very much like the ranch-style homes I'd seen so much of in Sylmar.

The system for visiting the animals is slightly different here than it was at The Gentle Barn. At Animal Acres, visitors can roam about on their own or take a guided tour. I'd noticed on the website that while all ages were welcome, the guided tours were limited to persons over the age of twelve, which I'd found interesting and of some concern because Michelle's niece and nephew were exceedingly smart and well-behaved, but not yet twelve.

We arrived fifteen minutes before the next guided tour would start, so we roamed about, petting the chickens, ducks, and turkeys that greeted us in the front lawn area. The birds had small kiddie swimming pools, fountains, and plenty of space. They seemed not in the least bit disturbed to have humans wandering about, and many of them came right up to us. Since we'd already been taught how to pet a turkey and a chicken, we obliged their requests. One turkey, Minerva, was particularly friendly and began to follow Michelle about. And in case you are wondering, a turkey waddling after a suddenly beloved human is endlessly amusing.

Once the guided tour started, it became obvious why small children were not encouraged. The volunteers at the Farm Sanctuary were more graphic in their descriptions of what had happened to these animals, or animals like them, and more direct in their advocating for a vegan lifestyle. It was not inappropriate—not in the least. It was reality. But it was also PG-13. Heck, I had nightmares over this stuff. How would a kid handle knowing that the sheep who produce Merino wool were bred to have wrinkly skin and are therefore vulnerable to fly larva infestations? And (graphic alert here) that to prevent this, farmers use a technique called "mulesing," where swatches of skin are sliced from the lamb's backside, without benefit of anesthesia or painkillers? (Yes, I'd stopped buying wool by then as well.)

If the tour guide didn't point it out, you might not notice that many of the turkeys and chickens had deformed feet from the living conditions they'd been subjected to, or that before their rescue their beaks had been hacked off so they would not, in tightly packed, stress-inducing cages, peck each other. And you perhaps wouldn't know that the pig in the pen tossing a ball about or the two lying on a mound of straw sunning themselves, although happy and safe now, still battled the deformities and health problems from their previous lives. The volunteers shared the information that is also provided on the website. But, as I'd begun to spare myself the gruesome details, I'll spare you too. But here's the deal—if you ever tell me or another vegan how wonderful bacon is, I reserve the right to describe to you in very graphic detail the life of the factory-farmed breeding sows and piglets who become that bacon. Because it's far more heinous than bacon is good. Deal?

But to watch these rescued pigs was a joy. If there was any doubt that pigs have personalities, watching the pigs at Animal Acres clears it up. A six-hundred-pound pig playing with a beach ball is a sight to behold. "Girls" that large cuddling with each other in the hay, safe inside their barns, is equally heartwarming.

Cows taller than me—a lot taller—were definitely not something I'd ever seen before. Yet they were friendly and calm, allowing us to pet and photograph them. And the fact that the Farm Sanctuary had rescued cows they'd named William and Harry is amusing in its own right. Goats roaming the hills seemed a bit suspicious of the humans, but who could blame them? I was by then pretty leery of the human race myself.

At the end of the tour we chose to roam about a bit more (inspired by the goats, perhaps?). Michelle loved on Minerva a bit, and Minerva continued to follow her around, asking for still more. (Minerva made her point; Michelle said she could never eat turkey again.) Finally, we made our way over to the gift shop. I perused the books, of course, and bought a few more, along with a T-shirt and a wineglass with the Farm Sanctuary logo (if ever there was a "must-have" souvenir of my day, this was it). Then I looked through the free educational materials they had available—brochures, flyers, and information sheets. I looked through it all, as I had at The Gentle Barn (where I also bought a T-shirt, and a book, and…oh never mind, Chris might be reading this). I considered what to take:

Sanctuary, Farm Sanctuary's compassionate quarterly magazine? Why yes, please.

Something Better: Why Millions of People Are Changing What They Eat? Absolutely, I need to know this!

The Truth Behind "Humane" Meat, Milk, and Eggs? May I have a thousand of these so I can hand them to everyone who tells me they eat this way? It'd be so much easier than explaining that these are meaningless terms and not in the least what any decent human thinks of as "compassionate" or "humane."

And that lovely brochure for *Recipes for Life: Simple Palate-Pleasers for the Aspiring Vegan*? Yep. I could use that.

Ooh, and the brochure showing a happy, plump mama chicken and her chicks pecking at grass under a bright blue sky, with the yellow lettered caption proudly declaring *Compassionate Choices—Making a Difference for Animals*? Yes! Yes! And yes! I was interested in all of it. I wanted to do all of it—be better, be more helpful, be more…*compassionate! Where was the tribe sign-up sheet?!*

I'm sure I looked like a hoarder—not of animals, but of information. When I saw the rainbow-colored peta2 "Free for All" flyer that said, simply, "Go Vegan & Save 100 Animals," I paused. A *hundred* animals? I turned the flyer over and read.

"Going vegan" helped the environment: "You can save more water by *not* eating a pound of beef than by *not* showering for *six months*!" Given the comments I'd received since turning vegan, I wondered which action would be more objectionable to the world at large, but I was not about to find out.

Vegans are also, according to my new favorite flyer, "less likely to be fat" than people who eat meat. This came with a completely gratuitous illustration of two purple silhouetted bodies, the vegan being of normal weight and the meat eater being of, um, well, of Homer Simpson proportions.

The brochure was only six-by-eight inches but still managed to mention the gory details of how the animals are slaughtered. Some of those particularly gruesome clauses were highlighted in a cheery turquoise font.

But the point—my point—what I'd suddenly focused on was *not* the gruesome reality of the torture, or the killing, but this one fact: I'd saved a hundred animals by having been on a plant-based diet for a year. *One hundred animals! Me! Fantastic!* Sure, a drop in the bucket, given the billions slaughtered annually, but still…a hundred animals saved! Wait…I'd certainly gotten Chris eating fewer animals. He regularly drank a vegan breakfast now, so let's say that's another twenty animals saved over the year. And we'd saved Daphne and Percival! So one hundred and twenty-two animals saved. This was no small thing. I loved animals, and my actions now demonstrated that.

Maybe my year hadn't been so bad after all.

Chapter 26

TRIBAL DRUMS

Percival saw Chris reach for the harness and hightailed it to the dining room "safe zone." Many of his toys, or, more precisely, shreds and remains of his toys, were scattered about under the table in a gruesome tableau of squeak-carnage, and he was in the middle of the mess staring at us while also clearly hoping we somehow couldn't see him. He loved walks but still hated car rides, and thus the harness was something to be wary of. Until we strolled past the door leading to the garage and out the front gate to safety, Percival did not relax and enjoy the idea of a walk. Daphne, on the other leash, began jumping up and down and heading for the front door the moment she felt us thinking about a departure of any kind. Be it walk or car ride, Daphne was game, as always.

"Sorry, buddy," Chris said. He maneuvered the harness onto the uncooperative dog. "It will be fun, I promise."

Percival's face registered both doubt and betrayal as he looked up at Chris. Unmoved, Chris scooped him up.

Daphne danced her way out to the courtyard and raced up to the garage door. I let her in and opened my car door. She hopped in immediately and turned, facing forward, waiting while I seat-belted her in. Chris placed a rigid, unhappy Percival on the blanket in the backseat and latched him in as well. I handed treats to both dogs, and while Percival took it, his mood was unchanged. *Not happy!* his whole countenance screamed.

We were going to a dog birthday party. Unfortunately for Percival that meant an hour drive to Los Angeles. Since I myself didn't fully understand what a "Zoom Room" was, I could not adequately explain it to the beagles (and yes, I recognize the futility of explaining things to dogs anyway). Daphne was willing to trust that wherever we went would be fun. But Percival…well, understandably, Percival had trust issues. And car sickness issues. Mostly, that.

Driving to Los Angeles is always an adventure, and that's the best spin I can put on it. It takes anywhere from an hour to three days, depending on—all together now—TRAFFIC. It's difficult to plan for, even on a Sunday. Thus, it's difficult to decide whether to risk stopping and letting the dogs out for fresh air, or if that will cause us to miss that narrow window where traffic was tolerable. Also, there's that whole thing about risking one's life getting out of the car in East Los Angeles, which is what happens to be between us and West Los Angeles. Thus, we decided to take advantage of the open freeway and keep driving. Percival rewarded our decision by spewing his breakfast across the backseat. Daphne moved aside and leaned up against the car door, her disgust and embarrassment over the little brother evident.

We endured it until we arrived. Then Chris and I both sprang from the car.

"You walk them around the parking lot. I'll go inside and get paper towels," I said.

"You'd think by now we'd travel with them. Note to selves."

I lifted the green, stiffened Percival from the backseat and put him on the ground. He remained perfectly still. I reached over him to leash the wiggling, barking Daphne Doodlebutt, who was making absolutely certain she did not miss one moment of the excitement, even if she had to walk through vomit to get there. This might be our first and last L.A. doggie birthday party. We'd be the family that arrives sick, smelly, and cranky. Fun! At least we'd remembered gifts—toys for the birthday girl and wine for her parents.

The birthday beagle was Indie, who had been rescued at four weeks of age by Beagle Freedom Project, along with her siblings and their mama, Grace. Mom and babies had been subjected to toxicity testing by a laboratory that at least turned the animals over to BFP when the tests were over. Indie's humans, Roy and Laurie, had come to our Words, Wine, and Wags fund-raiser for Beagle Freedom Project, and we'd hit it off immediately. Anybody who loves beagles and wine is pretty much top-notch in my book (hmm…literally *in* my *book*!).

Laurie had been present at several of the BFP rescues, and she and Roy had five, six, seven dogs…depending on what day it was, since they also fostered dogs in need.

I let Daphne and Percival sniff about, but there isn't a lot for a beagle to get excited about in an L.A. asphalt parking lot—not when Pink's Hot Dogs scents were drifting over from across the street, and there were myriad doggie smells from inside the Zoom Room to inundate their nostrils. Daphne pulled to get inside the Zoom Room and commence with the zooming, and soon enough Percival came out of his transportation trance and did the same. I passed Chris on our way into the building as he came out with paper towels and a spray bottle.

"Best boyfriend ever!" I said.

He shook his fistful of paper towels at me in mock anger.

We walked through the reception area and small gift shop where Percival and Daphne demonstrated the non-zooming portion of the visit by stopping to sniff and strain in the direction of every biscuit, bull "pizzle," rawhide, jerky, and intricately decorated treat in the place. I finally got them to the gate for entrance to the Zoom Room. And it is well named.

Daphne tore through the gate, announcing her arrival in a series of howls, barks, and jumps. Percival held back a bit, overwhelmed by the number of dogs who pounced on him, sniffing and wagging their tails. Percival ran, the dogs chased joyously, and Daphne chased after them all, barking and demanding…well, we didn't know what. But she seemed to be demanding something. And she was the only dog barking. Percival and his gang of furry hooligans tore about, going at full speed then cutting in sharp turns in the reverse direction. The room was covered in those black rubber mats usually found in smelly gyms frequented by huge muscle-bound men in tank tops throwing weights around. Instead of weights, this room had toys for zooming: canvas tunnels to run through; bendable pole slaloms to wind through; ramps to run up, over, and down; and hoops to jump through. None of these dogs were doing any of that, of course. Like the kids who play with the boxes their toys came in instead of the toys themselves, these dogs—mostly beagles and mostly Beagle Freedom

Project beagles at that—were making up their own games and running around the equipment.

Percival looked ecstatic and quickly made friends with the birthday girl, who, it was hard not to notice, looked an awful lot like Percival. They were nearly exactly a year apart in age—Indie was turning one that day and Percival would be two years old two days later. Both had been rescued from Northern California laboratories. They easily could have come from the same "breeder" and shared a parent. We'd never know. And it would never matter, any more than it mattered if Indie and her siblings could recognize Grace, their mama, when she arrived and joined in the frolicking.

The staff at the Zoom Room joined the dogs and enticed them to try the obstacle agility course. Wisely, they led the pack of beagles up over the ramp, across the bridge, and through the hoops by showing them a treat and moving the treat the direction they wanted the dogs to move. In no time at all, our beagles looked like agility champions. Until she gave them the treats and the beagle hysteria and doggie ADD broke out again.

The humans all stood back and watched, checking on their own dogs from time to time and photographing like we were parents at a child's first visit to Disneyland. Daphne was still doing her bossy bark, so we tried to quiet her. The Zoom Room staffer laughed.

"It's okay. We're a dog playground. We can handle barking. She's not threatening; she's just the referee. She wants everyone to behave."

"That's what she's doing? Just kind of bossing everyone around?"

"Not even that bossy. She's just keeping everyone in line."

Later I found Chris at the appetizer table with a glass of wine in hand (what kind of a one-year-old's birthday party would not have wine?). I told him the diagnosis of Daphne's behavior.

"Well, in that harness she does look like an umpire," he said. Daphne and Percival wore chest- and belly-padded harnesses with latches that could be attached to human seat belts when they traveled in the car with us. Daphne did look like an umpire, whereas Percival usually looked more like an insane asylum refuge—though that had more to do with the way he felt about car rides and less to do with the voluminous harness padding on his tiny frame.

"Ha. She does. I prefer to think of her as the umpire, instead of the antisocial one."

"Of course you do. Because she's like you. She's against fun."

"Not against fun. We just want good behavior. We're against out-of-control behavior."

"Right. Fun." He handed me the glass of wine. Maybe so I didn't smack him, but I prefer to think he just wanted me to enjoy the wine.

Most of the party was fellow Beagle Freedom Project adopters and fosters. Vanessa came to the party as well, and Percival got all kinds of extra lovin' from his former foster mom. She was thrilled to see him, and I hoped she saw he was happy and blossoming. Shannon was also there—the fairy godmother, devoted aunt, and savior of all these beagles. Her daily work must be exhausting and discouraging as often—or perhaps more often—than it was joyous and rewarding. So a day like this had to be heartwarming for her, and confirmation that her work—her mission—was solid and so very necessary. This birthday celebration would not have been possible without her tireless efforts.

As for me, I was happy to be able to spend time with other BFP folks to learn from them. Adopting one of these dogs is a joy, but it's not like adopting from a shelter or a litter of puppies where some background is known, or at least can be determined by behavior. These dogs have been through unknown trauma and thus need a lot of patience and understanding. What works with a lot of dogs—crate training for example—isn't going to work for a dog who had been kept in a cage his whole life and released only when needed for painful experiments. An adult dog who had never been potty-trained because he'd never been inside a house brings his own issues. So make that patience, pee pads, and paper towels that are required. We could share problems like Percival's fear of anything on wheels (trash cans, suitcases) and can discuss that with people who understand not just that it happens, but why: in the labs the carts that carry the equipment for the experiments are on wheels. And just as importantly, we could bask in the company of people who were doing something—doing all that they could—to *help*.

The menu was all vegan and the vibe was altruistic. I heard tribal drums calling.

Chapter 27

UNREMARKABLE ME

IT HAD BEEN WEEKS SINCE MY BRAIN MRI AND EVEN LONGER SINCE I'D had another restless brain…er, um, cognitive dissonance episode. I was so convinced the MRI would show nothing, and frankly so embarrassed that I'd even bothered to have the test done when it was now obvious that I'd allowed my stress to manifest itself physically (it was all in my mind; *all* of it!), that I almost forgot about getting the results. I would have forgotten if only my friends and family (and those wonderful Facebook followers) had forgotten. But *noooooooooooo*, it seems when one has an MRI, one is expected to find out the results. Chris also seemed to think this was important. And since we were toying with the idea of a "family trip" to Paso Robles, this time renting a dog-friendly house and taking both beagles, he suggested I find out if I was in the clear before we got too far along with our plans. This was a valid point. It would be very like me to plan a wonderful Alcohol, Books, Chris, and Dogs week only to learn that I would need to have brain surgery instead. Except it wasn't Christmas, so I should be totally fine.

I called the doctor's office. They put me through to the physician's assistant who immediately said the magic words every intelligent adult wants to hear: "Your brain is unremarkable."

I laughed. I'd certainly experienced enough medical tests and procedures to understand that in the medical world "negative" is positive. It's the one way I probably could have been a doctor. Hard as I try, I'm generally much more "negative" than "positive."

"So, I'm all good. No problems?"

"You're all good. We'll see you for your next checkup."

I reported the results to Chris, my father, my mother, and Facebook, in that order (that's my story). Chris and I naturally celebrated with a glass of wine in the hot tub.

"I knew it was going to be okay," I said. "I will admit it—I was stressing myself out."

"That you were. But you're going to have to continue to watch it. You can't let yourself get upset to the point of not functioning because of all of this animal rights stuff."

"I think I've got a much better grip on things now. I was reading the *Why We Love Dogs, Eat Pigs, and Wear Cows* book…"

"Wait, wasn't that the one you said gave you the worst nightmares?"

I took a sip of wine and set my glass down. "Maybe. They all did. But I remembered that the author talked about my now favorite theory—cognitive dissonance. So I picked it up to read again when I got home. She has some really good advice for dealing with all the trauma."

"Like don't read her book?"

"No author gives that advice."

"True. Okay, so, drink lots of wine?"

"Most authors give that advice. But no. Her advice was to look out for yourself too. Have compassion for yourself. I don't think I was doing that. I was so busy berating myself for all that I didn't know—all that I didn't do."

"And here I just thought you were busy throwing out all our household cleaning products and replacing them with products not tested on beagles."

"Percival thanks me for that."

"I'm sure he does."

"Also, the new products are nontoxic, in biodegradable containers, and won't cause cancer in us or the beagles."

"They're *super* products! They will cure *all* of the world's problems!"

Have I mentioned I love Chris's sarcasm? "Well, they're an improvement. And Percival isn't chewing his paws anymore."

I'd replaced our cleaning products but neglected to consider that our housekeeper brought her own supplies with her. Only after two housecleanings that left Percival chewing his back paw until it bled and then finding the cheap, generic cleaning spray left behind on my kitchen counter did I realize my mistake. I put all of our safe, nontoxic, cruelty-free products in a box and asked her to use only those in our house. I now had a "magic" box full of products with names like Ecover, Evolve, Seventh Generation, Earth Friendly, and Sun & Earth (they even sound better, don't they?). Percival never chewed his foot again, and our housekeeper commented how much better these products were. She was breathing easier herself.

Chris sipped from his glass of wine and then nudged the glass in my direction. "I think you may have strayed from your point."

"Right. My point. See how relaxed I am about all this? I can even digress on cute little tangents."

"Toxins! So cute." He wrinkled his nose playfully.

"My point was that I had to remember to have a little perspective. I can't focus on all the horror or I'm no good to anybody. And you are going to laugh, but I'm remembering a Mother Teresa quote I read in India."

"Um, are you about to quote Mother Teresa to me? I'm going to need more wine."

"I am. Are you ready?"

He faked guzzling his wine from his already empty wineglass. "Sure. Hit me with it."

"It was a quote in relation to numbers and numbing—how we get numb to violence and tragedy when it happens in huge numbers. Poverty, war, natural disasters…but when it's one or two people—one starving child, one wounded veteran, one buried earthquake victim, we feel it more. We have empathy. We want to help and often we do help."

"That's a quote?"

"No. That's a conversation. The quote was 'If I look at the mass, I will never act. If I look at the one, I will.' And that quote appears in the *Why We Wear Cows* book too. The 'mass' in this case being the billions of animals slaughtered for our consumption every year."

"And the point is?"

"Well, sort of like when I went to India. I wasn't thinking about helping everyone. Or saving all of the animals. And Buddha knows I was terrible with the group aspect. But I was doing what I *could* do. That's probably why I liked Mother Teresa's so much. It was one-on-one, doing what I could do with no expectation that I was going to end disease or suffering. I loved that *everyone*—every one of the women there—did all that they were capable of. Whatever that was." It was my turn to sip my wine. "That idea of doing to the best of one's abilities has really stayed with me. I can't save the world, but I can bring a little joy to a disabled woman in a home for the destitute and dying by painting her toenails red, or reading to her, or playing catch. And I can't save all of the animals in the factory farms, but I can save a hundred of them every year by staying vegan. And I can rescue beagles."

"This seems very logical. Finally. Well, except that beagle part."

"It *is* logical. But that's not to say I'm not going to keep trying to do more."

"Oh, I'm well aware of that."

"I need to help where I can. And find more ways to help. I loved being at The Gentle Barn. I love what the Farm Sanctuary is doing. I love knowing those people exist, and it's better for me to focus on that."

"*Focus on the cookie.*"

We both laughed. It was our favorite lesson from Seamus. Focus on the cookie at the end of the medical procedure—not the chemo, not the cancer, *the cookie*.

I smiled. "Obviously Mother Teresa and Seamus shared a philosophy. So The Gentle Barn, Farm Sanctuary, Beagle Freedom Project, the hundred-plus animals I save every year—those are the cookies I can focus on. The torture and slaughter of the animals—that's the cancer."

"Good thing that's not the cookie. That would be a terrible cookie."

At hearing the word *cookie*, Daphne ran outside and climbed up on the steps to the hot tub. She thumped her tail against the side and peered in at us. Percival followed her out and reached his paws up on the side of the hot tub. Chris's side of the hot tub, of course.

Chapter 28

GREAT LOVE

W E'D HAD PERCIVAL FOR THREE MONTHS AND DAPHNE FOR FOUR when we loaded them up into our rented Ford Explorer and headed for our week in Paso Robles wine country. This would be Daphne's second trip to wine country, which I was pretty sure made her a certified wine dog, especially since she'd also spent many days in Chris's wine shop as the unofficial greeter.

A half hour into the drive, I looked in the backseat to see that, even buckled into their harnesses, the two dogs had moved to the center of the backseat and were sleeping soundly, pressed up against each other.

"Awww, look. They're practically cuddling," I said.

"Awww, look, I'm driving," Chris said, gesturing to the road before him.

I turned back to the dogs and snapped a photo on my cell phone. Everyone on Facebook would see it before Chris, but he'd see it eventually.

We'd moved past détente with the dogs. We'd found peace. And maybe I was reading too much into it, but I think Percival felt better in the car with Daphne next to him. Daphne was so fearless about cars, and so many other things, it had to be rubbing off. Very shortly thereafter, we'd learn what other behavior Percival was learning from Daphne.

An hour and a half into the drive, Chris pulled off the freeway.

"Dog park number one!" he said as he lifted Percival out of the car.

Concerned about Percival's comfort on a five-hour drive, Chris had carefully mapped out dog parks and dog-friendly restaurants where we could stop along our way. It was a very compassionate and thoughtful thing to do, and if Percival wasn't already so madly, obsessively in love with Chris, this would have sealed the deal. Daphne hopped down and headed up the trail to the park, which was surprisingly empty for a Sunday afternoon. She burst through the gate and I removed her leash while Chris talked to Percival and coaxed him in.

Daphne ran the perimeter of the park, nose to the ground, white-tipped tail upright and flagging the hunters (not us, but somewhere in her bloodline, there was no denying this dog was bred to hunt). She got on the scent of something—Rabbit? Squirrel? Another dog long gone?—and raised her head, letting out a hearty *BÁAAAAARRRRRRRRRRRROOOOOOOOOOOOO*. And then again and again.

I looked back at Chris and laughed. "I'll never get tired of that sound."

"I know. Luckily no one else is here to hear it."

BAAARROOOOO!!! BAAARRRROOOO!! Daphne continued to howl and I continued to laugh, but then…

Roo…roo…rooo…aaarrrooo! Percival ran after Daphne, his mouth in the full beagle howl mode but the bay at about one-third the volume. Raspy, seal-like, but definitely a beagle howl.

I looked back at Chris. "He's howling!"

"I hear that." Chris was playing nonchalant, but this was a big deal. Percival had been debarked by the breeder who sells beagles to the labs. He hadn't howled for the first part of his life and had never been around other beagles that could howl. He wasn't supposed to be *able* to howl. We had been so used to first Seamus and his constant, demanding, and hilarious whiskey howl, and then Daphne and her umpire's shout, that Percival's silence had been surprising. We called him Stealth Beagle because he made so very little noise. He was tiny, so his walk didn't make much noise, he didn't snore (Daphne did enough of that for both of them), and he didn't growl, bark, or howl. The only noise we'd ever heard out of him were the yips and yelps from his night terrors (which were rapidly becoming a thing of the past) or the fights with Daphne, and then it was hard to tell which dog was making which noise. Now, though, it was clear which howl was Daphne's (*BAAARRROOOOOOOOOOOOOO!*) and which was Percival's (a tenuous and raspy *roo? roo? aaarrrooo!!*)

"Good boy, Percival! Good boy!" I shouted.

"Oh, great. Reward the dog for barking! That's going to be terrific when we get him back home."

"True. But I'm so excited to hear him howl. Look how proud of himself he is!"

Percival was following Daphne around the dog park, sniffing where she sniffed, howling on occasion, and periodically dropping down into play position in a futile effort to engage The Commissioner in a little fun. He was quite the happy little clown.

Chris and I moved to a park bench and watched them roam about for a bit, but very quickly Percival noticed Chris's available lap and ran across the grounds to hurl himself into Chris. Chris picked him up, turned him on his back, and held him on his lap, rubbing his belly. Dog parks were fun, but not nearly as much fun as the jungle gym that is Chris, as far as Percival was concerned.

When Percival batted Chris's face with his little paw (and probably because we'd been in the car with the radio on for quite some time), he earned another theme song. This one was courtesy of Lady Gaga's "Applause":

My paws, my paws
I beat you with my paws, paws,
Beat you with my paws, paws
Live for the way that you cheer and scream for me
The paws, the paws, the paws.

———————

We had five days of blissful indulgence in Paso Robles, easily now one of our favorite places in the world. Daphne and Percival got used to wine tasting rooms with us, and quickly learned to sit or lie down in the sun spots in any of the tasting rooms, patiently waiting for either a treat or for us to finish and take them back outside to roam the vineyards, the gardens, and the lawn areas, Daphne howling after the bunnies, vineyard workers, or, heaven forbid, other dogs, and Percival pulling backward to gain any leverage that took him in whatever random direction he felt the need to go.

At night they slept together on the couch, not exactly curled up together and sometimes not even touching, but they seemed to enjoy being together. When Chris and I retired to bed, Daphne usually

followed us but Percival stayed on the couch. In keeping with our philosophy of letting them each be who they were, we let him be. In the
mornings, he usually made his way into the bedroom for a little family
cuddle time. And then I'd quickly take him and Daphne both outside—
the house did not have a doggie door.

Dining out with one omnivore, one vegan, and two beagles was
not difficult in Paso. There were several restaurant options, a farmer's
market, and of course, well-stocked grocery stores. We were even able to
take the dogs out to lunch at a country club that had a patio and boasted
a doggie menu.

But toward the end of our week, we decided to stay in and cook
dinner at home. We bought "Smart Dogs" (vegan hot dogs) and potato
chips (still vegan! But yeah, some habits die hard). Then we realized
we forgot mustard. And what's a hot dog without mustard? At the last
winery we visited that day, I picked up a jar of caramelized onion mustard in the gift shop. Perfect.

I was about halfway through my hot dog, smeared with the mustard,
when Chris mused, "I wonder what they whip the mustard with?"

"A whisk?"

"I mean what ingredient." He headed into the kitchen to get the jar.

"Does it have to be with another ingredient? Don't they just whip it
and make it fluffy? –er?"

He read the back of the jar: "Mustard seed, white wine vinegar,
onion, and…there we have it. Cream cheese."

"Cream cheese? In mustard?" *Always read the ingredient list!! I blame
the wine…*

"Yep. That's what they whip it with to give it that texture. And
creamy taste."

"Great." I put my hot dog down. "So I'll be having chips for dinner.
It's like old times."

"Sorry, baby."

Well, it's not like I was going to burn in hell, or break out in a rash,
or have some sort of allergic reaction. (I did have one heck of a stomach
ache all night, though.) Vegan is a choice. Not a religion or a medical
condition. Or a cult. A tribe, sure, but not a cult.

The "cheese incident," however, stirred Chris. All summer I'd been making cashew nut "cheese" from one of the vegan cookbooks I'd picked up in the past year, and it was very good—Chris enjoyed it too—but we'd both wanted to find a recipe for vegan blue cheese. He was convinced such a recipe existed and, surprisingly, convinced it would be delicious. We'd been talking about it again since he'd had a blue cheese burger for lunch. While I went to the kitchen for more chips, Chris searched online for a vegan blue cheese recipe.

"I found one. I don't understand some of the ingredients but I found one," he said as I joined him on the couch and looked at his computer screen.

"Okay, I understand sauerkraut. And the cashews, of course. And yep, lemon juice. Even tahini I get. But um, blue-green algae culture? And acidophilus? Are we making cheese or conducting a science experiment?" I was reminded of a roommate long ago who used to clean out my refrigerator from time to time, calling it a "science project sweep."

"I don't know what acidophilus is or where to buy it. That's going to be the problem with this recipe. But that's what Google is for!"

"You Google. I'll get the wine."

I walked across the room to the kitchen, and as I popped the cork out of the wine, I heard Chris burst out laughing.

"This is either awesome or horrifying," he said.

"That shouldn't be a tough distinction."

"I give you the Mayo Clinic definition of acidophilus…" He read to me in a mock-serious announcer's voice, "*Lactobacillus acidophilus* belongs to a group of bacteria that normally live in the human small intestine and vagina."

"*What?*"

"Oh you heard me correctly."

"And we're supposed to make *cheese* with that?"

Chris started laughing again. "But suddenly it all makes sense."

"What makes sense?"

"Remember the art exhibit you went to? *The Blue Vagina* painting? It was an ode to vegan cheese! Save the cows, eat blue vagina cheese." He convulsed in laughter.

"This might be why people think vegans are weirdos."

He gasped for air. "*Might* be?"

We spent the last two nights of our family vacation farther south in the Santa Rita hills with Roy and Laurie and their six dogs on their beagle ranch. It has a real ranch name, but it will forever be "Beagle Ranch" to us and "Heaven" to Daphne and Percival. Roy and Laurie had invited us to join them and bring the dogs. We could leave the dogs at the ranch and head with them into the area of Santa Rita dubbed the "wine ghetto" with them for a day, and that was an opportunity too good to pass up. The section was called the wine ghetto because it was a series of industrial park tasting rooms set up by smaller, artisan winemakers, rather than the large gorgeous wineries set amongst vineyards. Their focus was on the wines, not the views.

Indie and Percival ran about the fenced area of the ranch—acres within a larger parcel—like long-lost siblings. In the blurs that they were when running and chasing, it was hard to tell who was who. And they stuck by each other. They were the youngest of the eight dogs, and it was as if each had been waiting for someone to keep up with their energy. Now that they'd found each other, they kept running, side by side or taking turns chasing each other.

Daphne found her personality doppelgänger too. Their beagle Homer was older, sturdier, and much more serious about patrolling the grounds and ridding the property of any intruders of the rodent or hopping variety. He and Daphne headed for the hills and trees and bushes, howling their demands.

I can't think of a better way to spend an evening than sipping wine on a patio at sunset, watching eight rescue dogs ranging in age from one to seventeen play and romp around wild and free on a ranch. There were a few scuffles (Daphne naturally had to challenge the alpha female of the beagle ranch) and a few scares (*where is Percival??*), but not enough to make it less than a thoroughly enjoyable evening. Made better only by the fact that Roy and Laurie are also vegan and talented chefs. I'd noticed that most people affiliated with Beagle Freedom Project were vegans. When you see the effects of exploitation of animals up close like we all had, your tolerance is lowered. It gets much tougher to rationalize certain behaviors.

Everyone was content on our drive home, and the beagles slept hard curled up right next to each other on the backseat. They'd likely sleep for days after their time at the ranch. I hoped they weren't too disappointed to return to their life in the suburbs.

"You look happy," Chris said.

"I am. That was a great vacation."

"You rested. You needed that. You don't look stressed anymore."

"Right. I feel very happy." I paused for a moment and took a deep breath. "I figured out something else I can do. And I'm feeling good about it."

"Go on. I'm only mildly afraid."

"Understandably. But I think this one's good. You'll be okay." I looked back at the beagles and then at Chris. "I think I can help by telling my story. By telling their story." I gestured toward our sleeping beagles.

"The book you're working on now?"

"That's the one."

"I like it."

"I do too. And I have another Mother Teresa quote to thank."

Chris laughed. "Weird, but okay. Go ahead."

"It goes, 'We can do no great things—only small things, with great love.'"

"Awww."

"I know. But it helps to think like that."

"See, it all worked out. The dogs are good. You're good. You'll save the world one page at a time. You had nothing to worry about."

"I'm pretty sure you were the one who thought it wasn't all going to work out with the dogs. I was just upset nothing was going according to *my* plan."

"Mmm."

"Right, I know. My plan. I should just not bother planning. My plans don't really work out."

"No, I like your plans. You just have to be a little more flexible."

He squeezed my thigh. But I knew this wasn't a reference to my lapsed yoga practice.

"I have to be more 'in the moment.' More golden dog at the Taj. I'm getting better at just letting things be."

"Sometimes."

"Well, not everything should be left alone."

"And therein lies life's great dilemma."

We were quiet for a few miles of our drive.

"So speaking of plans…" I said.

"We were?"

"We were."

"And you have another one?" Now he rested his hand on my knee.

"I do." I turned toward him in my seat and focused on his profile as he drove. He glanced at me briefly.

"Let's hear it."

"So you know our five-year plan for moving to Paso that's really just been a five-year dream?"

"And the five years have stayed five years, even though we've been talking about it for two years?"

"That plan."

"Okay. I love that plan."

"Me too. So, the years should stop sliding. And it shouldn't be five years. We can do it sooner."

"Funny you should mention that…" During our trip he'd been talking to the winery owners about his plans to specialize in Paso Robles wines. And he'd bought the domain name PasosBestWines.com.

"I hear there's wine in Paso Robles," I said.

"Wine? Like for someone with an online wine business?"

"*Exactly* like that."

He was smiling and laughing with me. "And what about a writer? Could a writer write in Paso?"

"Huh. That's a good question. Let's see, there's air. And water. And wine. So I'm going to say yes. A writer could write in Paso. And I'm guessing as much as I'm doing things online these days, a lawyer could lawyer in Paso too."

"If she went easy on the wine."

"That." *Dang it!*

"We'd need acreage."

"Definitely." Now that we'd shown the beagles the country life, I was fairly certain they'd want more.

"For some vines."

Vines? "Oh, right. Vines. And then some acres for the beagles."

"How many are we talking about?"

I looked at the two in the back, so happy, healthy, and well-adjusted now—kind of like me, I liked to think. "We'll see about that. We'll see."

I'd do what I could do.

And then I'd try to do a little more…with great love.

RESOURCES

"We must never permit the voice of humanity within us to be silenced. It is man's sympathy with all creatures that first makes him truly a man."

—*Albert Schweitzer*

So you want to know what's in my cupboards? Here are a few of my favorite cruelty-free vegan brands and resources. I hope you'll check them all out…for the animals. But first, buy the smartphone app Cruelty Cutter, developed by Beagle Freedom Project. You can scan the bar code of any item and instantly learn if it's tested on animals.

Cosmetics/Personal Care
Alba

Burt's Bees (also available at Target and many other retailers; BurtsBees.com)

E.L.F. (Eyes, Lips, Face; available at Target)—Cruelty-free and inexpensive cosmetics that feel and look great. Can't beat that!

Gud

Kiss My Face

LUSH cosmetics—They support Beagle Freedom Project! And the products are indeed lush.

NYR Organics

Pacifica (PacificaPerfume.com)—I love their products and don't know how I lived without their Coconut Pearls Lip Quench before.

Tarte—Love their lash conditioner and mascara.

Urban Decay

Household Products

Citra Solv

Ecover

Method

Mrs. Meyer's

Seventh Generation

Food

ChooseVeg.com

CompassionateCook.com

NativeFoods.com

ShopHumanitaire.com

Sprouts

Trader Joe's

TreelineCheese.com—Yes, cheese! Vegan nut cheeses to live for!

VeganEssentials.com

Viva La Vegan Grocery

Whole Foods

Clothing/Shoes

AlternativeOutfitters.com—My shoe habit didn't have to slow down at all.

HerbivoreClothing.com—Also has great books and fun jewelry.

Lulus.com—Search the vegan section.

And one day when I can afford it: Stella McCartney.

Also, stores you normally shop (just avoid leather, Merino wool, and silk).

Books

Beg—A Radical New Way of Regarding Animals by Rory Freedman

The Complete Idiot's Guide to Plant-Based Nutrition by Julieanna Hever

The Dog Cancer Survival Guide by Dr. Demian Dressler and Dr. Susan Ettinger

Eat Like You Care: An Examination of the Morality of Eating Animals by Gary L. Francione and Anna Charlton

Farm Sanctuary: Changing Hearts and Minds about Animals and Food by Gene Baur

*The Imperfect Environmentalist: A Practical Guide to Clearing Your Body,
Detoxing Your Home, and Saving the Earth (Without Losing Your Mind)*
by Sara Gilbert

Living Cruelty Free by Jennifer Thomson

*Main Street Vegan: Everything You Need to Know to Eat Healthfully
and Live Compassionately in the Real World* by Victoria Moran (with
Adair Moran)

*My Gentle Barn: Creating a Sanctuary Where Animals Heal and Children
Learn to Hope* by Ellie Laks

*The Plant-Powered Diet: The Lifelong Eating Plan for Achieving Optimal
Health, Beginning Today* by Sharon Palmer and David L. Katz

*Vegan for Life: Everything You Need to Know to Be Healthy and Fit on a
Plant-Based Diet* by Jack Norris and Virginia Messina

We Animals by Jo-Anne McArthur

Why We Love Dogs, Eat Pigs, and Wear Cows: An Introduction to Carnism
by Melanie Joy and John Robbins

Magazines

Animal Wellness
Dogs Naturally
LAIKA
VegNews

Documentaries/Films

Behind the Mask—Produced by Shannon Keith
Blackfish
The Cove—Graphic.
Cowspiracy
Earthlings—This one is also graphic; I couldn't watch the whole thing.
Fat, Sick, and Nearly Dead—This one got Chris to join me on a twelve-
day juice fast; this one in particular appears to appeal to men.
Food, Inc.
Forks Over Knives
The Ghosts in Our Machine
Maximum Tolerated Dose

Speciesism
Vegucated

Sanctuaries

They're springing up all over. Find one near you (Sanctuaries.org has a listing) and visit. It will transform your life.

Best Friends Animal Sanctuary*—Kanab, Utah

Farm Sanctuary—Orland, California; Watkins Glen, New York; Los Angeles, California

The Gentle Barn—Santa Clarita, California

Kindness Ranch*—Hartville, Wyoming (a sanctuary for lab research animals)

Woodstock Farm Animal Sanctuary*—Woodstock, New York

I haven't been to these, but they're on my dream vacation list.

Websites for More Information

BeagleFreedomProject.org

HappyCow.net (for finding vegan restaurants)

JLGoesVegan.com (also a wonderful vegan lifestyle coach)

LeapingBunny.org

OneGreenPlanet.org

PlantBasedDietitian.com

ShopHumanitaire.com

TheVeganWoman.com

Vegan.org

VegGuide.org

VegNews.com

Beagle Freedom Project, of course, is particularly near and dear to my heart. They've recently launched a campaign to build a Rescue & Outreach Center (the ROC). The ROC will provide temporary care for laboratory dogs and animals as they transition and get the veterinary care, love, and psychological assistance they need to begin their new life. For many of these animals, just like Percival, this bright new world they are experiencing can be overwhelming and scary—until they learn that they are safe. The ROC will provide this initial TLC until they are placed into loving family homes. If Percival's story has inspired you to want to help, we ask you to join us in making a contribution to "Percival's Place" at the ROC—we're trying to raise ten thousand dollars to name a portion of the center in Percival's honor. Find out more at www.beaglefreedom.org/teresarhyne. We thank you (and Percival says, *Roooo rooooo.*)

ACKNOWLEDGMENTS

W HEN MY FIRST BOOK WAS PUBLISHED, I ACKNOWLEDGED JUST about everyone I'd ever met, just in case I never got the chance to publish a second book. I'll try to be a bit more succinct this time (but really, *thanks everyone!*).

In many ways, and unbeknownst to her, Julieanna Hever and her glow set me off on this journey to a compassionate lifestyle, and for that I'm forever grateful.

My heartfelt thanks to the people who inspire me every day with their work on behalf of animals—Shannon Keith and everyone involved with Beagle Freedom Project; Ellie Laks and her team at The Gentle Barn; the folks at Farm Sanctuary; and the staff and board of directors at Mary S. Roberts Pet Adoption Center, where my work on behalf of animals began and I hope will always continue.

My beagle-loving, beagle-rescuing, beagle-crazed friends inspire me and keep me from feeling I might be too obsessed with my dogs (it's normal if we all do it, right?)—special thanks to Kelle and Manos Phoundoulakis, Leela Ruiz, Roy and Laurie Gentry, Juliana and Seamus Dever, Beverly Thomas, Christine Haro, Mari-Louise Guernsey, Tiffany and Todd Leaverton, Lisa Drew, Karal Gregory, and Matt Friedlander.

To the Delhi Dozen 2013, and Terri Wingham of A Fresh Chapter, you all inspired me more than you'll ever know and, um, I'm sorry about that first week. I hope this explains it a little bit. And in memory of Melissa Carroll, with whom we were all so privileged to travel. She is gone far too soon but will never be forgotten.

My family watched first in stunned silence as I turned vegan, and then with mirth and laughter (but respect…I'm pretty sure) as I stumbled through. Your willingness to still dine with me and even try a few vegan dishes yourselves made the journey that much more worth-while. So thank you again, Mom and Ted, Dad and Nancy, Jay, and Shawna and Eli.

I must again thank Norm Martin and Susan Medel, for the use of their lucky beach house in La Jolla where I finished *The Dog Lived (and So Will I)* and where I began *The Dogs Were Rescued (and So Was I)*. Who knows if I could write without the inspiration of Windansea Beach, but I hope to never find out. And in a not-unrelated note, thanks always to Jane Gideon and Lori Lacefield for your inspiration, your beverage selections, and all the laughter. Maui awaits us.

Writing is solitary work, making writers' groups necessary to one's sanity. I'm lucky to have a group of writers to gather with over fine wine and vegan foods to discuss our work. This book is that much better for the input of Michelle Ouellette, Barbara Shackelton, Dulce Pena, Kristin Tillquist, Patti Cotton McNeily, Susan Knock, and, still with me from my days in a Los Angeles writers' group, Eileen Austen. And my tell-it-like-it-is, spot-all-the-issues, premier beta reader, Sara J. Henry—thank you wholeheartedly once again. And, of course, I must acknowledge and thank my optimistic and always positive friend and fellow author (and sometimes stalker) Dodinsky.

As with the first book, my tirelessly supportive agent, Sarah Jane Freymann, helped me find my way with this story and again found it a home with the book- and dog-loving folks at Sourcebooks. She has my gratitude always. My editor, Shana Drehs, once again made the editing process enjoyable (and she even had a kale smoothie or three in the process), and I'm thrilled at the chance to work with her again, as well as the entire Sourcebooks team. Thank you all.

Additional thanks to the creative people who've photographed my adorable dogs (no easy task with beagles who never stand still!)—David and Sylvaine at Dogma Pet Portaits and Kimberly Saxelby of True Emotions; and to Jason "Stub" Stubblefield, who produced a heartfelt trailer for this book. And speaking of energy and creativity, thank you, Dawn LoCascio, for all of your support!

Of course, the health and care of my beagles is of paramount importance to me, so I must thank their long-term vet Dr. Wayne

Davis, the good folks of Veterinary Cancer Group, and Eye Care for Animals in Upland, whose love and support of Seamus will never be forgotten.

So right, this wasn't so short. But finally, my love and thanks always to all the beagles I've known, and to Chris, a true beagle man and the best part of my life. Here's to more adventures, planned or not.

ABOUT THE AUTHOR

Teresa J. Rhyne is a work in progress. She knows that now more than ever. For the moment, she is a lawyer, writer, speaker, animal advocate, wine aficionado, and, for always, breast cancer survivor. She lives in Riverside, California, with her boyfriend, soul mate, and partner in all things, Chris Kern, and their two mischievous beagles, all of whom keep her laughing. The four of them are actively plotting to move to Paso Robles wine country one day to continue some of the above-mentioned pursuits. And yes, she's still vegan.